Biographical Note

ROBERT LANGBAUM is James Branch Cabell
Professor of English and American Literature at
the University of Virginia. He received his A.B.
from Cornell University and his M.A. and Ph.D.
from Columbia University. During World War II
he served in Military Intelligence as a translator
of Japanese documents. He taught English at Cornell
from 1950 to 1960, when he moved to the University of Virginia. He is married, has a daughter,
and has with his family spent much time in Europe,
especially in England and Italy.

Professor Langbaum is a well-known writer of
articles and reviews. His doctoral dissertation
The Poetry of Experience was published in 1957, and
reissued in paperback in 1963 and 1971. His
edition of Shakespeare's *The Tempest* appeared
in 1964, and *The Victorian Age* in 1967. In 1964–
65 he published in Britain, Denmark and the
United States *The Gayety of Vision: A Study of Isak
Dinesen's Art*, which was reissued in paperback in
1975 as *Isak Dinesen's Art*. In 1970 he published
*The Modern Spirit: Essays on the Continuity of Nineteenth-
and Twentieth-Century Literature*; and in 1977 he
published *The Mysteries of Identity: A Theme in
Modern Literature*, reissued in paperback in 1982.

To my students of
Victorian literature

THE VICTORIAN AGE

Essays in History
and in
Social and Literary Criticism

Edited with an Introduction
and Commentary by
ROBERT LANGBAUM

Academy
Chicago
Publishers

Copyright © 1969, 1983 by Robert Langbaum

THIRD EDITION, REVISED

Published in 1983 by
Academy Chicago Publishers
425 N. Michigan Ave.
Chicago, IL 60611

Library of Congress Cataloging in Publication Data
Main entry under title:
The Victorian age.

   Originally published: Greenwich, Conn.:
Fawcett Publications, 1967.
   Bibliography: p. 315.
   Includes index.
   1. English literature — 19th century — Addresses,
essays, lectures.   2. Great Britain — 19th century —
History and criticism — Addresses, essays, lectures.
I. Langbaum, Robert Woodrow. 1924–

PR463.V52   1983   941.081   83-6415
ISBN 0-89733-055-2 (pbk.)

PREFACE

The books cited throughout comprise a select bibliography, which can be supplemented by the bibliographies in the books themselves. See *The Victorian Poets: A Guide to Research* (1968), published by Harvard University Press, and the Guides to Research in *Victorian Prose* (1973) and *Victorian Fiction* (1978), published by the Modern Language Association of America.

Possibly obscure terms are explained; the Index shows in darker type the pages where the explanations appear. I have selected and regularized the footnotes (my own notes are bracketed), corrected minor errors, and modernized the punctuation of the older texts.

Thanks to my research assistants, Miss Shelby Grantham and Mr. Vincente Mier; and to the University of Virginia Research Committee for financial help. Special thanks to Professors Jerome H. Buckley of Harvard and Cecil Y. Lang of the University of Virginia, who read my introduction and commentary and offered valuable suggestions.

NOTE TO ACADEMY CHICAGO EDITION

This edition has been revised and updated. To supplement the books already cited, I have added a list of some noteworthy books on topics covered in THE VICTORIAN AGE. Almost all these books were published since the year of the last edition.

R.L.

University of Virginia, May 1983

CONTENTS

Part Three

THE MODERN LITERARY VIEW

Introduction

To understand what the Victorian age means to us today, let us take the case of E. M. Forster. Two recent books on Forster see the story of his family as characteristic of the century-long migration of English liberal intellectuals from Clapham to Bloomsbury. Forster is the great-grandson of the Evangelical and Utilitarian M.P., Henry Thornton of Clapham; and Clapham, near London, was at the beginning of the nineteenth century the home of the so-called Clapham Sect —wealthy lay leaders of the Evangelical or Low Church reforming party within the Church of England. At Clapham resided Hannah More, who wrote pious tracts and did philanthropic work among the poor, and William Wilberforce, who led the campaign to abolish the slave trade and was aided in the campaign by such other residents as Zachary Macaulay, father of Thomas Babington, later Lord Macaulay, and James Stephen, grandfather of Leslie Stephen and great-grandfather of Virginia Woolf. These families gradually connected through marriages with Trevelyans, Huxleys, Arnolds, Darwins, Keyneses, Stracheys—all the families who, according to Noel Annan in his biography of Leslie Stephen (London, 1951) constitute the intellectual aristocracy of modern England.

The point is that in the early nineteenth century the upper middle-class elite believed in piety, reform of Church and State, moral action and laissez-faire economics. Their early twentieth-century descendants, however, as represented by the so-called Bloomsbury Group (Leslie Stephen's four children formed the nucleus; Lytton Strachey and J. M. Keynes belonged; Forster was a frequent visitor), disbelieved in religion and moral action, and did believe in government regulation or ownership of industry and in refinement of sensibility. Between Clapham and Bloomsbury stands Matthew Arnold with his admonition to liberals to be less Hebraic or moral and more Hellenic or aesthetic; for the Victorian experience had shown that moral action without self-understanding and inner refinement resulted in the hypocrisy and the damaging forms of philanthropy Dickens is so good at exposing. Forster himself, in *Two Cheers for Democracy*

9

(London, 1951), sums up the paradoxical position of liberal intellectuals nowadays in Britain and America. We believe in government regulation of the economy, he suggests, but in a laissez-faire of the spirit; we believe in political democracy, but in an aristocracy of the spirit. Since this is the position toward which the whole Victorian literary enterprise has led us, we can see why Victorian literature matters. And indeed, the concerted revaluation of the period that has gone on since 1940 has quite reversed the old sneering attitude exemplified by Lytton Strachey's *Eminent Victorians* (London, 1918).

The order of perception that lay behind Arnold's attack is expressed by the remark of Arnold's contemporary, Walter Bagehot, that "Nothing is more unpleasant than a virtuous person with a mean mind. A highly developed moral nature joined to an undeveloped intellectual nature, an undeveloped artistic nature, is of necessity repulsive." In the 1850's, the younger members of the prosperous middle class were becoming aware of the narrowness and meagerness of the middle-class tradition. The word "Victorian" or "early Victorian" began at this time to appear in its pejorative sense, to refer to the middle-class Evangelical and Utilitarian spirit. Since the best Victorian writers were on the whole anti-"Victorian," we have to read backward from their writings to discern the assumptions and tastes of the articulate public. Thomas Babington Macaulay is the one outstanding writer who does speak for the middle class or (as Arnold was to call them) Philistines; and it is to give the side against which the literary men were reacting that I reprint a selection from Macaulay's attack on Southey.

Southey and the other two Lake poets, Wordsworth and Coleridge, were considered renegades, because they had started in the 1790's as radicals, supporters of the French Revolution, and later turned into Tories. But leaving aside their personal crotchets, they are, I think, to be understood as the first Victorians, in that they realized long before Queen Victoria's accession that the nature of the enemy had changed —that the enemy was no longer feudalism but rather the laissez-faire industrialism that threatened to destroy the countryside and men's souls. From what Mill here says about Coleridge, and Macaulay about Southey, we see the makings of a peculiarly Victorian phenomenon—that the movement against laissez-faire and toward the present-day welfare state came largely from the political right, from Tories harking back nostalgically to a unified and more humane agrarian order. In the early Carlyle of *Sartor Resartus* (1833-34) and *Past and Present* (1843), we see a radical Toryism; for Carlyle wanted radical institutional changes in order to revivify the permanent responsibility of all societies to look after the physical, moral and spiritual welfare of their citizens. The economists were mistaken, said Carlyle, in supposing that they had found a new formula through which society could now shirk its responsibility, could send its citizens into the "free market" with the pious hope that the general good would somehow be served if each man looked after his own interest without minding the other fellow's.

The characteristics we think of as Victorian were well established by the time of the Queen's accession in 1837. Some historians consider the era as starting with the 1832 Reform Bill, which opened the way for the eventual political ascendancy of the middle class and ushered in a rapid succession of legislative reforms. Certainly the laissez-faire ideology reached its high-water mark just before the Factory Act of 1833—which was the first act regulating hours and conditions of work that had teeth in it, because it provided for inspection. There followed a succession of regulatory laws; so that Victoria's reign saw a steady retreat from laissez-faire. Again, if we associate Victorianism with prudery, gloomy Sundays and fear of the senses, of pleasure and art—with, in other words, the Evangelical spirit—then it is also true that the Evangelical spirit had triumphed by 1833, the year of Wilberforce's death and the Abolition of Slavery, and that Victoria's reign saw a slow retreat from it, a retreat that became apparent with the rise of aestheticism after the mid-century. By the 1890's, the cultivated minority was in full rebellion against prudery.

The apparent exception to the above line of development is the Free-Trade principle, which did not win out until 1846 with the repeal of the Corn Laws, the tariff on wheat that seemed to protect the aristocratic or landed interest. The Free-Trade principle, which had acquired the magical sanction of a religious dogma, maintained its ascendancy for the rest of the century, even though British agriculture suffered badly in the last three decades from the competition of American wheat.

Another Victorian characteristic, well established before the Queen's accession, resulted from the unprecedented statistical surveys that accompanied the reform movement of the thirties. The thirties was the decade of the Blue Books, the reports of Parliamentary Committees or Royal Commissions on every aspect of English life except agriculture. Engels and Marx, who settled in England in 1849 (Engels had already visited in 1843-44), used these Blue Books— Engels for *The Condition of the Working Class in England in 1844* and Marx for *Das Kapital,* the first volume of which was published in 1867. The guiding spirit behind the Blue Books was that of Bentham and his Philosophic Radicals or Utilitarians; and they, through the Blue Books, taught the English reading public to worship—as Dickens was to put it satirically in *Hard Times*—"Facts . . . Facts . . . Facts."

The Philistine worship of facts went along with a literary reaction against Byronism that followed Byron's death in 1824. The literary reaction, as summed up by Carlyle's injunction in *Sartor,* "Close thy Byron; open thy Goethe," was against self-preoccupation and for the social responsibility that Goethe's Wilhelm Meister and Faust finally arrive at. As summed up by Sir Henry Taylor in the preface to his verse drama *Philip Van Artevelde* (1834), the reaction was against too much feeling and imagination at the expense of realism, intellect and morality. Passing on to Shelley, Taylor condemns him for a too exclusive pursuit of beauty and for a visionary quality that presents us forms "never to be seen through the mere medium of eyesight."

It was into this hostile atmosphere that Tennyson and Browning sent their still romantic poems of 1830, with unhappy results. Tennyson, particularly, wavered throughout his career between his impulse to write poetry of private sensation and his genuine interest in writing on public issues and joining in the march of progress. In reviewing Tennyson's 1830 *Poems,* Arthur Hallam praises Tennyson for just the qualities Taylor condemns in Shelley; for Hallam classes Tennyson with Keats and Shelley, with "poets of sensation" as distinguished from a "reflective" poet like Wordsworth. Hallam's position was taken up again in the aesthetic movement—especially the later phase, beginning with Pater in the seventies, that defined itself in opposition to ideas and dogmatic commitments. The opposing impulses that Tennyson along with Browning and Arnold contained within themselves were polarized by the end of the century between, on the one hand, the extreme aestheticism of Yeats and his friends, the poets of the nineties, who sought to empty their poetry of content, and, on the other hand, the socially responsible naturalism of Ibsen and Shaw. Yeats in his *Autobiography* (New York, 1938) writes that he and his friends could not escape the antithetical Ibsen, because "we had the same enemies." The enemies were, of course, the middle-class Philistines—which suggests that both sides were revolutionary and had in common a principle of progress opposed to that of the Philistines, a principle based on more complex criteria than the rise in national wealth and population. To this larger principle of progress the nineteenth century gave the elusive name of "culture."

In the Introduction reprinted here from *Culture and Society 1780-1950* (New York, 1958), Raymond Williams tells us that of the key words that first became operative in the nineteenth century, "culture" presents the most important and complex cluster of concepts. Williams goes on in the rest of the book to investigate the development and ramifications of these concepts through studies of major figures from Burke through the Victorians to Lawrence, Eliot, the Marxist critics and Orwell. He locates the idea of culture in the principle held in common by such contrasting pairs as the late eighteenth-century conservative Burke and the radical Cobbett, and the early nineteenth-century Tory Southey and the socialist Robert Owen. Both sides "attacked the new [industrializing] England from their experiences of the old England," and were concerned with what had been lost.

Such reconciliation of opposites relates to John Stuart Mill's advice to his contemporaries, in the essay reprinted here, to "master the premises and combine the methods" of Bentham and Coleridge. Bentham was a radical, utterly irreverent of the past, who thought all laws and institutions ought to be subjected to the test of utility, "the greatest happiness of the greatest number"; while the later Coleridge, the Coleridge of the prose writings who exercised so much influence on the Victorians, was a romantic conservative, who was mainly out to rehabilitate old institutions. By absorbing into his own inherited Benthamism the opposite Coleridgian view, Mill worked out for himself what was to be the characteristic Victorian synthesis—the absorption, that is, into a progressivist philosophy of a new respect for the past and for those institutions and values of the past that could not have been frauds, as the Benthamites thought, since they had engaged the best minds and hearts of so many centuries.

When Mill goes on to say that the Germano-Coleridgian school has made the largest contribution "towards the philos-

ophy of human culture," he means that the school of Herder
and Goethe, with its influence on Michelet in France and
Coleridge in England, has taught us to view alien societies,
whether past or present, as manifestations of national *character* at a particular phase of development. Societies are not,
in other words, to be judged by a fixed abstract standard, but
are to be understood as *characteristic* and therefore self-
justifying—once we understand how they came to be as they
are and how their parts cohere to make an organism adapted
to its geographical and historical environment.

I use the biological metaphor to make a point Mill does
not make—that the central idea of the nineteenth century is
the organicist or evolutionary idea, launched in England by
Burke's answer to the French Revolutionists who wanted to
wipe out the past and start over with an abstract blueprint
for the perfect society. Burke's answer was to say that the
state is in some respects like a plant, that it is organized
according to a living principle of continuity that cannot be
abrogated and that transforms separate persons into a People
—into an entity greater than and different from the sum of
its parts. The state is an artificial creation, but one which
functions for man, who is a reasonable being, *like* a natural
organism—for "Art is man's nature."

That paradox of Burke's—"Art is man's nature"—helps
us understand the nineteenth-century concept of culture—the
concept behind the attempt of the Victorians reprinted here
to reconcile change with continuity and order. The Latin
cultura means cultivation of the soil; and the obvious emphasis, the emphasis one still finds in Arnold, is on education,
on the things man adds to nature. But Arnold is aware that
culture is also an unconscious inevitable growth; and Carlyle
insists that the principles that really hold society together are
unconscious.

In our own time, when sociologists, anthropologists and
depth psychologists have further expanded the concept of
culture, the word is seldom used in serious discussions to
mean *belles lettres,* but comprehends every characterizing
aspect of a people, their *whole* way of life. The most trivial
characteristics—the ones of which we are not conscious—
may be most fundamental, because indicative of that internal
life of a people that survives political change. It is internality,
if not subconsciousness, that stands behind Coleridge's distinction between cultivation, or culture, and civilization: "a
nation can never be a too cultivated, but may easily become

an over-civilized, race"; or behind Mill's criticism of Bentham: "Man is never recognized by Bentham as a being capable of pursuing spiritual perfection as an end." T. S. Eliot, however, has both internality and subconsciousness in mind in *Notes towards the Definition of Culture* (London, 1948). Since "culture cannot altogether be brought to consciousness," says Eliot, it cannot be dominated or directed by politics or education. "The culture of which we are wholly conscious is never the whole of culture: the effective culture is that which is directing the activities of those who are manipulating that which they *call* culture." Like Burke, Eliot uses the concept of culture to oppose the engineered or totally manipulated society.

One has to understand that the word *culture* was from the beginning charged with a world-view and a battle cry. In a revolutionary age, the word was used to define a principle of continuity underlying political, economic and even social change. It was used, in an industrial age which measured progress by numbers, to ask about the *quality* of life—especially since quality seemed to be declining. Since the economy required specialization and dehumanization, the word *culture* was invoked as an argument for the harmonious development of all our human faculties. Since the dominating middle class viewed art as useless and therefore as a mere luxury product, the antithetical concept of culture came to include the idea that the art of a period is an index to its quality and that aesthetic judgments are therefore inextricably related to moral and social judgments. This was the lesson taught, as regards architecture and the visual arts, by Pugin, Ruskin and Morris; and, as regards literature, by Matthew Arnold. "For the creation of a master-work of literature," says Arnold, "two powers must concur, the power of the man and the power of the moment, and the man is not enough without the moment; the creative power has, for its happy exercise, appointed elements, and those elements are not in its own control." Style came to be regarded as organic to a society and therefore as an index to its real or subconscious character.

Because the Victorians' attack on their own age is so largely expressed through the concept of culture, an anthology such as this is especially relevant—an anthology dealing with the meeting ground between history and social criticism, on the one hand, and literature on the other. For the concept of culture was the product of the literary mind when it was turned upon the unprecedented conditions of the nineteenth century. Indeed the literary mind, with its memory of other world views and of "the best [in Arnold's words] that is known and thought in the world," offered the one hope of escape, that was not a mere return to stale orthodoxy, from the latest shibboleths—"the greatest happiness of the greatest number" or "doing as you like with your own."

It took a mind stored with cultural memory to see, as Coleridge does in *Constitution of Church and State* (1830), how unprecedented was the manufacturers' refusal of responsibility for the excess workers whom they had "virtually called into existence" through the lure of increased jobs; or to see as Carlyle does, in the powerful opening chapter of *Past and Present,* that England in the "hungry forties" lay under a Midas enchantment—dying of starvation with wealth all around. The enchantment was the paralyzing laissez-faire dogma that forbade tampering with the free market; so that men could not reach out and distribute the wealth they were producing. It required cultural memory to see in the case of the pauper Wragg who strangled her unwanted baby on the bleak Mapperley Hills, to see in the case, as Arnold does in the essay I have been quoting, not so much the age-old story of poverty but, through the ugliness of the names and setting and the impersonal newspaper account, an unprecedentedly dismal cultural situation.

In this essay, "The Function of Criticism at the Present Time," Arnold means by "criticism" just such a turning of the literary mind upon public affairs. Not only has the literary mind access to a high and wide tradition by which to judge the current scene, but it has the "disinterestedness," the ability to play freely with ideas and possibilities, which is the peculiar reward of literary study. Because of this disinterestedness, the literary mind can give assent to opposite positions—as, according to Arnold, Burke did when he concluded his arguments against the French Revolution as follows:

"If a great change is to be made in human affairs, the minds of men will be fitted to it; the general opinions and feelings will draw that way. Every fear, every hope will forward it; and then they who persist in opposing this mighty current in human affairs, will appear rather to resist the decrees of Providence itself, than the mere designs of men. They will not be resolute and firm, but perverse and obstinate."

Like Arnold, who though a liberal spent most of his career criticizing liberals, Burke paid allegiance to a principle of culture that can be served by a properly informed liberal or conservative position. The conservative Coleridge, for example, influenced the Christian Socialist and the Broad-Church or liberal Anglican movements. And Arnold, in *Culture and Anarchy*, connects the working-class movement of the sixties with Newman's Oxford or High Church movement which, in promoting thirty years earlier the dogmatic, Catholic character of Anglicanism, helped undermine the Protestant, liberal individualism of the middle class.

Perhaps the most important advantage of the literary mind is that its figurative way of reading events and using language enables it to deal at once with external and internal matters. This advantage accounts for a peculiar phenomenon of the age. I mean the so-called Victorian prophets or sages—prose writers like Carlyle, Newman, Arnold, Ruskin (I would add Pater and the discursive Morris; Shaw and Lawrence are in the same tradition), who, whether they wrote on history, or on political, social or economic subjects, religion, literature or the visual arts, wrote under a governing principle of culture that connected any one of these subjects with all the others and with a demand for action, either personal or social. The most distinctive thing about these discursive prose writings is that they ranked with the poetry and fiction of the age as literature.

In a brilliant introduction to his book, *The Victorian Sage* (New York, 1953), John Holloway shows why these discursive writings can be regarded as literature. Like the poet and novelist, the Victorian sage persuades not by logical argument but by projecting a coherent vision of life into which his argument fits. "The methods traced here persuade because they clarify, and clarify because they are organic to a view presented not by one thread of logical argument alone, but by the whole weave of a book." To judge the argument, "one must have a critic's sense of how the parts of a book unite in what is not a logical unity." The views of the Victorian sages cannot be judged by summaries; for "what gave their views life and meaning lay in the actual words of the original . . . to work by quickening the reader to a new capacity for experience is to work in the mode of the artist in words." Thus Holloway extends the term *Victorian sage* to cover novelists like Disraeli, George Eliot and Hardy, who deal with the same subjects as the discursive

writers through "illustrative incidents in a story" analogous
to the latter's "illustrative examples in an argument." It
should be clear from the literary criticism reprinted here
that all the major poets and novelists dealt like the Victorian
sages with the same cluster of subjects, subjects related to
each other through a governing concept of culture.

Victorian writers dealt with the fragmentation of life in
the nineteenth century, just because they carried in their
heads an ideal of cultural unity. But the ideal in their heads
was itself a result of fragmentation, of their being forced to
internalize those values of the superseded agrarian, aristocratic and Christian society, the loss of which in the public
domain produced the feeling of fragmentation. Thus the
Victorian writers established what remains the special knack
of modern intellectuals—the knack of inhabiting two or more
cultures at the same time. We can appreciate in literary or
historical discussion the virtues of noblemen and peasants, or
of an age of faith, or of exotically primitive peoples, at the
same time that we vote for more democracy and social
welfare and, crowning irony, the industrialization of agrarian
societies. That is how we arrive at the paradoxical position
described by E. M. Forster. For we have appropriated
to the realm of the spirit the aristocratic pursuit of distinction and the bold individualism of the laissez-faire
ideology, even though we have abolished the aristocracy from
our political life and the laissez-faire ideology from our
economic life.

The Victorian writers have taught us that culture can and
should be antithetical to the prevailing ideology—not so
much to destroy the ideology (though that may at times be
necessary) as to complete it. In teaching us that the mind
must inhabit and judge from a much larger sphere than any
ideology can supply, the Victorian writers have bequeathed
us the crucial principle by which societies in our time might
be differentiated. For now that in politics the democratic
ideology is universally acknowledged even if it is not universally in effect, and now that the distinction is dissolving
between capitalist and socialist economies, the crucial difference ought to be between open and closed societies—between
societies that respect the autonomy of culture and those that
use culture to close up all avenues of intellectual escape, to
reinforce the dreary clichés of political and economic bosses.

I say *ought to*, because the concept of culture is hard to
maintain after all we have been through in the first half of

the twentieth century. Auschwitz might be read as a portent of the future; and if we read it so, what happens to our faith in the organically inevitable enlargement of consciousness? Besides, the organic metaphor, which derives everything from the soil, may be inappropriate to a time when man is taking off from Earth itself. More immediately discouraging is the spectacle of the open societies of the West, where life is more impersonal than ever and the autonomy of culture has led to a binge of "consumerism" and a taste for intellectual pap —to a freely chosen intellectual sleep.

Orwell's *Nineteen Eighty-Four* (New York, 1949) projects the nightmare future of a technologically advanced socialist society without culture—without the individuality, spirituality and intellectual freedom, without the whole heritage of the past that originally produced the technology and socialism. To achieve total tyranny, to make consciousness identical with ideology, the Party reduces the area of private life by discouraging sexual and family love, and reduces the range of consciousness by reducing available vocabulary and obliterating all memory of the past. The one glimmer of hope is in the hero, an obsolete man who still has some primitive instincts and some cultural memory.

Similarly, to the extent that we can think optimistically about the future, our thoughts are necessarily based on the cluster of ideas connected with the word *culture*—ideas that give coherence to much of the material reprinted here. This little book is designed to be suggestive only—to provide an entry into Victorian literature for those who are new to it, and to offer those who have read or are reading in the literature a mode of organizing their reading. The book should be used as an index finger pointing to those other Victorian works, and those other modern works on the period, which will enable the reader to fill out the picture sketched in here and to go on to find for himself still other orders of coherence.

ROBERT LANGBAUM

Part One

THE HISTORICAL VIEW

In the wittiest, most trenchant and most readable portrait of the Victorian age yet written, G. M. Young suggests that the early-Victorian period is characterized by "the parallel operation of Evangelicalism and Utilitarianism." He describes these two movements in such a way as to evoke the spirit of the thirties and forties. When "in the great peace of the fifties," he goes on to say, "the word 'Victorian' was coined," it registered the reaction of a new generation against the Evangelical and Utilitarian spirit of the early Victorians.

G. M. Young

VICTORIAN ENGLAND: PORTRAIT OF AN AGE

A boy born in 1810, in time to have seen the rejoicing after Waterloo and the canal boats carrying the wounded to hospital, to remember the crowds cheering for Queen Caroline, and to have felt that the light had gone out of the world when Byron died, entered manhood with the ground rocking under his feet as it had rocked in 1780. Paris had risen against the Bourbons; Bologna against the Pope; Poland against Russia; the Belgians against the Dutch. Even in well-drilled Germany little dynasts were shaking on their thrones, and Niebuhr, who had seen one world revolution, sickened and died from fear of another. At home, forty years of Tory domination were ending in panic and dismay; Ireland, unappeased by Catholic Emancipation, was smouldering with rebellion; from Kent to Dorset the skies were alight with burning ricks. A young man looking for some creed by which to steer at such a time might, with the Utilitarians, hold by the laws of political economy and the greatest happiness of the greatest number; he might simply believe in the Whigs, the Middle Classes, and the Reform Bill; or he might, with difficulty, still be a Tory. But atmosphere is more than creed, and, whichever way his temperament led him, he found himself at every turn controlled, and animated, by the imponderable pressure of the Evangelical discipline and the almost universal faith in progress.

Evangelical theology rests on a profound apprehension of the contrary states: of Nature and of Grace; one meriting eternal wrath, the other intended for eternal happiness. Naked and helpless, the soul acknowledges its worthlessness before God and the justice of God's infinite displeasure, and then, taking hold of salvation in Christ, passes from darkness into a light which makes more fearful the destiny of those unhappy beings who remain without. This is Vital Religion. But the power of Evangelicalism as a directing force lay less

G. M. Young, VICTORIAN ENGLAND: PORTRAIT OF AN AGE, Second Edition (New York: Oxford University Press, 1953), pp. 11-13, 15-26. Reprinted by permission of the publisher. See also G. M. Trevelyan, *Illustrated English Social History*, 4 vols. (London, 1952), *Volume Four: The Nineteenth Century.*

in the hopes and terrors it inspired, than in its rigorous logic, "the eternal microscope" with which it pursued its argument into the recesses of the heart, and the details of daily life, giving to every action its individual value in this life, and its infinite consequence in the next. Nor could it escape the notice of a converted man, whose calling brought him into frequent contact with the world, that the virtues of a Christian after the Evangelical model were easily exchangeable with the virtues of a successful merchant or a rising manufacturer, and that a more than casual analogy could be established between Grace and Corruption and the Respectable and the Low. To be serious, to redeem the time, to abstain from gambling, to remember the Sabbath day to keep it holy, to limit the gratification of the senses to the pleasures of a table lawfully earned and the embraces of a wife lawfully wedded, are virtues for which the reward is not laid up in heaven only. The world is very evil. An unguarded look, a word, a gesture, a picture, or a novel, might plant a seed of corruption in the most innocent heart, and the same word or gesture might betray a lingering affinity with the class below. . . .

The Evangelicals gave to the island a creed which was at once the basis of its morality and the justification of its wealth and power, and, with the creed, that sense of being an Elect People which, set to a more blatant tune, became a principal element in late Victorian Imperialism. By about 1830 their work was done. They had driven the grosser kinds of cruelty, extravagance, and profligacy underground. They had established a certain level of behaviour for all who wished to stand well with their fellows. In moralizing society they had made social disapproval a force which the boldest sinner might fear.

By the beginning of the Victorian age the faith was already hardening into a code. Evangelicalism at war with habit and indifference, with vice and brutality, with slavery, duelling, and bull-baiting, was a very different thing from Evangelicalism grown complacent, fashionable, superior. Even its charity had acquired what a Yorkshire manufacturer once grimly styled a "diffusive, itinerant quality." The impulses it had quickened showed at their best in the upper ranks of society, where they had been absorbed into an older tradition of humour, culture, and public duty; or at the Universities, where they blended with new currents of intellectual eagerness and delight. The piety of a fine scholar like Peel or a

haughty Border lord like Graham, of Gladstone or Sidney
Herbert, had not much in common with the soul-saving theology of the money-making witness-bearers, those serious
people whose indifference to national affairs Bright was one
day to deplore. But, morally, their way of life was the same.
Evangelicalism had imposed on society, even on classes
which were indifferent to its religious basis and unaffected
by its economic appeal, its code of Sabbath observance, responsibility, and philanthropy; of discipline in the home,
regularity in affairs; it had created a most effective technique
of agitation, of private persuasion and social persecution. On
one of its sides, Victorian history is the story of the English
mind employing the energy imparted by Evangelical conviction to rid itself of the restraints which Evangelicalism
had laid on the senses[1] and the intellect; on amusement, enjoyment, art; on curiosity, on criticism, on science.

The Evangelical discipline, secularized as respectability,
was the strongest binding force in a nation which without it
might have broken up, as it had already broken loose. For a
generation and more the static conception of society[2] had
been dissolving because society itself was dissolving. "A nobleman, a gentleman, a yeoman," Cromwell told one of his Parliaments, "that is a good interest." But the good interest was
splitting into a hundred aristocracies and a hundred democracies, button-makers and gentlemen button-makers,[3] all heels
and elbows, jostling, pushing, snubbing, presuming. On the
whole, the articulate classes, whose writings and conversation
make opinion, were gainers by the change—it has been estimated, for example, that between 1815 and 1830 purchasing
capacity of the classes above the wage-earning level was all
but doubled—and the Victorian belief in progress was bot-
tomed on the complacency which comes of steadily rising
incomes and steadily improving security. Mixed with this, no
doubt, was the vulgar pride in mere quantity, the thoughtless

---

[1] Kingsley (who described Shelley as a lewd vegetarian) correctly
diagnosed Byron as an Evangelical gone wrong. Byron's objection to
mixed bathing, even when the parties are married, as "very indeli-
cate," comes from his Venetian period.

[2] As explained, for example, by an Irish judge in 1798. "Society consists of noblemen, baronets, knights, esquires, gentlemen, yeomen,
tradesmen and artificers." The jury found that, as the subject had
ceased to be a breeches maker without becoming a gentleman, he
must be a yeoman.

[3] For whom there were separate doors in the Birmingham taverns.

exultation of a crowd in motion. But no one can read for long in the literature of the thirties and forties without touching a finer and deeper pride, portentously draped in tables of trade and revenue and the publications of the Useful Knowledge Society, but glowing with the authentic sense of war and victory, man against nature, and reason against the traditions of the elders.

Great things are done when men and mountains meet.

To travellers descending from the moorlands, the smoke and roar of Lancashire seemed like the smoke and roar of a battle-field, and the discipline of the factories like the discipline of a great army. It is hardly an accident that the first history of the Renaissance came from Liverpool and that the most conspicuous memorial of the Utilitarians is a History of Greece.[4] Across the ages, the modern Englishman recognized his peers.

But we must be careful if we are to keep the picture true, not to view the early Victorian age of production through that distorting medium, the late Victorian age of finance. Science touched the imagination by its tangible results. It was immersed in matter, and it conformed directly to the Augustan canon of historic progress by its immediate contribution to the "order, regularity, and refinement of life." Romance and the Revolution bred ideas of human purpose which only slowly permeated the English mind. Even in 1830 —far more powerfully in 1840—they were beginning to work. But the common intelligence was still dominated by the solid humanism of the Augustans, to which the Eighteenth Proposition of Oxford Liberalism would have seemed a self-evident truth:

Virtue is the child of Knowledge: Vice of Ignorance: therefore education, periodical literature, railroad travelling, ventilation, and the arts of life, when fully carried out, serve to make a population moral and happy.[5]

"The objects of this Society," so ran the prospectus of the Rochdale Pioneers,[6] "are the moral and intellectual advance-

---

[4] [William Roscoe's *Life of Lorenzo de' Medici* (1795) and *Life and Pontificate of Leo the Tenth* (1805); George Grote's *History of Greece*, 12 vols. (1846-56).—Ed.]

[5] Newman, *Apologia*, Note A. But what does *serve* mean? The almost magical effect of ventilation on the moral habits (temper and sobriety) of a poor quarter was demonstrated again and again.

[6] [First successful consumers' co-operative, founded in 1844.—Ed.]

ment of its members. It provides them with groceries, butcher's meat, drapery goods, clothes and clogs." Gas-lighting of the streets was hardly an improvement so much as a revolution in public security;[7] cheap cotton goods in personal cleanliness, colza lamps in domestic comfort. Finance, the manipulation of wealth and credit as things by themselves, three or four degrees removed from the visible crop or ore, was an adjunct. Production was the thing itself.

A generation which has come to take invention for granted and is, perhaps, more sensitive to its mischief than its benefits, cannot easily recover the glory of an age when knowledge, and with it power, seemed to have been released for an illimitable destiny.[8] The Englishman might reluctantly allow that in social amenity the French, in care for the well-being of the people the Prussians, went beyond him. He might at moments be chilled by the aesthetic failure of his time, so profuse and yet so mean: alienated by its ethical assurance, at once so pretentious and so narrow. In a petulant mood, he would talk, with Grote, of the Age of Steam and Cant, but all the while he knew that in the essential business of humanity, the mastery of brute nature by intelligence, he had outstripped the world, and the Machine was the emblem and the instrument of his triumph. The patriotism of early Victorian England, not yet blooded by the Crimean War and the Indian Mutiny, irritated by Napoleon III, or exalted by the vision of empire, was at heart a pride in human capacity, which time had led to fruition in England; and in the great humanist, who brought all history to glorify the age of which he was the most honoured child, it heard its own voice speaking.[9]

---

[7] Without presuming to play on words," said the Lambeth magistrate, "I regard gas as essential to an enlightened police." It was once proposed to illuminate thieves' quarters with lamps of a special construction so that law-abiding pedestrians should pass by on the other side.

[8] The admiration of Bacon, almost amounting to a rediscovery, is very characteristic of the period. So is the Utilitarian preference for the more scholastic, less imaginative Hobbes. When his editor, Molesworth, stood for Southwark the populace paraded the streets shouting NO OBBS.

[9] *Il a son orgueil d'homme.* Taine's fine saying of Macaulay is true of his whole age. "That wicked XVIII century" died hard: under his Romantic ornament Macaulay is through and through Augustan; and contemporary critics (Brougham and Harriet Martineau are examples) reproduce against him the charges which the early Romantics had laid against Gibbon—materialism and want of philosophy.

To articulate the creed of progress, to state its evidences and draw out its implications, was the mission of that remarkable group of men variously known as the Utilitarians, or the Philosophic Radicals. In discipleship or reaction no young mind of the thirties could escape their influence. Bentham's alliance with James Mill, Mill's friendship with Malthus and Ricardo, had created a party, almost a sect, with formularies as compact as the Evangelical theology, and conclusions not less inexorable. However far the Benthamite disciple went, he would find the old sage had been there before him; every trail was blazed, every pitfall marked, and in every path stood a lion, the Sinister Interest of Privilege. Between rulers and ruled there exists an inherent antagonism[10] which can only be resolved if rulers and ruled are identified by means of universal suffrage and the ballot-box, and the identity is preserved by publicity and a cheap press.[11] The sovereignty thus created is to be exercised through a carefully balanced system: of Parliament to legislate, central organs to direct, local organs to execute. On the question of Women's Suffrage, the Utilitarians were somewhat inconsistently divided; Bentham, a flirtatious old bachelor, being more logical than James Mill, who, in spite of Malthus, had begotten more children than he could afford on a female whom he despised. On all other matters, above all on the sovereign authority of Economic Law, they spoke with one voice.

Reduced from an aspiration to a schedule, progress might seem a gloomy business for the mass of mankind. It rests on competition, and always and everywhere competition is reducing the profits of the employer, and the wages of the workman, to the level of bare subsistence. Only the landowner, the common enemy of all, continually profits by the growing demand for sites, and for food, because, always and everywhere, population is pressing on the means to live. Such is the law. But Nature has not left her children without all

[10] Translate this into economic terms, substitute for the antagonism of rulers and ruled the antagonism of employers and employed, and some curious conclusions will follow which the Socialists of the next age were ready to draw.

[11] The principle of human nature, upon which the necessity of government is founded, the propensity of one man to possess himself of the objects of desire at the cost of another, leads on, by infallible sequence, not only to that degree of plunder which leaves the members (except the instruments and recipients) the bare means of subsistence, but to that degree of cruelty which is necessary to keep in existence the most intense terrors."—James Mill on Government.

hope of escaping the fate to which her mathematics seem to have consigned them. By industry, and abstinence, the employer may enlarge the market for his goods; by industry, and continence, the workman may increase the purchasing power, and limit the numbers, of his class: progress, like salvation, is the reward of virtue; of diligence and self-education; of providence and self-control; and all the evolutionary speculation of the next age has for background Malthus's Stoic vision of that remote, austere, divinity "whose purpose is ever to bring a mind out of the clod."

In the early thirties the Philosophic Radicals were a portent, men whose meetings were watched, the spearhead of a revolution beginning with the ballot and going on, Heaven knew how far, to compulsory education and a federated Empire. Then, frigid and scholastic, as a party they fade from the view. The popular Radicals, hotter against Church and Lords, and readier champions of the unprivileged and the oppressed, made more noise; the people preferred the Tories. Grote lived to decline a peerage; when the ballot was at last conceded in 1872 John Mill had decided that he did not want it and had moved on to proportional representation instead; Leader vanished into an aesthetic Italian exile; Molesworth's features are more familiar at Ottawa than his name at Westminster. The case for Free Trade was taken out of their hands by men who had learnt their economics in the counting-house, their logic on the platform, and their rhetoric in the pulpit.[12] But they had done inestimable service. They came down into a world where medieval prejudice, Tudor Law, Stuart economics, and Hanoverian patronage still luxuriated in wild confusion, and by the straight and narrow paths they cut we are walking still. The Gladstonian Liberals have gone where the Peelites followed the Canningites; the Evangelical creed long ago foundered on the Impregnable Rock of Holy Scripture, and the great Whig name has not been heard for fifty years. But it would be hard to find any corner of our public life where the spirit of Bentham is not working to-day.

It is dangerous to force historic movements into exaggerated symmetry. But the parallel operation of Evangelicalism and Utilitarianism cannot be ignored. Their classics, Malthus on *Population* and Wilberforce's *Practical View,* appeared almost simultaneously, one in 1797, the other in 1798.

[12] The supersession of Charles Villiers by Cobden, Bright, and W. J. Fox is typical.

Their greatest victories in public affairs, the Abolition of
Slavery and the Reform of the Poor Law, were won in 1833
and 1834. When a distracted Government threw the Old
Poor Law at a Royal Commission, the Benthamites rose to
the height of their opportunity. The Secretary of the Commission was Edwin Chadwick, whom the Patriarch had selected to be his apostle to the new age, and in his hands
there was no fear lest the faith should grow cold. Born in
1800, in a Lancashire farmhouse where the children were
washed all over, every day, the mainspring of Chadwick's
career seems to have been a desire to wash the people of
England all over, every day, by administrative order. In
practical capacity Chadwick was the greatest, in the character of his mind, in the machine-like simplicity of his ideas
and the inexhaustible fertility of his applications, the most
typical of the Benthamites. Napoleon III once asked him
what he thought of his improvements in Paris. "Sir," he
answered, "it was said of Augustus that he found Rome brick
and left it marble. May it be said of you that you found
Paris stinking and left it sweet." It might stand for Chadwick's epitaph. He found England stinking. If he did not
leave it sweet, the fault was certainly not his. Through the
Poor Law Commission, the Benthamite formula—inquiry,
legislation, execution, inspection, and report—was incorporated in our working constitution. It was rounded off by
the invention of the Public Audit and the Grant-in-aid to
tighten central control and stimulate local activity. But the
corresponding formula for unofficial effort—information,
agitation, the parent society, the local branch, the picture,[13]
and the handbill—had been discovered by the Evangelicals
and humanitarians in their warfare against slavery, and by
them it was imported to the Chartists[14] and the Free Trade
League.

The Evangelical and Utilitarian movements both rested
on a body of doctrine which to question was impious or

[13] For example, the fine colour prints by Smith after Morland, of
the shipwrecked crew entertained by natives, whom they return to
carry into slavery.

[14] [The first national working-class movement in Britain, Chartism
wanted to extend the 1832 Reform Bill to gain political representation
for labor. The People's Charter of 1838 presented six demands: universal manhood suffrage, secret ballot, annual parliaments, equal
electoral districts, no property qualifications for House of Commons
and payment of members. Considered the radical threat of the "hungry forties," Chartism faded away after 1843, probably because prosperity had arrived.—Ed.]

irrational; in both cases the doctrine was the reflection of an exceptional experience, the religious experience of a nation undergoing a moral revival, its social experience during a revolution in the methods of production; and in both cases a larger view was certain to show that neither was a more than provisional synthesis. In the meantime they furnished England with a code and a great company of interpreters: with their almost Genevan rigour, and almost Latin clarity, they imposed themselves like foreign task-masters on the large, ironic English mind, and their great doctrines were all too readily snipped into texts for the guidance of those who did not wish to think at all, and the repression of those who wished to think for themselves, into Cant for Practical Men and Cant for Serious Men. Finally, they were alike in this, that each imparted its peculiar virtue: the Evangelicals their zeal for holiness, the Utilitarians their faith in reason, to the movements, even to the reactions which sprang out of them, to Tractarians and Agnostics who denied their introspective ethic, to Tories, and Socialists who challenged their conception of the competitive State.

Kitson Clark suggests a division of Queen Victoria's reign (1837-1901) into three periods: *early*, 1830's and '40's, characterized by depression, unrest and much reform; *mid*, from roughly 1846 to 1866, characterized by prosperity, complacency and a lull in reform; *late*, starting with the second Reform Bill of 1867 and continuing through the great depression of 1873 to the end of the century, characterized by even more drastic changes than in the *early* period.

Kitson Clark is revisionist, in that he questions the doctrinaire image of the age that has emerged from nineteenth-century political battles—particularly from the hostility to industrialism, capitalism and the middle class. Reminding us that the enormous increase in the population of western Europe preceded industrialization, he makes us realize how much worse the hardships of the early nineteenth century would have been without industrialism. The brutality of the first entrepreneurs, he says, was not caused by industrialism; it was inherited from the past. But the nineteenth century had the means of discovering atrocities and the humanitarian capacity to react with indignation.

G. KITSON CLARK

THE MAKING OF VICTORIAN ENGLAND

I

Progress and Survival in Victorian England

1848 is on the eve of my chosen period [mid-Victorian], and the situation in that year makes it evident that at least part of the legacy of the past to Victorian England is deeply seated social discontent and the thrust of an unsatisfied demand for change. Two years before there had been the great Liberal victory of the repeal of the Corn Laws. It is true that during 1848 it became clear that the Chartist agitation was in obvious dissolution, but to a reasonable reformer that was an advantage for it meant that the claim to change could be pressed without being compromised by futile appeals to violence and the distractions of social disorders. Therefore a man standing on the threshold of the new age might well have been pardoned for thinking that the work of fundamental change must now go swiftly forward, that the citadel of privilege would soon fall and the disinherited classes enter to take their rightful places in the community.

This was what John Bright expected in 1848. But in the sequel he was mistaken. The new bill for Parliamentary reform, the real Reform Bill, for which Bright passionately hoped in 1848, did not come till 1867, and even then it was a very imperfect instrument for reform. After 1848 the classes which had flourished and monopolized power under the old régime showed no intention to retreat from a world in which they should have been anachronisms. In fact, after 1848 their position was stronger than it had been before, for they had abandoned what was indefensible in their position and retained what was material for their power. It would have been impossible to have defended for much longer the palpable

G. Kitson Clark, THE MAKING OF VICTORIAN ENGLAND (Cambridge, Mass.: Harvard University Press, 1962), pp. 42-58, 64, 88-97. Reprinted by permission of the publisher, copyright 1962 by G. Kitson Clark. See also Elie Halévy, *A History of the English People in the Nineteenth Century*, tr. E. I. Watkin and D. A. Barker, 6 vols. (New York, 1961).

absurdities of the electoral system that had existed before 1830; what had taken its place was more tolerable and yet left the controlling power where it had ever been. The hatred of the Corn Laws had proved an effective rallying point for the enemies of the aristocracy, but the Corn Laws had been repealed, the forces that had mustered on that point were dissipated, and yet the aristocracy had in general retained, indeed they were increasing, their wealth.

So in the middle of the nineteenth century, instead of a period of rapidly accelerating reform there seems to be a lull, a centre of indifference, an interlude of relative quiescence and indecision between the political activities of the first half of the century and the even more drastic changes that marked its close. Reforms for which men had clamoured were left incomplete or not passed at all, though some of them were debated often enough. The Dissenters had got rid of the Test and Corporation Acts in 1828, and in 1836 had been relieved of their need to be married in the parish church, but they still remained till after 1867 subject to Church Rates, they still could not secure burial with their own rites in the parish churchyard and though in the fifties they gained the right to take degrees at Oxford and Cambridge it was not till 1871 that all posts and prizes at the older universities were opened to them. Other reforms which had been pressed in the thirties were not conceded till after 1867. Vote by ballot at Parliamentary elections was not imposed by law till 1872. Flogging remained a peacetime punishment in the Army till 1868. The sale of commissions in the Army had been a standing abuse the dreadful results of which were evident in the Crimea, but it was not abolished till 1871. Violent attacks had for long been made on the recruitment of the Civil Service by aristocratic or political nomination, and the cure, entry by competitive examination, was proposed by the Trevelyan-Northcote report in 1854, but this expedient was not generally used for the Home Civil Service till after 1870.

This period of indecision and delay in the middle of this century of progress and growth had serious results. Probably the most serious loss of opportunity was as ever in Ireland. In his last ministry Peel had tried to get to the root of the Irish troubles, he had appointed the Devon Commission to deal with the basic problem of Irish land tenure and he had attacked the problem of Irish Education; then there had come the tragedy of the potato famine, and Peel's energies were diverted. The sequel was disastrous. In the period after the famine years of 1845-47, when Ireland at least enjoyed the peace of exhaustion and in due course some prosperity, nothing was done, no other statesman turned to the problems of Ireland with the resolution which Peel had shown until his pupil Gladstone took up the matter in 1868, and then nemesis was very near at hand. Only a little less disastrous was the neglect of public education. As sometimes seems to be forgotten, there was a system of public education in England in the middle of the nineteenth century, through the agency of the religious societies, and the general standard of literacy was far higher than it sometimes seems to be believed; but taking England for what she was, the richest and in some ways the most liberal country in Europe, compared to what was provided in Prussia, in Switzerland or in France, what educational facilities were provided for the mass of the people in England were disastrously meagre and poor. It is true that development was impeded by the difficult problem of religious education and the quarrels of the Church, but that problem existed in most countries and it seems to be unquestionable that a determined attack on the problem could have achieved something better for public secondary education and an elementary school for every child before 1870.

There is something of the same pattern in the development of the problem of public health. This was of the greatest importance, for the sanitary condition of the great towns could only be made tolerable by strenuous efforts on the part of the public authorities, otherwise they would remain places where reasonable human lives could not be lived. The great pioneer in this matter was Edwin Chadwick, the secretary of the Poor Law Commission, whose reports awakened the public mind on the subject. In 1848 the first general public health Act was passed under which a Board of Health was set up upon which Chadwick and Lord Shaftesbury served. They did good work, but they excited opposition, and in 1854 both Shaftesbury and Chadwick were driven from their position. The Board of Health itself was abolished in 1858. As a matter of fact, the effects of these actions were less serious than they might appear to be, for in these middle years, as will be shown, the initiative in matters of public health was largely taken up by enlightened local authorities. Indeed, in judging this middle period it is important to remember how far in such matters as social reform the effective action was still, and by prevailing theory ought to have been, in private hands, or, if public action were needed, localized in scope, the result of the initiative not of a ministry nor of the legislature but of those directly concerned. Nevertheless, the ineffectiveness of Parliament in this middle period is very remarkable, as is also the failure of the concerted forces of Liberalism to dispossess the old rulers of the land. This had two results. In the Victorian mixture, in which progress and liberalism are such important elements, conservatism and the survival of habits, types of human being and institution from earlier, and one might have thought irrelevant, centuries remain important also. The other result was that when the change did come what developed in the end was very different from what the idealists of the first half of the century had shaped in their dreams.

Obviously such frustrations, such delays and such hesitations on the part of Parliament require explanation; and for the hesitations of Parliament at least there is a comparatively simple explanation. Unfortunately for itself this period in the middle of the nineteenth century was the golden age of the private member of the House of Commons. The House of Commons now controlled the legislation of the country, the working of government and the lives of ministries, but there was at the moment no power which could adequately control the members of the House of Commons. In the eighteenth century the members of the House of Commons had been controlled by the power of patronage and the authority of the Crown, in the late nineteenth century and in the twentieth century the Commons were to be kept under discipline by party. Immediately after the Reform Bill there had been a two-party system which closely resembled what was to come, but when Peel repealed the Corn Laws he broke the Conservative party into two. The larger section of it came to be led by Lord Derby and Disraeli, and remained the best organized party in the country; but it was only a fragment and never large enough in these middle years to obtain a majority in the House of Commons and maintain a government. The other section, the immediate followers of Peel, simply added to the number of independent groups that served to confuse politics. On the other side there could not be said to be a coherent Whig or Liberal party. There was usually a Whig Government supported by the traditional apparatus of Whips probably attached to the person of the Prime Minister, but beyond their influence was a shifting mass of individuals or of independent groups like the Peelites or the Manchester men,[1] who might or might not support the Government and its measures.

The result was politics without effective discipline and therefore politics without effective purpose. The House could debate a matter, re-debate it and debate it again and never get anywhere; so it debated Parliamentary reform, so it debated public education. The policy of the ministry, and too often its life, were at the mercy of the whim of the House of Commons. Between 1850 and 1860 there were no less than six different administrations, called into existence to meet Parliamentary necessities and ending their lives because dismissed by the House of Commons sometimes for reasons which would appear to us today to be trivial enough.

If politics were in this condition, small wonder that action was hampered and that reform fell into arrear. That however only throws the question back one stage: why were politics in this condition? An explanation of a situation such as this, which refers solely to the behaviour of politicians or the nature of the organizations which they operate, is likely to be a superficial, or at least a partial, explanation. What politicians do at a particular period is likely to be in part the result of the action of forces operating beyond the control, and normally beyond the knowledge, of the politically conscious, but which provide the conditions under which they act. In many periods a rather difficult and rather complicated social analysis is necessary to discover what these forces may be, though when they are discovered they seem to shew how superficial and unreal is the historical work which explains the course of events entirely in the terms of the day-to-day events which are thrown up in the ordinary commerce of politics. But in this case an explanation of the situation has already suggested itself which is neither abstruse or remote. This interlude was the result of the anodyne of prosperity. Chartism had been the politics of suffering and despair, but now large sections of the working classes were enjoying an improvement of their conditions and a modicum of hope. The Anti-Corn Law League had been to a large extent the product of the depression of the late thirties and early forties, but that depression was slipping back into history. Even in Ireland after the tremendous clearance of the famine there was probably for a fleeting moment less distress than there had been for years. Most important of all, the prosperity of these middle years was shared by industry and agriculture,

[1] [The Free-Trade party had its headquarters in Manchester.—Ed.]

so that politics were not disturbed by the discontent of the landed interest as they had been before 1836, or by the warfare between agriculture and industry as they had been between 1838 and 1846. In fact, there was a relaxation of tension, and the passions and the insistent needs that had given shape and direction to politics had for a season lost their strength.

This did not mean that the nature of the country was fundamentally altered or that any of the forces which had made for change had been eliminated. This is a period of hesitations and confusions but not of reaction; men still believed in progress and reform, they had no desire to go back to the old régime, though they sometimes tolerated strange survivals from the eighteenth century as a matter of custom or because they did not see how to remove them. The tone of the country seems to have been liberal, probably more definitely and generally liberal than when Peel wrote to Croker [about the new liberal tone—Ed.], thirty years before. The Governments of the period normally reflected this condition; they were normally Whig, with a strong liberal tincture, the Conservatives never gained a majority in the House of Commons till 1874. There was no going back on protection, the foreign policy of the country was in its way liberal, and in the House of Commons members were prepared to debate liberal reforms, if, too often, there was not enough political discipline, or common resolution, available to secure that they were passed into law.

But even outside the House of Commons the acceptance of liberal principles did not in the third quarter of the century always carry with it an urgent desire for drastic change. Probably at that time most intelligent and educated men held beliefs which may be called liberal, beliefs in the right to freedom, the virtue of mutual toleration and in the effective powers of reason and common sense. For some men the natural corollaries of those beliefs were the promotion of an effective programme of Radical reform, the abolition of the special privileges of the established Church, or of any other way in which the State gave preference to any particular opinion, and the extension of the franchise to anyone who could use it. Such indeed was the creed which John Stuart Mill expounded with great lucidity and all the force of a deeply sincere man with unusually intense emotions. But in the middle of the century there were a good many educated men with generally liberal principles who did not follow him.

In particular there were what may be called liberal realists, men like Anthony Trollope, Walter Bagehot or James Fitz-James Stephen and the other contributors to the *Saturday Review,* who accepted many basic liberal principles but were not always altogether convinced of the value or safety of popular democratic government. Such men would often be naturally on the liberal side in politics for they would feel no temptation to share the Conservative benches with the well-fed cohorts of the country gentry. They would wish to further administrative reform, fiscal reform or legal reform; but they would feel no reason to welcome the probable results of the next extension of the franchise, if that was to mean the submergence of the educated few beneath the confused and ill-considered rule of the uneducated many.

In the circumstances of the middle of the nineteenth century such an attitude was not unnatural. Except for the American system, which seemed to possess some very unattractive characteristics, and for France during brief and dangerous periods of revolution, there was little experience of the working of democratic government, and the prospect at home was not encouraging. What was most popular in the British form of government, the electoral system in urban constituencies, was often the most unpleasant and corrupt part of it, as Thackeray, Trollope and Bagehot all found to their cost when they tried unsuccessfully to get into Parliament. Indeed, it was to electoral facts and to popular habits of which many of his fellow-members in the House of Commons must have been acutely conscious that Robert Lowe appealed when opposing the Reform Bill of 1866. No doubt there was much to be said against the system of government that existed in Britain in the middle of the nineteenth century; it gave too much power to the landed gentry, it gave too much power to the aristocracy; but it was reasonably liberal, it was government by debate in which educated opinion played its part, and an intelligent man might well consider matters very seriously before he became anxious to change all this for the clumsy tyranny which seemed very likely to result from the direct rule of the people.

Such an attitude of mind did not promise any but the most minor changes in the political system, it certainly held out no expectation that some force would be introduced which would be strong enough to break the spell of indecision and set matters moving again, and the men who inclined to it were men of such intellectual force that they are apt to conceal

from us the sources from which an impulse to change might
come; for it is difficult not to see mid-nineteenth-century
England through their eyes—through the eyes of Trollope
in his political novels, and particularly through the eyes of
Walter Bagehot in the terms of what is still the best book
on the English Constitution that has yet been written. Nothing could be better than the humane and brilliant realism of
Bagehot's ringside account of Parliamentary life, and the
temptation is to believe that nothing more is to be learnt
about the political system of Britain in the middle of the
nineteenth century; so clear is the view that it is easy to
forget how close is the horizon he has accepted. Yet, in fact,
beyond Bagehot's field of vision, in the constituencies and
among the unenfranchised, forces were there gathering head
while he was yet writing which would make very drastic
differences to the game that was being played so prettily at
Westminster.

They were possibly not forces which he and those like him
found it easy to understand or even to detect. It may not
have been easy for those whose eyes were used to the brightly
lit professional and Parliamentary world of London to see the
growth of new classes in the provinces or to understand the
social and economic needs which those classes were likely to
propose to the body politic, and even where the eye could see
it is possible that the mind could not assess the importance of
what was seen because of a complete incapacity to sympathize. To Bagehot, very reasonably, the most satisfactory
result of political evolution was government by discussion.[2]
Government by discussion seems to imply the civilized exchange of reasonable views in language which one educated
man might use to another. But many of the contributions to
public discussion in the middle of the nineteenth century did
not seem to be couched in such language, many particularly
of the contributions of the leaders of nonconformity. They
seemed to be inflated and rhetorical, heavy with clichés, often
grossly sentimental with an irresistible tendency towards
bathos. Against this the clear masculine intelligence of the
educated mid-Victorian reacted strongly; what they thought
about it can still be read in the trenchant pages of the *Saturday Review,* or in the contemptuous language with which
Matthew Arnold describes the modes of thought of the
Philistines. Whether these attacks were altogether fair could
only be decided after a careful study of the words of the men

[2] See W. Bagehot, *Physics and Politics* (London, 1906), pp. 156-204.

they scarified, which few but the most devoted students are ever likely to undertake. Nor is it necessary to do this in order to understand the mistake of which those who made them were likely to have been guilty, for it is one that is very often made by intelligent and highly educated men. They underestimate the force and significance of opinions, which are habitually framed in terms which seem to them to be absurd, and by so doing they neglect what are going to be the springs of power.

But in the years immediately after 1850 the possibility of any considerable force gathering head in the constituencies or among the disenfranchised was remote; indeed for most of the period between 1846 and 1866 the description of the English Constitution in Bagehot's book suffices. The people he does not describe had not enough unity of purpose or sense of urgency to intrude often into the game at Westminster. The one point which he does notice about the electorate remains for most of the period probably the most important point. He noticed that it was to a curious extent a "deferential" electorate, and this was true; the most important single political fact in Britain in the middle of the century was the power of the old proprietary classes entrenched in the traditional structure of the countryside, protected by the habit of deference on the part of many sections of the community and using for their own purposes many of the institutions of the State. Britain was Liberal because many of the nobility were Liberal, or knew that they ought to work with Liberals, but it was not a Liberalism that promised an early change in the kind of people who controlled the sinews of power. The pre-revolutionary rulers of the country were still stronger than any force that might try to dispossess them.

There is something of a parallel in the history of Europe. In 1848 the forces of Liberalism, nationalism, romanticism and democracy boiled over, but after a sharp struggle the forces of order and tradition proved to be strong enough to contain the revolutions. As the result during these middle years many political movements were frustrated and dissipated, many emergent nations remained in chains. Italy was neither liberated nor united, Poland, Bohemia and Hungary could not win their freedom, and further east Christian nations still remained under the Turk. On the other hand the Austrian Empire was reprieved, German liberalism failed and German nationalism began to make its dangerous alliance with the power of Prussia. Even in France, the country which was the natural leader of the Liberal forces of Europe, the revolution which started in 1848 ended in the Second Empire—that strange compromise between what claimed to be liberal and democratic and what was certainly authoritarian supported uneasily by what was traditional. Though there were striking differences, the situation in France in the third quarter probably resembled that in Britain more closely than did that of any other great European power. Many Englishmen felt a stronger affinity for the Germans, but German forms of government and society were often more remote from ours than was generally realized, and there was much in German nationalism that was misunderstood, indeed unknown, in England. Britain and France were the two great liberal powers on this side of the Atlantic, and in 1854 as such they fought Russia, which appeared at that time to be the strongest reactionary power in Europe. After that Britain wisely contented herself with making a good deal of noise from the safe side of the touch-line, but the Emperor thought it to be necessary to fight Austria in Italy in 1859, and thereby he destroyed the European balance and opened the way for the Prussian victories of 1866 and 1870. These victories not only destroyed his own régime but they led towards that witches' sabbath in the twentieth century during which so much that was bad, and so much that was good, in Victorian Europe was for ever consumed.

This however raises this difficult question: when did this interlude come to an end and what brought it to an end? Obviously part of the answer has been given. As far as the old Europe is concerned, it was largely brought to an end by war followed by revolution, war largely engineered by the old diplomacy trying to use, or trying to thwart, the power of nationalism. In 1870 the Second Empire went down into irremediable defeat, though the forces that had combined to support it continued to be powerful in the republic of Thiers and MacMahon and were strong enough to be in large part responsible for the Dreyfus case; the rest of Victorian Europe in large part ground itself to pieces between 1914 and 1918. Yet it may be doubted whether, even in the case of Europe, diplomacy and war were the only agents of destruction; certainly they cannot have been so in Britain, where the pattern of change starts sometime before Britain became again fatally involved in the tragedy of Europe.

In fact, as far as politics are concerned in Britain, the

beginning of change can perhaps be seen in the same year as it was in France, in 1859, and by a curious coincidence it was a beginning in which the Italian question played a part. In 1859 Gladstone, partly apparently to enable himself to do what he could for Italy, definitely went over to the Whig-Liberal side in politics and joined Lord Palmerston's administration. The period of Peelite hesitation was over, politics could become simpler and more effective, and what was most important from this time onwards the Cabinet contained in Gladstone one who possessed, uniquely, certain characteristics which gave to him the key to the situation. Gladstone could work with the old ruling classes, with whom he had always passed his life, he was not a Whig but he was connected with them by marriage; he had been trained in what had been the best school for statesmen in nineteenth-century English history, Peel's Conservative administration of 1841-46, and yet by 1859 his opinions were definitely liberal, indeed, for that period, radical. Most important of all, however, for the task which history had set him, he was developing a way of speaking that could move the hearts of men who were entirely beyond what might be deemed at that time to be educated circles, a power which possibly evinced itself in him for the first time in his visit to Newcastle in 1862.[3] At first, after 1859 there straddled right across the path of Gladstone the Prime Minister Lord Palmerston, who maintained the old Whig compromise with surprising vigour into what seemed likely to be an indefinitely prolonged old age. In 1865, however, it was proved against all expectation that Lord Palmerston was in fact mortal, Lord John Russell succeeded him as Prime Minister with Gladstone as his chief lieutenant and they produced the Reform Bill of 1866. This did not pass, but was followed by the Conservative Bill of 1867 which did, and that in turn was followed by the election of 1868 which brought Gladstone back into power as Prime Minister himself, this time at the head of what has been reasonably called the first truly Liberal administration.[4]

A sense of purpose had returned and with it effective party

[3] For the significance of the Newcastle visit, see Stuart J. Reid, *Memoirs of Sir Wemys Reid 1842-1885* (London, 1905), pp. 54-57.

[4] See *1859: Entering an Age of Crisis,* edited by Philip Appleman, William A. Madden, Michael Wolff (Bloomington, Ind., 1959), particularly pp. 115-96 for Gladstone. W. E. Williams, *The Rise of Gladstone (1859-68)* (Cambridge, 1934). Sir Philip Magnus, *Gladstone: A Biography* (London, 1954), pp. 141-95.

politics. Gladstone passed his long list of overdue reforms and then the Conservatives won the next general election in 1874, thereby producing the first Conservative majority in the House of Commons since the majority returned in 1841 to support Robert Peel. A new epoch had begun. In 1872 Walter Bagehot, in the introduction to the second edition of his *English Constitution* compared the state of affairs in that year with what it had been in the year 1865 and 1866, which was what he had originally described, and he found the difference very striking indeed. "A new world," said he, "has arisen which is not as the old world; and," he added, "we naturally ascribe the change to the Reform Act. But this is a complete mistake. If there had been no Reform Act at all there would, nevertheless, have been a great change in English politics."[5] He did not, as a matter of fact, mean by that that the Reform Act of 1867 had made no difference at all to the kind of House of Commons elected in 1868, on the contrary he believed that the names of the members returned to the new House suggested that the Act of 1867 was completing the work of 1832 and was turning an aristocracy into a plutocracy. There is little means of knowing how exact or how casual his calculations were; later analyses seem to suggest they cannot have been conclusive. What was remarkable about that election was the number of members returned who were prepared to disestablish the Church, a fact which he does not mention. But he was probably completely justified when he said that the change which had taken place in politics was not to be ascribed to the Act of 1867.

The Reform Act of 1867 is an important Act, it enfranchised a good many new voters in the boroughs, and more in the counties than are usually credited to it. In many of the boroughs the new voters were working men, though in some boroughs they seem to have been mainly shopkeepers, clerks, and the like—classes already well represented in the electorate. These large additions to the size of urban constituencies were to have important results for the development of party organization and, in certain cases, on the type of Liberal returned to the House. This, however, was not likely to make an immediate change in the course of politics. To secure an immediate political result it is not enough to increase the number of voters, it is necessary so to distribute them that they can control an increased number of seats.

Nothing is effected if the numbers voting in a radical majority in an already radical constituency is increased by many thousands, if the members so returned can still be out-voted by the representatives of a much smaller constituency. The amount of redistribution and disenfranchisement effected at the time of the Act of 1867 was not decisive. In 1867 and 1868, 17 boroughs lost their members entirely, 4 of them for gross corruption. Thirty-five members were taken from other English boroughs, but 87 boroughs with approximately less than 2,000 electors apiece still returned 105 members, 35 of these had in fact less than approximately 1,000 electors.[6] Some of the surviving boroughs were certainly collectors' pieces for connoisseurs in the more picturesque phases of electoral history, but they had little else to commend them. For instance, Bridgewater and Beverley were notorious for their corruption even in mid-nineteenth-century England. In 1866 Bagehot had been the inevitably unsuccessful Liberal candidate for Bridgewater, in 1868 Anthony Trollope was foolish enough to stand for Beverley. He did not of course get in, it was his money not his person they wanted, but he described the matter afterwards in his novel *Ralph the Heir*, so the effort was not entirely wasted. Both Bridgewater and Beverley were spared by the Act of 1867, as also were certain very small proprietary boroughs like Calne and Woodstock, the preserves of Lord Lansdowne and the Duke of Marlborough respectively. If, therefore, some very large boroughs had been called into being by the Act, there were plenty of others of another sort to balance them when it came to a division in the House of Commons. Meanwhile the countryside was still carefully sealed off from the town and the county franchise carefully limited so that there should be no dangerous infiltration of new voters to disturb the country gentleman's control of his shire.[7]

An Act so devised was not likely to work an immediate political revolution. If as Bagehot asserted a new world had come into existence by 1872, if, as he declared, by that time laws were being passed which would have been unthinkable five years before, then the Reform Act of 1867 can only have been in very small part the cause. Indeed, for the passage

---

[6] I owe these figures to Mr. F. B. Smith of Trinity College, Cambridge. It should be pointed out that it is not always easy to find out how many electors had been enfranchised in a particular borough.

[7] For the results of the Act of 1867, see H. J. Hanham, *Elections and Party Management. Politics in the time of Disraeli and Gladstone* (London, 1959) *passim*. I have also gained much knowledge from Mr. Hanham's unpublished thesis.

of one important Act the Reform Act of 1867 can have been in no way responsible and that was the Reform Act itself, passed after sixteen years' hesitation in apparently such a hurry that the minister in charge, Disraeli, seems not to have understood all its clauses. If, therefore, there had been a change, and it seems there had been a change, it is necessary to look beyond the Act of 1867 to find the explanation. Bagehot characteristically looked inwards to the game at Westminster. He said that there had been a change of generation, that certain key personalities had died or retired and so the face of politics had changed. There is probably something in this; there is no doubt that the death of Palmerston made a considerable difference, but there is as little doubt that as an explanation it is incomplete. It is not to be conceived that the death of one old man or of several old men was the sole motive cause in the profound change in politics which Bagehot himself had noticed. In fact, the purely political explanation is again unsatisfactory. The behaviour and fortunes of politicians have no doubt very important results on the course of events, but the situations they have to handle, the forces they must strive to direct must to a very large extent be not of their making, but rather the result of broader movements in the community—social, economic, spiritual—which lie outside the game of politics. Indeed, the nature of these movements does not only affect the fortunes of the statesmen involved: it may mould the statesman himself. Much has been written about the various men and events that influenced Gladstone's mind in the critical ten years between 1858 and 1868, but there is one influence that is not often mentioned though in all probability it was as potent with him as anything else, it was the influence of the popular audiences which were responsive to him. Indeed, study of his opinions from now onwards suggests that these people had an increasing effect on the ways he thought. It was this characteristic that made him seem to be a renegade from the educated classes.

If this be so, an explanation of what Gladstone said and thought must be sought not only in the history of Gladstone's mind but also in the social history which explains the nature of the crowds who came to hear him and were prepared to applaud certain particular statements in a speech and to enjoy the way in which he said them. But there are other things which require explanation in the political history of this period. There is the Liberal victory of 1868. It cannot, as has been seen, be wholly put down to the changes made by the Reform Act of 1867, the old naïve statement that the "new electors were grateful to Mr. Gladstone" does not seem to survive a detailed analysis of what happened in particular constituencies. There are indeed signs of a change in earlier elections but 1868 is obviously a critical election, significant not only for the size of the Liberal victory but also for the type of Liberals returned, and even more significant for the phase of politics it seems to have initiated.

What in fact requires an explanation is twenty years of political revolution starting in 1866, and since this is the sequel of the twenty years between 1846 and 1866 it is tempting to give an explanation which is the sequel of the explanation given of the lull in politics in that earlier period. In the middle of the nineteenth century it has been suggested that tensions relaxed because of the development of general prosperity in this period, possibly tension reappeared because that prosperity got less. Probably, again, there is something in this suggestion. In about 1873 what is called the great depression may be said to have started; there is controversy about its nature, but certainly about this time the old confident industrial predominance was challenged and the old unbounded optimism began to disappear. More serious still, after 1874 a series of devastating blows struck British agriculture, starting with those sections of it which were primarily dependent on the price of corn. There is little doubt that the disasters to agriculture affected the structure of politics. The stability of the mid-Victorian period had in part rested upon the balance of prosperity between industry and agriculture. After 1874 that balance was permanently upset, for what happened to agriculture was more serious and more lasting in its results than any set-back which commerce or industry suffered, and the disastrous conditions in the countryside helped to shake the aristocratic control of the county constituencies with results evident in the general elections of 1880 and 1885.

But any study of conditions in the counties makes it clear that the disasters to agriculture were not the only cause of the crumbling away of the political power of many of the landowners, and it is hard to see in what ways the great depression affected the political history of towns. It may have left some members of the middle class with inflated demands on life and diminished incomes to meet them, but it is difficult to see clearly what effect that would have upon their politics, it was not likely to make them more radical; and the general effect of the depression on working-class prosperity as a whole is much more doubtful. There seems indeed to be evidence that considerable sections of the people were enjoying a rising standard of life. But in any case the political change in the towns seems to start too early to be attributed to a breakdown of prosperity. There are notable signs of change in the general election of 1868, in years when things on the whole were going well.

Moreover, if what happened in and after 1868 is to be attributed to some important change having taken place over large enough areas of the country to affect the course of politics, it cannot be a change that happened overnight; it must be something the origins of which can be traced back to some point much earlier in the century. But if that is possible, it is obviously necessary to look more carefully at the period between 1850 and 1866. It may be a period of social peace, and apparently of political stagnation, but is it possible that all the time powerful spiritual and social forces were at work under the surface which were changing the structure of society and preparing the way for the more obvious changes of the last thirty years or so of the nineteenth century? Perhaps one may be too ready to believe that social disturbances are the best evidence of radical social developments, that broken water is the only sign that the current is moving fast. However, to detect such changes it must obviously be necessary to consider the community in England in that period much more closely than I have yet done and perhaps to try to disregard a little that self-conscious, self-confident minority who seem to have made history and certainly have normally written it, whose voices, unless we are careful, are the only ones we are likely to hear from the past. . . .

The struggle for political progress was conscious, its advocates were struggling for an object the nature of which they fully understood, and the advocates for conservatism often knew what they were doing and what it was they feared; the apostles of religion knew what they desired, so did the humanitarians. But there were also at work in the country blind forces of great power, the agents for which were not directed or controlled by any conception of the results of their actions for humanity in general. These forces are very significant, in fact two of them must be of primary consideration in any assessment of the Victorian situation for they are of basic importance in every part of it; they are the nineteenth-century increase in the population and the nineteenth-century increase in the powers of production. . . .

II

The New Industry and the New State

There were . . . good reasons for two sharply contested views about the Industrial Revolution in the early 1840's. On the one hand there were those who looked at the wonderful progress that had taken place since the beginning of the century and felt that if only the power that had done these great things could be liberated from the obstacles placed upon it by a stupid protectionist system, fit instrument of a selfish and parasitic aristocracy, particularly if the Corn Laws could be repealed, it would surely recover its old force and bring almost illimitable advantages to all humanity. On the other hand the Chartist, or the Tory, conscious of the revelations of the commissions of enquiry on child labour, repelled by the ugliness and inhumanity of the factory districts at any time and surveying the stricken field of Britain in the black depression that prevailed, not unreasonably took another view. Many of them felt that something evil had intruded itself into British life, something not only avaricious and cruel but dangerously reckless and unreliable as well. Many joined in a bitter attack on the mill owners, and even moderate men, who were not disposed to speak violently, read a very serious warning in what had happened.

For many men could not accept the statement that the depression had been caused by the obstruction of the Corn Laws. The Corn Laws were not new, they had been in operation all through the period of mounting prosperity; a more likely cause might well be the speculative activities of the manufacturers themselves. Trusting to the infinite possibilities of an expanding market, factory after factory had been built each equipped with ever more potent machinery. The result of this was to flood the markets of the world with British goods and to involve the manufacturers in cut-throat competition, to make them reduce the price of goods below what could possibly be remunerative and to bring down wages below starvation point. The end of this process was a situation in which the markets of the world had become glutted with unsaleable produce. Many of the manufacturers had been ruined, and the men and women they had employed reduced to unemployment and starvation or the tender mer-

cies of the Poor Law bastilles,[1] which a thoughtful Whig
Government, with the support of the factory owners, had
provided for them.

Taken with what other matter could be put on the charge
sheet it was a formidable indictment and it was natural that a
good many men should be impressed by it, as natural in fact
as that others should be impressed by the tremendous poten-
tialities of the new machines. The conflict of views is reflected
in much that was written and spoken in the great battle over
the Corn Laws and also in the controversy which seemed very
important to men at the time but which has been rather
neglected by historians, the controversy over the question
whether the development of machinery brought advantage
or disaster to mankind. It was a conflict which men on both
sides were inclined to see in moral terms, as is normally
the case with conflicts which are emotional and personal and
likely to have an outlet in politics, for it is easier in such
cases to conceive that an evil has been caused by the mis-
behaviour of people you know and dislike than that it is the
result of impersonal historical forces which possibly no man
can control.

The desire to assign personal responsibilities normally leads
to a dangerous oversimplification of issues and it would have
been as well if in due course so important a problem as the
results of the Industrial Revolution could have been separated
from its emotional context and more cooly and more objectively considered. This, however, was not likely to happen,
for though the recovery of the fifties relieved many of the
tensions of the forties, the issues that had been raised did not
disappear. There remained much that was very wrong in the
heart of the great cities, and in the last twenty years of the
nineteenth century they began increasingly to challenge the
public conscience. Nor did the conflict between capital and
labour disappear. On the contrary, after a period of relative
quiescence it became more sharp, more important, more
effectively pressed by better organized trade unions and became the reason for the existence of a new political party.
All this affected the way men thought about the Industrial
Revolution. The growth of a city like Manchester was clearly
associated with the Industrial Revolution and therefore it was
felt that its slums had been created in all their horror by the

---

[1] [The New Poor Law of 1834 abolished relief at home and required
paupers to live in workhouses. In *Past and Present*, Carlyle attacks
"Poor-Law Prisons . . . the workhouse Bastille."—Ed.]

Industrial Revolution, the promoters of which ought to bear full responsibility for them. "Industrialism," undefined or only vaguely defined, and the "Industrial Revolution" were the creations and the tools of "capitalism" and must share the same condemnation. As a result of this tendency the whole conception of the Industrial Revolution began to change, men began to think less and less of the usefulness and importance to mankind of its inventions, or of the human genius displayed in their development, and to consider it almost wholly as if it were an event in the sphere of morals to be judged, and condemned, according to the supposed motives of those who promoted it.[2]

Whatever truth there might be in this view, it has had unfortunate results for historical thought. It oversimplified the diagnosis of what have been the causes of suffering and cruelty in early nineteenth-century Britain and obscured the importance of two factors. One was the inherited tradition of callousness, brutality and degraded conditions which went far back into history, the results of which were now much more obvious because the nineteenth century had opportunities of learning what was going on which were denied to earlier centuries and humanitarians were teaching men to note these things and object to them. The other was the strain resulting from the rapid growth of the population. And apart from that, this view of the Industrial Revolution has suggested that it is easier than in fact it is to dogmatize with certainty about the motives of a large number of people who lived a long time ago and to compare their moral standards with those who lived before or after them. In fact, it is not easy to discern and describe with any confidence the motives of a man about whom there exists a great deal of evidence, and it is much more difficult to rest an argument on the presumed motives of men who have left very little direct record and to compare them satisfactorily with other men in other ages who have probably left behind even less. It would require more evidence than I believe is likely to exist to prove that the Industrial Revolution was caused by the fact that those who promoted it were more callous and ruthless than men who have lived before it happened or since, or perhaps that its conditions caused them to become so.

It is possible that the fast-developing conditions of the

[2] For a discussion of the various ways of looking at the Industrial Revolution, see R. M. Hartwell, *The Journal of Economic History*, "Interpretations of the Industrial Revolution in England: a Methodological Inquiry," Vol. XIX, No. 2 (New York, June 1959), 229-49.

nineteenth century increased the opportunities for men on the make, themselves the product of harsh conditions, to indulge in such abuses as payment of wages in truck and to exploit cruelly those who worked for them, particularly when they were relatively defenceless women and children; it is possible that those conditions increased their temptation to do so. It is possible that the development of the factory system by dividing the great mill owner or capitalist from the artisan destroyed a natural sympathy which had existed between the small master and the man who worked at his elbow. But it is well to remember that probably the worst abused child labour in the country was that of the climbing boys, the wretched children apprenticed to chimney sweeps, small masters who were only too close to those they employed for they beat them when they would not go up flues in which they might be suffocated; or that the unhappy sempstresses, like the one celebrated in Tom Hood's "Song of a Shirt," also seemed to have been normally working for small-scale employers who were not mechanized at all. Even in the factories and mines the children were often not directly employed by the factory owner but by the worker himself, while some of the worst cruelties were inflicted by the overseer. This is not said to deny the responsibility of the factory owners, but it may suggest a reflection which any knowledge of the conditions of the time confirms, that neither the possession of capital nor the extensive use of machines was needed to make men callous and brutal in the early nineteenth century. Too many of them were like that by nature and had been so from time out of mind.

However, the worst result of the attempt to judge the Industrial Revolution primarily from a moral standpoint is that it deflects attention from what is after all the most important question, which is not a question of motive but of results. What matters most is the result of these developments in mechanization on the life which was offered to contemporary men and women. In fact, there can be little doubt that in very many cases these results were beneficial, sometimes immediately, sometimes ultimately. There is certainly a reasonably sharp controversy among experts whether in general real wages improved in the first half of the century. To one who is in no way an expert it would appear to be a controversy which it is not going to be easy to resolve, especially in so far as it refers to the actual lives of particular groups of workers. For one thing not enough would seem to be known about retail prices, which for those who live in the back streets of towns are probably the only significant prices. Moreover, there seems to be a doubt as to how frequently and how continuously what might be deemed to be the standard rates of wages were actually earned.[3] If, however, this issue is to be made a touchstone to test whether in fact the Industrial Revolution benefited or harmed humanity, another question must be asked even though it is one which cannot be answered. What would have happened to the wages of large sections of the working class if there had been no Industrial Revolution? This question should not only refer to those whose special skills and fortunate positions gave them peculiar opportunities to benefit by the Industrial Revolution, but also to humbler unskilled workers who got jobs for whom otherwise, as far as can be seen, there would have been no employment. What would have happened for instance to the Irish immigrant if there had been no railways to construct? Indeed this question might as well be extended over the whole century; it seems to be agreed by most people that in the second half of the century there was a general or continuous advance in real wages, it might be asked whether there would have been any chance of this if there had been no mechanization and industrialization on the scale achieved in the early nineteenth century. The answer here surely is No.

Nor did the Industrial Revolution only benefit the working classes as wage earners, it benefited them as consumers also. As the century went forward it produced even for poor people, if they had any money to spend at all, goods in a profusion and a variety which would have been beyond men's wildest expectations in earlier ages. The hastiness and carelessness of the manufacture of so much that was put on the market, the poorness in design, materials and workmanship which are often so painfully evident in what has survived, the silliness of a great deal of the reading matter which the new steam presses ran off, the obvious discomforts of a cheap railway excursion, all these considerations may make one forget how much was being added to the richness of

---

[3] On this see Clapham, *An Economic History of Great Britain. The Early Railway Age*, pp. 536-602. T. S. Ashton, *Journal of Economic History* Supplement IX, (September 9, 1949), 19-38. E. J. Hobsbawm, *Economic History Review*, 2nd Series, Vol. 10, No. 1 (1957), 46-48. S. Pollard, *Economic History Review*, 2nd Series, Vol. 11, No. 2 (December 1958), 215-26. R. M. Hartwell, *Economic History Review*, 2nd Series, Vol. 13, No. 3 (April 1961).

life. And when such things as washable clothes and soap are provided for those who would have had in the past little chance for such luxuries, the advantages to health and comfort are incalculable.

Yet none of this establishes the fact that the Industrial Revolution was a benevolent movement designed by far-sighted philanthropists for the good of humanity. It probably should be considered as nearly as void of moral significance as a change in the weather which happens to produce in some years a good harvest; probably the human agents who promoted it were in many cases as innocent of any far-sighted visions for humanity as the human agents who caused the increase in population. It was in fact morally neutral. It was not directed with any certainty to any particular end. It might bring good and might bring evil. Indeed, as men realized from the beginning, it did bring good and did bring evil to different people or to the same people at different times, and if it were to be made safe for humanity its propensities for evil must be brought under control or compensated.

It cannot be said that the attempts to do this were at first strikingly successful. As has been seen, one of the dangers which the new forces at work produced was that of recurrent financial crises producing ruin and widespread distress and unemployment. Even through the period of greatest prosperity men remained aware of this danger, in fact they experienced it in such years as 1847, in 1857 and in 1866. But it cannot be said that they discovered any satisfactory way of dealing with it: probably their understanding of the issues at stake was too limited and their monetary mechanism too clumsy to enable them to do so. Fortunately the buoyancy of the economy in the middle of the century seems to have been always strong enough to pull them out of the difficulties which they encountered. Nor did they prove themselves to be more capable of dealing with the very difficult problem of technological unemployment, the problem of those skilled craftsmen whom new mechanical developments have put out of business. They investigated the lot of the hand-loom weavers at considerable length, but they could do nothing more for them. At first they were almost equally unsuccessful in the attempt to control conditions in the factories and to protect the overworked factory children. Up to 1833 the legislation passed on the subject was largely inoperative and very little was done. Even after 1833, as Lord Shaftesbury was to find, the way of the factory reformer was hard and very frustrating, he had to face excessively bitter opposition and often enough the sickening experience of success being forfeited when it had seemed to be assured.

But the Act of 1833 was a turning-point, not because it gave the factory reformers what they wanted, it certainly did not do that, it was only passed after Shaftesbury's motion for a Ten-Hours Bill had been rejected, but because it contained provision for the appointment of a board of inspectors with executive powers to put into effect and to report on the way it worked. Both functions were important; on the one hand the reports were evidence of the inspectors' growing specialized knowledge of the problem in hand upon which all future legislation was in part necessarily based, on the other hand the discretionary power confided to the inspectors looks forward to the immense delegated powers which were to be given in the twentieth century to ministers to be in fact exercised by civil servants. Indeed, the lesson seems to be this. Though the tremendous power which was being developed by the Industrial Revolution could and did work for the good of humanity, there could be no security that that was what it would do unless it was brought under conscious discipline, and that discipline could only be imposed by the assumption by the public of constantly increasing discretionary powers to be exercised under the direction of experts who would draw upon the growing experience which only work in that particular department of government could give. It was a lesson pregnant with importance for the future.

The same lesson was very soon to be repeated in the history of the cities and towns of Britain in the first half of the nineteenth century. Something has been already said of the flood of humanity which was pouring into them and of the conditions they created when they got there. The force at work here was the increase of population, not the Industrial Revolution. As I have observed, it is often said that the cities of early nineteenth-century Britain were what they were as the result of industrialism, but it is important to think carefully what those words can mean. The condition of nineteenth-century British towns was very largely the result of the incursion of a very large number of poverty-stricken immigrants. Industrialism had not called these people into existence, nor had it made them poor. They were born so. It is not even clear that it was, at least in many cases, industrialism that drew them into the towns. They flocked into non-industrial

towns such as Brighton and they seem in many cases to have
come to the towns for no better reason than that they had nowhere else to go. After all, a town is most likely to be where
the displaced or surplus countryman will end, he is less likely
to find a permanent resting-place in another countryside unless it is an empty one that he can colonize. The city offered
the chance of survival to many who would otherwise not have
survived, and possibly life in a cellar in Manchester was
better than death by the roadside in Connemara, though not
much better. At the least, while there was life there might be
hope, and there would be hope if the industrial development
of the country was to go forward with unchecked speed and
force.

However, even though in due course industrial development might give them employment and a place in the community, it would not by itself make the cities of nineteenth-
century Britain places in which human beings might live with
self-respect or even perhaps live at all for long. As a matter
of fact, the actual lethal character of what was happening in
Britain has apparently been exaggerated. It is a remarkable
fact that the death rate in England in the first half of the
nineteenth century seems on the whole to have been a good
deal lower than what it was in other countries which were as
yet less mechanized and less urbanized.[4] It is possible that
part of the cause of this as far as England—not of course
Scotland—is concerned was the existence in England of a Poor
Law which however badly administered did at least reduce
the possibility of death from starvation, but it suggests also
that the new cities which were coming were at least not more
deadly than what had existed before. This, however, should
probably not be counted to the credit of the new urban areas,
but as a measure of the badness of conditions in the old cities,
and often enough in the countryside, old or new. There are
enough accurate descriptions of what it was like in the worst
sections of the towns in early nineteenth-century English
cities to make it clear that as far as such areas were concerned, whatever the force behind it, their extension in size
meant merely the extension of large suppurating masses of
degradation and disease. Perhaps if such were to remain forever the living conditions of large numbers of people in

[4] See Sir John Clapham, *Economic History*, pp. 316-17, and also the
*Fiftieth Annual Report of the Registrar-General of Births, Deaths
and Marriages in England* (reports from commissions, etc., 1888,
Vol. XXX), pp. lxxvii-lxxxviii, Tables 39-56.

Britain it would after all have been better if nineteenth-century developments had led not to life on such terms, but to more merciful death.

It is true that industrial development might produce what was necessary to improve these conditions. It produced the steam-pumps and iron pipes which were necessary to convey sufficient water necessary for a civilized life; it might help to train the civil engineers to make reservoirs and drainage systems; it might, but this was in the future, produce the local transport needed to spread the congested populations; above all things it would produce the wealth without which all urban improvement is impossible. But without conscious directions, privately directed industrial development was not likely to do any of these things. There would be exceptions, of course, there would be model areas planned by benevolent factory owners, but left to itself industrial development might produce wealth, some of which might even be enjoyed by the working classes, or sections of them; but to the terms on which life would be lived in the areas in which it was most active, its main contributions would be smoke and dirt and haphazard congestion in ill-built and brutally utilitarian streets. Power and knowledge to discipline and to direct and utilize these forces was needed if life was to be lived in tolerable conditions, let alone to improve in quality. That power could only be developed and directed to the right ends by the public authority.

This eye-witness description, by Marx's closest collaborator, of London slums in 1844 shows us what Carlyle was referring to, and makes us understand how realistic were Dickens's London scenes. In describing the endless stream of people in the London streets, their "brutal indifference, the unfeeling isolation of each in his private interest," Engels indicates that condition of modern alienation discussed by Marx and exemplified, according to Dorothy Van Ghent, in Dickens's rendition of character. In his 1892 Preface to this translation, Engels refers us to the first volume of Marx's *Das Kapital* for a "description of the state of the British working-class, as it was about 1865, that is to say, at the time when British industrial prosperity reached its culminating point."

FRIEDRICH ENGELS

THE CONDITION OF THE WORKING CLASS IN ENGLAND IN 1844

A town such as London, where a man may wander for hours together without reaching the beginning of the end, without meeting the slightest hint which could lead to the inference that there is open country within reach, is a strange thing. This colossal centralisation, this heaping together of two and a half millions of human beings at one point, has multiplied the power of this two and a half millions a hundredfold; has raised London to the commercial capital of the world, created the giant docks and assembled the thousand vessels that continually cover the Thames. I know nothing more imposing than the view which the Thames offers during the ascent from the sea to London Bridge. The masses of buildings, the wharves on both sides, especially from Woodwich upwards, the countless ships along both shores crowding ever closer and closer together, until at last only a narrow passage remains in the middle of the river, a passage through which hundreds of steamers shoot by one another; all this is so vast, so impressive, that a man cannot collect himself, but is lost in the marvel of England's greatness before he sets foot upon English soil.[1]

But the sacrifices which all this has cost become apparent later. After roaming the streets of the capital a day or two, making headway with difficulty through the human turmoil and the endless lines of vehicles, after visiting the slums of the metropolis, one realises for the first time that these Londoners have been forced to sacrifice the best qualities of their human nature, to bring to pass all the marvels of civilisation which crowd their city; that a hundred powers which slumbered within them have remained inactive, have been suppressed in order that a few might be developed more fully and multiply through union with those of others. The very turmoil of the streets has something repulsive, something against which

[1] This applies to the time of sailing vessels. The Thames now is a dreary collection of ugly steamers.—F. E.

Frederick Engels, THE CONDITION OF THE WORKING-CLASS IN ENGLAND IN 1844, tr. Florence Kelley Wischnewetzky (London: Swan Sonnenschein, 1892), "The Great Towns," pp. 23-32. See also Henry Mayhew, London Labour and the London Poor, 4 vols. (London, 1861-62).

human nature rebels. The hundreds of thousands of all classes
and ranks crowding past each other, are they not all human
beings with the same qualities and powers, and with the same
interest in being happy? And have they not in the end to seek
happiness in the same way, by the same means? And still they
crowd by one another as though they had nothing in common, nothing to do with one another, and their only agree-
ment is the tacit one that each keep to his own side of the
pavement so as not to delay the opposing streams of the
crowd, while it occurs to no man to honour another with so
much as a glance. The brutal indifference, the unfeeling isolation of each in his private interest becomes the more repellent
and offensive, the more these individuals are crowded together within a limited space. And however much one may
be aware that this isolation of the individual, this narrow
self-seeking is the fundamental principle of our society everywhere, it is nowhere so shamelessly barefaced, so self-
conscious as here in the crowding of the great city. The
dissolution of mankind into monads of which each one has
a separate principle, into the world of atoms, is here carried
out to its utmost extreme.

Hence it comes, too, that the social war, the war of each
against all, is here openly declared. Just as in Stirner's recent
book, people regard each other only as useful objects; each
exploits the other, and the end of it all is that the stronger
treads the weaker under foot and that the powerful few, the
capitalists, seize everything for themselves, while to the weak
many, the poor, scarcely a bare existence remains.

What is true of London, is true of Manchester, Birmingham, Leeds, is true of all great towns. Everywhere barbarous
indifference, hard egotism on the one hand, and nameless
misery on the other, everywhere social warfare, every man's
house in a state of siege, everywhere reciprocal plundering
under the protection of the law, and all so shameless, so
openly avowed that one shrinks before the consequences of
our social state as they manifest themselves here undisguised,
and can only wonder that the whole crazy fabric still hangs
together.

Since capital, the direct or indirect control of the means
of subsistence and production, is the weapon with which this
social warfare is carried on, it is clear that all the disadvantages of such a state must fall upon the poor. For him no man
has the slightest concern. Cast into the whirlpool, he must
struggle through as well as he can. If he is so happy as to find

work, *i.e.*, if the bourgeoisie does him the favour to enrich itself by means of him, wages await him which scarcely suffice to keep body and soul together; if he can get no work he may steal, if he is not afraid of the police, or starve, in which case the police will take care that he does so in a quiet and inoffensive manner. During my residence in England, at least twenty or thirty persons have died of simple starvation under the most revolting circumstances, and a jury has rarely been found possessed of the courage to speak the plain truth in the matter. Let the testimony of the witnesses be never so clear and unequivocal, the bourgeoisie, from which the jury is selected, always finds some backdoor through which to escape the frightful verdict, death from starvation. The bourgeoisie dare not speak the truth in these cases, for it would speak its own condemnation. But indirectly, far more than directly, many have died of starvation where long continued want of proper nourishment has called forth fatal illness, when it has produced such debility that causes which might otherwise have remained inoperative, brought on severe illness and death. The English workingmen call this "social murder," and accuse our whole society of perpetrating this crime perpetually. Are they wrong?

True, it is only individuals who starve, but what security has the workingman that it may not be his turn tomorrow? Who assures him employment, who vouches for it that, if for any reason or no reason his lord and master discharges him tomorrow, he can struggle along with those dependent upon him, until he may find some one else "to give him bread"? Who guarantees that willingness to work shall suffice to obtain work, that uprightness, industry, thrift, and the rest of the virtues recommended by the bourgeoisie, are really his road to happiness? No one. He knows that he has something today, and that it does not depend upon himself whether he shall have something tomorrow. He knows that every breeze that blows, every whim of his employer, every bad turn of trade may hurl him back into the fierce whirlpool from which he has temporarily saved himself, and in which it is hard and often impossible to keep his head above water. He knows that though he may have the means of living today, it is very uncertain whether he shall tomorrow.

Meanwhile, let us proceed to a more detailed investigation of the position in which the social war has placed the non-possessing class. Let us see what pay for his work society does give the workingman in the form of dwelling, clothing, food, what sort of subsistence it grants those who contribute most to the maintenance of society; and, first, let us consider the dwellings.

Every great city has one or more slums, where the working class is crowded together. True, poverty often dwells in hidden alleys close to the palaces of the rich; but in general a separate territory has been assigned to it where, removed from the sight of the happier classes, it may struggle along as it can. These slums are pretty equally arranged in all the great towns of England, the worst houses in the worst quarters of the towns; usually one or two-storied cottages in long rows, perhaps with cellars used as dwellings, almost always irregularly built. These houses of three or four rooms and a kitchen form throughout England, some parts of London excepted, the general dwellings of the working class. The streets are generally unpaved, rough, dirty, filled with vegetable and animal refuse, without sewers or gutters, but supplied with foul, stagnant pools instead. Moreover, ventilation is impeded by the bad, confused method of building of the whole quarter; and since many human beings here live crowded into a small space, the atmosphere that prevails in these workingmen's quarters may readily be imagined. Further, the streets serve as drying grounds in fine weather; lines are stretched across from house to house, and hung with wet clothing.

Let us investigate some of the slums in their order. London comes first, and in London the famous rookery of St. Giles which is now, at last, about to be penetrated by a couple of broad streets. St. Giles is in the midst of the most populous part of the town, surrounded by broad, splendid avenues in which the gay world of London idles about, in the immediate neighbourhood of Oxford Street, Regent Street, of Trafalgar Square and the Strand. It is a disorderly collection of tall, three or four-storied houses, with narrow, crooked, filthy streets, in which there is quite as much life as in the great thoroughfares of the town, except that here people of the working class only are to be seen. A vegetable market is held in the street, baskets with vegetables and fruits, naturally all bad and hardly fit to use, obstruct the sidewalk still further, and from these, as well as from the fish-dealers' stalls, arises a horrible smell. The houses are occupied from cellar to garret, filthy within and without, and their appearance is such that no human being could possibly wish to live in them. But all this is nothing in comparison with the dwellings in the narrow courts and alleys between the streets, entered by covered passages between the houses, in which the filth and tottering ruin surpass all description. Scarcely, a whole windowpane can be found, the walls are crumbling, doorposts and window frames loose and broken, doors of old boards nailed together, or altogether wanting in this thieves' quarter, where no doors are needed, there being nothing to steal. Heaps of garbage and ashes lie in all directions, and the foul liquids emptied before the doors gather in stinking pools. Here live the poorest of the poor, the worst paid workers with thieves and the victims of prostitution indiscriminately huddled together, the majority Irish, or of Irish extraction, and those who have not yet sunk in the whirlpool of moral ruin which surrounds them, sinking daily deeper, losing daily more and more of their power to resist the demoralising influence of want, filth, and evil surroundings.

Nor is St. Giles the only London slum. In the immense tangle of streets, there are hundreds and thousands of alleys and courts lined with houses too bad for anyone to live in, who can still spend anything whatsoever upon a dwelling fit for human beings. Close to the splendid houses of the rich such a lurking place of the bitterest poverty may often be found. So a short time ago, on the occasion of a coroner's inquest, a region close to Portman Square, one of the very respectable squares, was characterised as an abode "of a multitude of Irish demoralised by poverty and filth." So, too, may be found in streets such as Long Acre and others which, though not fashionable, are yet "respectable," a great number of cellar dwellings out of which puny children and half-starved, ragged women emerge into the light of day. In the immediate neighbourhood of Drury Lane Theatre, the second in London, are some of the worst streets of the whole metropolis, Charles, King, and Park Streets, in which the houses are inhabited from cellar to garret exclusively by poor families. In the parishes of St. John and St. Margaret there lived in 1840, according to the *Journal of the Statistical Society*, 5,366 workingmen's families in 5,294 "dwellings" (if they deserve the name!), men, women, and children thrown together without distinction of age or sex, 26,830 persons all told; and of these families three-fourths possessed but one room. In the aristocratic parish of St. George, Hanover Square, there lived, according to the same authority, 1,465 workingmen's families, nearly 6,000 persons, under similar conditions, and here, too, more than two-thirds of the whole number crowded

together at the rate of one family in one room. And how the
poverty of these unfortunates, among whom even thieves find
nothing to steal, is exploited by the property-holding class in
lawful ways! The abominable dwellings in Drury Lane, just
mentioned, bring in the following rents: two cellar dwellings,
3s.; one room, ground-floor, 4s.; second-storey, 4s. 6d.; third-
floor, 4s.; garret-room, 3s. weekly, so that the starving occupants of Charles Street alone pay the house-owners a yearly
tribute of £2,000, and the 5,336 families above mentioned
in Westminster, a yearly rent of £40,000.

The most extensive working-people's district lies east of
the Tower in Whitechapel and Bethnal Green, where the
greatest masses of London working people live. Let us hear
Mr. G. Alston, preacher of St. Philip's, Bethnal Green, on
the condition of his parish. He says:

> It contains 1,400 houses, inhabited by 2,795 families, or
> about 12,000 persons. The space upon which this large
> population dwells is less than 400 yards (1,200 feet)
> square, and in this overcrowding it is nothing unusual to
> find a man, his wife, four or five children, and sometimes
> both grandparents, all in one single room, where they eat,
> sleep, and work. I believe that before the Bishop of London
> called attention to this most poverty-stricken parish, people
> at the West End knew as little of it as of the savages of
> Australia or the South Sea Isles. And if we make ourselves
> acquainted with these unfortunates, through personal ob-
> servation, if we watch them at their scanty meal and see
> them bowed by illness and want of work, we shall find
> such a mass of helplessness and misery, that a nation like
> ours must blush that these things can be possible. I was
> rector near Huddersfield during the three years in which
> the mills were at their worst, but I have never seen such
> complete helplessness of the poor as since then in Bethnal
> Green. Not one father of a family in ten in the whole
> neighbourhood has other clothing than his working suit,
> and that is as bad and tattered as possible; many, indeed,
> have no other covering for the night than these rags, and
> no bed save a sack of straw and shavings.

The foregoing description furnishes an idea of the aspect
of the interior of the dwellings. But let us follow the English
officials, who occasionally stray thither, into one or two of
these workingmen's homes.

On the occasion of an inquest held Nov. 14th, 1843 by Mr.
Carter, coroner for Surrey, upon the body of Ann Galway,

aged 45 years, the newspapers related the following particulars concerning the deceased. She had lived at No. 3 White Lion Court, Bermondsey Street, London, with her husband and a nineteen-year-old son in a little room, in which neither a bedstead nor any other furniture was to be seen. She lay dead beside her son upon a heap of feathers which were scattered over her almost naked body, there being neither sheet nor coverlet. The feathers stuck so fast over the whole body that the physician could not examine the corpse until it was cleansed, and then found it starved and scarred from the bites of vermin. Part of the floor of the room was torn up, and the hole used by the family as a privy.

On Monday, Jan. 15th, 1844, two boys were brought before the police magistrate because, being in a starving condition, they had stolen and immediately devoured a half-cooked calf's foot from a shop. The magistrate felt called upon to investigate the case further, and received the following details from the policeman. The mother of the two boys was the widow of an ex-soldier, afterwards policeman, and had had a very hard time, since the death of her husband, to provide for her nine children. She lived at No. 2 Pool's Place, Quaker Court, Spitalfields, in the utmost poverty. When the policeman came to her, he found her with six of her children literally huddled together in a little back room, with no furniture but two old rush-bottomed chairs with the seats gone, a small table with two legs broken, a broken cup, and a small dish. On the hearth was scarcely a spark of fire, and in one corner lay as many old rags as would fill a woman's apron, which served the whole family as a bed. For bed clothing they had only their scanty day clothing. The poor woman told him that she had been forced to sell her bedstead the year before to buy food. Her bedding she had pawned with the victualler for food. In short, everything had gone for food. The magistrate ordered the woman a considerable provision from the poor-box.

In February 1844, Theresa Bishop, a widow 60 years old, was recommended, with her sick daughter, aged 26, to the compassion of the police magistrate in Marlborough Street. She lived at No. 5 Brown Street, Grosvenor Square, in a small back room no larger than a closet, in which there was not one single piece of furniture. In one corner lay some rags upon which both slept; a chest served as table and chair. The mother earned a little by charring. The owner of the house said that they had lived in this way since May 1843, had gradually sold or pawned everything that they had, and had still never paid any rent. The magistrate assigned them £1 from the poor-box.

I am far from asserting that *all* London working people live in such want as the foregoing three families. I know very well that ten are somewhat better off, where one is so totally trodden under foot by society; but I assert that thousands of industrious and worthy people—far worthier and more to be respected than all the rich of London—do find themselves in a condition unworthy of human beings; and that every proletarian, everyone, without exception, is exposed to a similar fate without any fault of his own and in spite of every possible effort.

But in spite of all this, they who have some kind of a shelter are fortunate, fortunate in comparison with the utterly homeless. In London fifty thousand human beings get up every morning, not knowing where they are to lay their heads at night. The luckiest of this multitude, those who succeed in keeping a penny or two until evening, enter a lodging-house, such as abound in every great city, where they find a bed. But what a bed! These houses are filled with beds from cellar to garret, four, five, six beds in a room; as many as can be crowded in. Into every bed four, five, or six human beings are piled, as many as can be packed in, sick and well, young and old, drunk and sober, men and women, just as they come, indiscriminately. Then come strife, blows, wounds, or, if these bed-fellows agree, so much the worse; thefts are arranged and things done which our language, grown more humane than our deeds, refuses to record. And those who cannot pay for such a refuge? They sleep where they find a place, in passages, arcades, in corners where the police and the owners leave them undisturbed. A few individuals find their way to the refuges which are managed, here and there, by private charity, others sleep on the benches in the parks close under the windows of Queen Victoria. Let us hear the London *Times* (Oct. 12th, 1843):

It appears from the report of the proceedings at Marlborough Street Police Court in our columns of yesterday, that there is an average number of 50 human beings of all ages, who huddle together in the parks every night, having no other shelter than what is supplied by the trees and a few hollows of the embankment. Of these, the majority are young girls who have been seduced from the country by the soldiers and turned loose on the world in all the destitution of friendless penury, and all the recklessness of early vice.

This is truly horrible! Poor there must be everywhere. Indigence will find its way and set up its hideous state in the heart of a great and luxurious city. Amid the thousand narrow lanes and bystreets of a populous metropolis there must always, we fear, be much suffering—much that offends the eye—much that lurks unseen.

But that within the precincts of wealth, gaiety and fashion, nigh the regal grandeur of St. James, close on the palatial splendor of Bayswater, on the confines of the old and new aristocratic quarters, in a district where the cautious refinement of modern design has refrained from creating one single tenement for poverty; which seems, as it were, dedicated to the exclusive enjoyment of wealth, that *there* want and famine and disease and vice should stalk in all their kindred horrors, consuming body by body, soul by soul!

It is indeed a monstrous state of things! Enjoyment the most absolute that bodily ease, intellectual excitement or the most innocent pleasures of sense can supply to man's craving, brought in close contact with the most unmitigated misery! Wealth, from its bright saloons, laughing—an insolently heedless laugh—at the unknown wounds of want! Pleasure cruelly but unconsciously mocking the pain that moans below! All contrary things mocking one another— all contrary, save the vice which tempts and the vice which is tempted!

But let all men remember this—that within the most courtly precincts of the richest city of God's earth, there may be found, night after night, winter after winter, women—young in years—old in sin and suffering—outcasts from society—ROTTING FROM FAMINE, FILTH AND DISEASE. Let them remember this, and learn not to theorise but to act. God knows, there is much room for action nowadays.

The most famous controversy of the Victorian age, the controversy between science and religion, came to a climax with the publication in 1859 of the book that did most to discredit the Biblical account of Creation—Charles Darwin's *On the Origin of Species by Means of Natural Selection, or the Preservation of Favoured Races in the Struggle for Life.* Darwin had behind him, as Noel Annan makes clear, a positivist tradition going back to Bacon. Among his more immediate predecessors were Malthus, from whose *Essay on the Principle of Population* (1798; 1803), Darwin got the idea of the struggle for existence; and Sir Charles Lyell, from whose *Principles of Geology* (1830-33), he got the idea of gradual development. Biblical authority was further challenged by the Higher (or historical) Criticism of the Bible that originated in Germany. Especially influential was D. F. Strauss's *Leben Jesu* (1835-36), translated by George Eliot in 1846, which treated the Gospels as myth rather than history.

In *Essays and Reviews* (1860), seven Broad-Church writers, who were later condemned in the ecclesiastical court, welcomed the new discoveries in natural science and Biblical scholarship as reinvigorating for faith.

NOEL ANNAN

Science, Religion, and the Critical Mind

Science, then as now, was feared. Today while we see in it the hope of human welfare, we fear it as the agent of our destruction. But it is not the subject itself but the use to which nation-states put it that we fear. In 1859 the Victorians were hardly beginning to take account of the political and international implications of science, but they were deeply suspicious of its effect upon individuals. Science was suspected of being a moral danger. Ruskin pointed to one type of corruption—the corruption of the craftsman. Newman, and after him Matthew Arnold, pointed to another—the impoverishment of the individual's mind if he were permitted to specialize in science and set aside the liberal arts. But in the popular imagination the greatest danger seemed to be whether science was going to contradict the whole tradition of European thought by substituting a totally different account of what life on this planet had been, was, and ought to be. How could the findings of science be reconciled with the history, the morality, the ideals, and the faith of Christian England? The situation was similar to that in the twelfth and thirteenth centuries, when men were forced to reconcile Aristotle to Christian theology. And this time no Aquinas was born to resolve the crisis.

The *Origin of Species* was not, of course, the sole great dissolver of faith in mid-Victorian England, and we would misinterpret the age if we saw it as such. To see the celebrated controversy between science and religion a century ago in perspective, we must stand back from the fifties and relate Darwin's book to a tradition of thought already long developed. The *Origin of Species* was simply another stage in the development of the positivist tradition—a tradition that owed something to Bacon but first took shape in the writings of Hobbes, Locke, and Newton. For over two centuries it was

Philip Appleman, William A. Madden, Michael Wolff, ed., 1859: ENTERING AN AGE OF CRISIS (Bloomington, Indiana University Press, 1959), pp. 32-37. Reprinted by permission of the publisher. See also William Irvine, *Apes, Angels and Victorians: The Story of Darwin, Huxley and Evolution* (New York, 1955); Lionel Stevenson, *Darwin among the Poets* (Chicago, 1932).

to be the most consistently powerful intellectual movement
in England. Its most original philosopher, Hume, might expose its limitations; the governing class might prefer prag-
matic reform and Burkean principles to Benthamism; the
Romantic poets and seers from Blake to Yeats pilloried its
methods and conclusions. But positivism called the tune and
forced other modes of thought to dance to it.

Positivism was both a method and a disposition of mind.
It claimed to be scientific because it applied to human behaviour the methods of inductive and deductive reasoning
that Newton had hallowed. The interplay of these methods
(which John Stuart Mill sketched in his *System of Logic*)
was put forward as the soundest way of discovering the truth
about all subjects. Today we think of knowledge as a set of
different subjects, each with its own discipline; but when in
1852 Cambridge, responding to demands to broaden its
curriculum, instituted the Natural Sciences and the Moral
Science Triposes, the names reflected the implicit assumption
that knowledge was a unity. In the nineteenth century, moreover, science meant pre-eminently the discovery of new laws:
great immutable hypotheses necessarily replete with profound
cosmological implications. There was nothing new in such
extrapolation. From Newton's laws not only had a new
physical universe been constructed; psychology and even
economics and religion were infused with Newtonian infer-
ences. And so, as each new scientific law in Victorian times
was propounded, men tried to apply it to society or the
universe. Tennyson, whose sensibility was so acutely tuned
to the dilemmas of his generation, was of course doing this
when he immortalised in *In Memoriam* the relation of ther-
modynamics to the ancient tale of the loving purposes of God
towards man.

There was every reason why such ideas should take root
easily. The eighteenth-century tradition of rationalism had
assumed that the words "scientific" and "rational" were
synonyms. The business of living in society—of choosing
between right and wrong, of choosing your objectives, of
choosing between different courses of action, of choosing the
means to achieve your goals—was described as a rational,
and, as men grew wiser, a scientific process. It was irrational
to prefer pain to pleasure; it was ascetic or unnatural to aim
at unattainable goals; it was superstitious to perform actions,
such as rituals, which were not directed towards a specific
end. Circumstances, "other people," and the situation in

which you found yourself of course influenced your conduct. But you could prevent circumstances dictating to you by acquiring facts about your situation and inferring—scientifically—from them how best to act. What prevented men from doing this? What impeded the march of mind and the progress of civilization? Ignorance, false doctrine, and anachronistic institutions. Here the positivist dispositon of mind deeply disturbed the conservatives and the orthodox: they were faced by something much more sweeping and alarming than a movement for political reform.

At the same time positivists recognized that the social sciences could not hold a candle to the natural sciences when it came to making claims that incontrovertible truths had been discovered. The basic premise about society—that its health and wealth rested on the pursuit of rational self-interest—was said to be implicit in Nature herself and to be confirmed by the most striking achievement in all the social sciences—the body of related conclusions about human behaviour constructed by the classical economists. And yet, difficult as it was to refute these conclusions, the abstract and deductive nature of the argument detracted from its prestige. The conclusions of Bentham or Comte or Buckle were not demonstrable to the same degree as those of Lyell. Lyell's work contained hypotheses in plenty but they rested on facts. Was there a branch of knowledge about human beings that could produce facts of comparable strength and validity?

There was indeed. History had suddenly become a much more impressive study and had acquired a new status. The critical study of sources which the Germans introduced became a science in itself and the material on which the conclusions of yesterday were based was exposed, at the worst as surmise, gossip, travellers' tales, and myth, and at the best as documents which carried a meaning for the original writer and his contemporaries quite different from the meaning which had traditionally been assigned to them by the churches and other self-interested parties. The techniques which Barthold Niebuhr had used on Livy began to be applied to the Bible, and it was these techniques, not the general philosophy of the individual historian, that impressed the English clerisy. Strauss, for example, was no eighteenth-century rationalist: his purpose was to expose the shallowness of the old-fashioned rationalist attack on the Bible: but his Idealist interpretation of Roman-Jewish history was insignificant beside the spectacle of his remorseless examination of every fact, every parable, and every incident in the Gospels. This new scientific treatment of evidence put Biblical history outside the orbit of any but professional scholars, and as a result bewildered and enraged the mass of the clergy in mid-Victorian England.

There was, then, a disposition of mind towards interpreting all natural and human phenomena in positivist terms; and it was continually gaining strength. No single thinker ever set out its assumptions and conclusions in their entirety (though Mill came nearer to it than any). Yet already by the 1830's the study of man could not be undertaken analytically without reference to utilitarianism, classical economics, and associationist psychology; and by the fifties the positivist interpretation of the history of man began to take a more formidable shape. Lyell's geology was all grist to the positivist mill, and the idea of development—the idea that the world and all that is in it has radically changed over the centuries and that nothing, not even our knowledge of God, is given once and for all and is immutable—was current long before 1859. Darwin confirmed more rigorously what positivism had for long asserted—that the history of the world is the history of progress and that there was no need of supernatural intervention during the ages to account for whatever had happened. The descent of man was incorporated into the positivist cosmology and the picture painted by the new scholars of Natural History was set up to mock the old picture of Creation which the churches implicitly upheld.

And yet we should be equally wrong to minimise the shock made by the publication of the *Origin of Species*. No doubt Francis Newman,[1] George Eliot, and others had lost their faith because they found Christian morality as preached by the churches deficient. No doubt J. A. Froude and Baden Powell were more affected by the Higher Criticism of the Bible than by science. No doubt Lecky or Herbert Spencer or Clough or W. R. Greg or Matthew Arnold or Browning or dozens of other mid-Victorians who moved on their different paths away from belief in dogmatic Christianity were impelled by many reasons. But Darwin remains a crucial name and 1859 a crucial year. The *Origin of Species* became the foundation of a new history of the world. Colenso's statistical

[1] [Not to be confused with his more famous brother, John Henry (later Cardinal) Newman whose opposite religious development, from Evangelicalism through the Oxford or High-Church movement to Roman Catholicism, is described in his spiritual autobiography, *Apologia pro Vita Sua* (1864).—Ed.]

enquiry into the arithmetic of the Pentateuch,[2] which so enraged his brother bishops, was influenced by Darwinism as well as by the Higher Criticism. The issue was not simply whether scholars might re-interpret the Bible but whether the beloved story of man's Creation and the Flood was rubbish. Darwin not only offended the Fundamentalists among all Christian communions . . . but all those attuned to believing in a world in which God was continually at work in a material way—in a world which He planned. Was Natural Selection part of God's design? It might indeed seem so to men who saw the principle at work in the ruthless competition of the early Industrial Revolution in which the weakest capitalists went to the wall and only a prodigious effort of Self-Help on Smilesian lines[3] could lift a man out of the squalor of the slums. But if this seemed morally repulsive, was not Huxley right in claiming that man's sole hope lay in "combatting the cosmic process" and defeating by his own efforts the blind determinism of evolution? A great chasm seemed to have opened between God and Nature. Darwin introduced the idea that *chance* begot order in the world, and today, whether in atomic physics or in the genetical properties of the nucleic acids, chance still rules in terms of any single individual particle, however much the laws of mathematical probability work in respect to any groups of particles. To the Victorians the metaphysical significance of this situation seemed of appalling importance. . . . It seemed to many of them that God had been banished from the world and that the new account of Creation foretold a spiritual and moral destiny for the human race incompatible with the story of God's dealings with man as depicted in the Bible. Belief in Divine intervention in the affairs of men was widespread and disasters in Nature were often held to be instances of God's justly provoked wrath. How could this be if mechanistic blind chance alone prevailed in the order of Nature? Despite the fact that Darwin denied that he intended to trespass on theological pastures, and despite the fact that he was to dissociate his work from Herbert Spencer's adaptation of the principle of evolution, the churches fell upon him. The rumpus perhaps

[2] [In his sensational book of 1862, *The Pentateuch and the Book of Joshua Critically Examined*, Bishop J. W. Colenso showed, for example, that the Congregation of Israelites, as he calculated its number, could not have fitted into the court of the Tabernacle, the dimensions of which are specified in Exodus.—Ed.]

[3] [Samuel Smiles's *Self-Help* (1859), a bestseller through 1905, used true success stories to teach the virtues of work, ambition, thrift, honesty, perseverance.—Ed.]

was inevitable, but it turned out to be singularly unfortunate for the churches. As sometimes happens when the established order in society decides to force an issue and crush out a lone danger, the dissident suddenly appears to gather strength from the soil itself and emerges as the leader of an army triumphant with banners flying.

The year 1859 was also the year in which Mill published his essay *On Liberty*. In it Mill confused two distinct propositions, but he confused them with incomparable power and fervour. He argued that all repression and restraint is bad because it frustrates human beings, and can be justified only if it can clearly be shown to prevent a demonstrably greater evil; and that only in a free society can men discover the truth and cherish it. The two propositions are not identical, but small wonder that later, with Darwin's experience before their eyes, the new English intelligentsia was convinced that they were. This intelligentsia, which was gaining power as it filled the Civil Service at home and in the colonies, which was providing teachers in the universities and Public Schools, which was editing and contributing to the growing numbers of periodicals that were such a stimulus to Victorian intellectual life, and which was establishing links in the governing class itself but was in no way dependent on aristocratic patronage, was in no mood to be called to order by bishops and country clergymen. When Darwin made his well known comment that Lyell's support for the *Origin of Species* was heroic in view of his age and his position in society, he underlined one of the main theses in Mill's book: the search for truth and hence the means of progress were being impeded not by the laws but by social pressures, such as the risk of losing respectability, or the pillorying and petty persecution of men in the ancient universities, or the requirement that men should be reticent or even prove their soundness by a prudent display of unction. Sometimes today we detect a strained note, an unattractive overemphasis, in the protestations of the mid-Victorian rationalists, but their plea for intellectual freedom was justified and carried all before it, not solely from the rightness of their cause, but because the treatment of Darwin's work was a simple touchstone. That is why 1859 marked a new phase in the development of positivism and led to the outburst of anti-clerical and rationalist books and articles in the seventies and to the secularisation of intellectual life.

Of the new words that came into use or changed their meaning at the turn of the nineteenth century, the word *culture,* says Raymond Williams in the Introduction to this book, is the most striking; for it comprehends in the development of its meaning all the revolutionary questions raised by the other new words. The book describes nineteenth- and twentieth-century intellectual and literary history by tracing the development of the idea of culture.

RAYMOND WILLIAMS

CULTURE AND SOCIETY 1780-1950

In the last decades of the eighteenth century, and in the first half of the nineteenth century, a number of words, which are now of capital importance, came for the first time into common English use, or, where they had already been generally used in the language, acquired new and important meanings. There is in fact a general pattern of change in these words, and this can be used as a special kind of map by which it is possible to look again at those wider changes in life and thought to which the changes in language evidently refer.

Five words are the key points from which this map can be drawn. They are *industry, democracy, class, art* and

Raymond Williams, CULTURE AND SOCIETY 1780-1950 (New York: Columbia University Press, 1958), pp. xiii-xviii. Reprinted by permission of the publisher. See also Walter E. Houghton, *The Victorian Frame of Mind* (New Haven and London, 1957).

culture. The importance of these words, in our modern structure of meanings, is obvious. The changes in their use, at this critical period, bear witness to a general change in our characteristic ways of thinking about our common life: about our social, political and economic institutions; about the purposes which these institutions are designed to embody; and about the relations to these institutions and purposes of our activities in learning, education and the arts.

The first important word is *industry,* and the period in which its use changes is the period which we now call the Industrial Revolution. *Industry,* before this period, was a name for a particular human attribute, which could be paraphrased as "skill, assiduity, perseverance, diligence." This use of *industry* of course survives. But, in the last decades of the eighteenth century, *industry* came also to mean something else; it became a collective word for our manufacturing and productive institutions, and for their general activities. Adam Smith, in *The Wealth of Nations* (1776), is one of the first writers to use the word in this way, and from his time the development of this use is assured. *Industry,* with a capital letter, is thought of as a thing in itself—an institution, a body of activities—rather than simply a human attribute. *Industrious,* which described persons, is joined, in the nineteenth century, by *industrial,* which describes the institutions. The rapid growth in importance of these institutions is seen as creating a new system, which in the 1830's is first called *Industrialism.* In part, this is the acknowledgement of a series of very important technical changes, and of their transforming effect on methods of production. It is also, however, an acknowledgement of the effect of these changes on society as a whole, which is similarly transformed. The phrase *Industrial Revolution* amply confirms this, for the phrase, first used by French writers in the 1820's, and gradually adopted, in the course of the century, by English writers, is modelled explicitly on an analogy with the French Revolution of 1789. As that had transformed France, so this has transformed England; the means of change are different, but the change is comparable in kind: it has produced, by a pattern of change, a new society.

The second important word is *democracy,* which had been known, from the Greek, as a term for "government by the people," but which only came into common English use at the time of the American and French Revolutions. Weekley, in *Words Ancient and Modern,* writes:

It was not until the French Revolution that *democracy* ceased to be a mere literary word, and became part of the political vocabulary.

In this he is substantially right. Certainly, it is in reference to America and France that the examples begin to multiply, at the end of the eighteenth century, and it is worth noting that the great majority of these examples show the word being used unfavourably: in close relation with the hated *Jacobinism,* or with the familiar *mob-rule.* England may have been (the word has so many modern definitions) a democracy since Magna Carta, or since the Commonwealth, or since 1688, but it certainly did not call itself one. *Democrats,* at the end of the eighteenth and the beginning of the nineteenth centuries, were seen, commonly, as dangerous and subversive mob agitators. Just as *industry* and its derived words record what we now call the Industrial Revolution, so *democracy* and *democrat,* in their entry into ordinary speech, record the effects, in England, of the American and French Revolutions, and a crucial phase of the struggle, at home, for what we would now call democratic representation.

Industry, to indicate an institution, begins in about 1776; *democracy,* as a practical word, can be dated from about the same time. The third word, *class,* can be dated, in its most important modern sense, from about 1772. Before this, the ordinary use of *class,* in English, was to refer to a division or group in schools and colleges: "the usual Classes in Logick and Philosophy." It is only at the end of the eighteenth century that the modern structure of *class,* in its social sense, begins to be built up. First comes *lower classes,* to join *lower orders,* which appears earlier in the eighteenth century. Then, in the 1790's, we get *higher classes; middle classes* and *middling classes* follow at once; *working classes* in about 1815; *upper classes* in the 1820's. *Class prejudice, class legislation, class consciousness, class conflict* and *class war* follow in the course of the nineteenth century. The *upper middle classes* are first heard of in the 1890's; the *lower middle class* in our own century.

It is obvious, of course, that this spectacular history of the new use of *class* does not indicate the *beginning* of social divisions in England. But it indicates, quite clearly, a change in the character of these divisions, and it records, equally clearly, a change in attitudes towards them. *Class* is a more indefinite word than *rank,* and this was probably one of the reasons for its introduction. The structure then built on it is in nineteenth-century terms: in terms, that is to say, of the changed social structure, and the changed social feelings, of an England which was passing through the Industrial Revolution, and which was at a crucial phase in the development of political democracy.

The fourth word, *art,* is remarkably similar, in its pattern of change, to *industry.* From its original sense of a human attribute, a "skill," it had come, by the period with which we are concerned, to be a kind of institution, a set body of activities of a certain kind. An *art* had formerly been any human skill; but *Art,* now, signified a particular group of skills, the "imaginative" or "creative" arts. *Artist* had meant a skilled person, as had *artisan;* but *artist* now referred to these selected skills alone. Further, and most significantly, *Art* came to stand for a special kind of truth, "imaginative truth," and *artist* for a special kind of person, as the words *artistic* and *artistical,* to describe human beings, new in the 1840's, show. A new name, *aesthetics,* was found to describe the judgement of art, and this, in its turn, produced a name for a special kind of person—*aesthete. The arts*—literature, music, painting, sculpture, theatre—were regrouped together, in this new phrase, as having something essentially in common which distinguished them from other human skills. The same separation as had grown up between *artist* and *artisan* grew up between *artist* and *craftsman. Genius,* from meaning "a characteristic disposition," came to mean "exalted ability," and a distinction was made between it and *talent.* As *art* had produced *artist* in the new sense, and *aesthetics aesthete,* so this produced *a genius,* to indicate a special kind of person. These changes, which belong in time to the period of the other changes discussed, form a record of a remarkable change in ideas of the nature and purpose of art, and of its relations to other human activities and to society as a whole.

The fifth word, *culture,* similarly changes, in the same critical period. Before this period, it had meant, primarily, the "tending of natural growth," and then, by analogy, a process of human training. But this latter use, which had usually been a culture *of* something, was changed, in the nineteenth century, to *culture* as such, a thing in itself. It came to mean, first, "a general state or habit of the mind," having close relations with the idea of human perfection. Second, it came to mean "the general state of intellectual development, in a society as a whole." Third, it came to mean "the general body of the arts." Fourth, later in the century, it came to mean "a whole way of life, material, intellectual and spiritual." It came also, as we know, to be a word which often provoked either hostility or embarrassment.

The development of *culture* is perhaps the most striking among all the words named. It might be said, indeed, that the questions now concentrated in the meanings of the word *culture* are questions directly raised by the great historical changes which the changes in *industry, democracy* and *class,* in their own way, represent, and to which the changes in *art* are a closely related response. The development of the word *culture* is a record of a number of important and continuing reactions to these changes in our social, economic and political life, and may be seen, in itself, as a special kind of map by means of which the nature of the changes can be explored.

I have stated, briefly, the fact of the changes in these important words. As a background to them I must also draw attention to a number of other words which are either new, or acquired new meanings, in this decisive period. Among the new words, for example, there are *ideology, intellectual, rationalism, scientist, humanitarian, utilitarian, romanticism, atomistic; bureaucracy, capitalism, collectivism, commercialism, communism, doctrinaire, equalitarian, liberalism, masses, medieval* and *mediaevalism, operative* (noun), *primitivism, proletariat* (a new word for "mob"), *socialism, unemployment; cranks, highbrow, isms* and *pretentious.* Among words which then acquired their now normal modern meanings are *business* (=trade), *common* (=vulgar), *earnest* (derisive), *Education* and *educational, getting-on, handmade, idealist* (=visionary), *Progress, rank-and-file* (other than military), *reformer* and *reformism, revolutionary* and *revolutionize, salary* (as opposed to "wages"), *Science* (=natural and physical sciences), *speculator* (financial), *solidarity, strike* and *suburban* (as a description of attitudes). The field which these changes cover is again a field of general change, introducing many elements which we now point to as distinctively modern in situation and feeling. It is the relations within this general pattern of change which it will be my particular task to describe.

The word which more than any other comprises these relations is *culture,* with all its complexity of idea and reference. My overall purpose in the book is to describe and analyse this complex, and to give an account of its historical formation. Because of its very range of reference, it is necessary, however, to set the enquiry from the beginning on a wide basis. I had originally intended to keep very closely to *culture* itself, but, the more closely I examined it, the more widely my terms of reference had to be set. For what I see in the history of this word, in its structure of meanings, is a wide and general movement in thought and feeling. I shall hope to show this movement in detail. In summary, I wish to show the emergence of *culture* as an abstraction and an absolute: an emergence which, in a very complex way, merges two general responses—first, the recognition of the practical separation of certain moral and intellectual activities from the driven impetus of a new kind of society; second, the emphasis of these activities, as a court of human appeal, to be set over the processes of practical social judgement and yet to offer itself as a mitigating and rallying alternative. But, in both these senses, culture was not a response to the new methods of production, the new *Industry,* alone. It was concerned, beyond these, with the new kinds of personal and social relationship: again, both as a recognition of practical separation and as an emphasis of alternatives. The idea of *culture* would be simpler if it had been a response to industrialism alone, but it was also, quite evidently, a response to the new political and social developments, to *Democracy.* Again, in relation to this, it is a complex and radical response to the new problems of social class. Further, while these responses define bearings, in a given external area that was surveyed, there is also, in the formation of the meanings of *culture,* an evident reference back to an area of personal and apparently private experience, which was notably to affect the meaning and practice of art. These are the first stages of the formulation of the idea of culture, but its historical development is at least as important. For the recognition of a separate body of moral and intellectual activities, and the offering of a court of human appeal, which comprise the early meanings of the word, are joined, and in themselves changed, by the growing assertion of a whole way of life, not only as a scale of integrity, but as a mode of interpreting all our common experience, and, in this new interpretation, changing it. Where *culture* meant a state or habit of the mind, or the body of intellectual and moral activities, it means now, also, a whole way of life. This development, like each of the original meanings and the relations between them, is not accidental, but general and deeply significant.

Part Two

VICTORIANS ON THEIR AGE

"Every Englishman of the present day is by implication either a Benthamite or a Coleridgian," says John Stuart Mill, who was brought up as a Benthamite. In *Westminster Review* essays on Bentham (1838) and Coleridge (1840), Mill shows how all the issues of the Victorian age can be understood by reference to the opposing world-views of the late eighteenth-century Utilitarian radical and the early nineteenth-century romantic conservative. Mill here urges his contemporaries to "master the premises and combine the methods of both" these seminal thinkers—to combine belief in progress with respect for the past. Victorian literature was on the whole on Coleridge's side; so that Mill, through his appreciation of Coleridge, places one foot in the literary camp. Since Mill's "Coleridge" contains enough discussion of Bentham to make the contrast clear, there is no better introduction to the intellectual climate of the Victorian age.

JOHN STUART MILL

Coleridge

The name of Coleridge is one of the few English names of
our time which are likely to be oftener pronounced, and to
become symbolical of more important things, in proportion
as the inward workings of the age manifest themselves more
and more in outward facts. Bentham excepted, no Englishman of recent date has left his impress so deeply in the
opinions and mental tendencies of those among us who
attempt to enlighten their practice by philosophical meditation. If it be true, as Lord Bacon affirms, that a knowledge
of the speculative opinions of the men between twenty and
thirty years of age is the great source of political prophecy,
the existence of Coleridge will show itself by no slight or
ambiguous traces in the coming history of our country; for
no one has contributed more to shape the opinions of those
among its younger men who can be said to have opinions
at all.

The influence of Coleridge, like that of Bentham, extends
far beyond those who share in the peculiarities of his religious
or philosophical creed. He has been the great awakener in
this country of the spirit of philosophy within the bounds of
traditional opinions. He has been, almost as truly as Bentham,
"the great questioner of things established"; for a questioner
needs not necessarily be an enemy. By Bentham, beyond
all others, men have been led to ask themselves, in regard to
any ancient or received opinion, Is it true? and by Coleridge,
What is the meaning of it? The one took his stand *outside*
the received opinion, and surveyed it as an entire stranger
to it; the other looked at it from within, and endeavored to
see it with the eyes of a believer in it: to discover by what
apparent facts it was at first suggested, and by what appearances it has ever since been rendered continually credible—
has seemed, to a succession of persons, to be a faithful interpretation of their experience. Bentham judged a proposition
true or false as it accorded or not with the result of his own

John Stuart Mill, DISSERTATIONS AND DISCUSSIONS, 3 vols. (Boston,
1864), II, 5-20, 35-78. See also Basil Willey, *Nineteenth Century Studies:
Coleridge to Matthew Arnold* (New York, 1949).

inquiries; and did not search very curiously into what might be meant by the proposition, when it obviously did not mean what he thought true. With Coleridge, on the contrary, the very fact that any doctrine had been believed by thoughtful men, and received by whole nations or generations of mankind, was part of the problem to be solved; was one of the phenomena to be accounted for. And as Bentham's short and easy method of referring all to the selfish interests of aristocracies or priests or lawyers, or some other species of impostors, could not satisfy a man who saw so much farther into the complexities of the human intellect and feelings, he considered the long or extensive prevalence of any opinion as a presumption that it was not altogether a fallacy; that to its first authors at least it was the result of a struggle to express in words something which had a reality to them, though perhaps not to many of those who have since received the doctrine by mere tradition. The long duration of a belief, he thought, is at least proof of an adaptation in it to some portion or other of the human mind: and if, on digging down to the root, we do not find, as is generally the case, some truth, we shall find some natural want or requirement of human nature which the doctrine in question is fitted to satisfy; among which wants the instincts of selfishness and of credulity have a place, but by no means an exclusive one. From this difference in the points of view of the two philosophers, and from the too rigid adherence of each to his own, it was to be expected that Bentham should continually miss the truth which is in the traditional opinions, and Coleridge that which is out of them and at variance with them. But it was also likely that each would find, or show the way to finding, much of what the other missed.

It is hardly possible to speak of Coleridge and his position among his contemporaries without reverting to Bentham; they are connected by two of the closest bonds of association—resemblance and contrast. It would be difficult to find two persons of philosophic eminence more exactly the contrary of one another. Compare their modes of treatment of any subject, and you might fancy them inhabitants of different worlds. They seem to have scarcely a principle or a premise in common. Each of them sees scarcely any thing but what the other does not see. Bentham would have regarded Coleridge with a peculiar measure of the good-humored contempt with which he was accustomed to regard all modes of philosophizing different from his own. Coleridge would probably have made Bentham one of the exceptions to the enlarged and liberal appreciation which (to the credit of *his* mode of philosophizing) he extended to most thinkers of any eminence from whom he differed. But contraries, as logicians say, are but *quæ in eodem genere maxime distant*—the things which are farthest from one another in the same kind. These two agreed in being the men who, in their age and country, did most to enforce by precept and example the necessity of a philosophy. They agreed in making it their occupation to recall opinions to first principles—taking no proposition for granted without examining into the grounds of it, and ascertaining that it possessed the kind and degree of evidence suitable to its nature. They agreed in recognizing that sound theory is the only foundation for sound practice; and that whoever despises theory, let him give himself what airs of wisdom he may, is self-convicted of being a quack. If a book were to be compiled containing all the best things ever said on the rule-of-thumb school of political craftsmanship and on the insufficiency for practical purposes of what the mere practical man calls experience, it is difficult to say whether the collection would be more indebted to the writings of Bentham or of Coleridge. They agreed, too, in perceiving that the groundwork of all other philosophy must be laid in the philosophy of the mind. To lay this foundation deeply and strongly, and to raise a superstructure in accordance with it, were the objects to which their lives were devoted. They employed, indeed, for the most part, different materials; but as the materials of both were real observations, the genuine product of experience, the results will in the end be found not hostile, but supplementary, to one another. Of their methods of philosophizing, the same thing may be said: they were different, yet both were legitimate logical processes. In every respect, the two men are each other's "completing counterpart": the strong points of each correspond to the weak points of the other. Whoever could master the premises and combine the methods of both would possess the entire English philosophy of his age. Coleridge used to say that every one is born either a Platonist or an Aristotelian; it may be similarly affirmed that every Englishman of the present day is by implication either a Benthamite or a Coleridgian—holds views of human affairs which can only be proved true on the principles either of Bentham or of Coleridge. In one respect, indeed, the parallel fails. Bentham so improved and added to the system of philosophy he adopted that, for his successors, he may almost be accounted its founder; while Coleridge, though he has left on the system he inculcated such traces of himself as cannot fail to be left by any mind of original powers, was anticipated in all the essentials of his doctrine by the great Germans of the latter half of the last century, and was accompanied in it by the remarkable series of their French expositors and followers. Hence, although Coleridge is to Englishmen the type and the main source of that doctrine, he is the creator rather of the shape in which it has appeared among us than of the doctrine itself.

The time is yet far distant when, in the estimation of Coleridge and of his influence upon the intellect of our time, any thing like unanimity can be looked for. As a poet, Coleridge has taken his place. The healthier taste and more intelligent canons of poetic criticism, which he was himself mainly instrumental in diffusing, have at length assigned to him his proper rank as one among the great (and, if we look to the powers shown rather than to the amount of actual achievement, among the greatest) names in our literature. But, as a philosopher, the class of thinkers has scarcely yet arisen by whom he is to be judged. The limited philosophical public of this country is as yet too exclusively divided between those to whom Coleridge and the views which he promulgated or defended are every thing, and those to whom they are nothing. A true thinker can only be justly estimated when his thoughts have worked their way into minds formed in a different school; have been wrought and moulded into consistency with all other true and relevant thoughts; when the noisy conflict of half-truths, angrily denying one another, has subsided, and ideas which seemed mutually incompatible have been found only to require mutual limitations. This time has not yet come for Coleridge. The spirit of philosophy in England, like that of religion, is still rootedly sectarian. Conservative thinkers and Liberals, transcendentalists and admirers of Hobbes and Locke, regard each other as out of the pale of philosophical intercourse; look upon each other's speculations as vitiated by an original taint which makes all study of them, except for purposes of attack, useless if not mischievous. An error much the same as if Kepler had refused to profit by Ptolemy's or Tycho's observations, because those astronomers believed that the sun moved round the earth; or as if Priestley and Lavoisier, because they differed on the doctrine of phlogiston, had rejected each other's chemical experiments. It is even a still greater error than either of these. For among the truths long recognized by Continental philosophers, but which very few Englishmen have yet arrived at, one is the importance, in the present imperfect state of mental and social science, of antagonist modes of thought, which, it will one day be felt, are as necessary to one another in speculation as mutually checking powers are in a political constitution. A clear insight, indeed, into this necesssity is the only rational or enduring basis of philosophical tolerance, the only condition under which liberality in matters of opinion can be any thing better than a polite synonym for indifference between one opinion and another.

All students of man and society who possess that first requisite for so difficult a study, a due sense of its difficulties, are aware that the besetting danger is not so much of embracing falsehood for truth, as of mistaking part of the truth for the whole. It might be plausibly maintained that in almost every one of the leading controversies, past or present, in social philosophy, both sides were in the right in what they affirmed, though wrong in what they denied; and that, if either could have been made to take the other's views in addition to its own, little more would have been needed to make its doctrine correct. Take, for instance, the question how far mankind have gained by civilization. One observer is forcibly struck by the multiplication of physical comforts; the advancement and diffusion of knowledge; the decay of superstition; the facilities of mutual intercourse; the softening of manners; the decline of war and personal conflict; the progressive limitation of the tyranny of the strong over the weak; the great works accomplished throughout the globe by the co-operation of multitudes: and he becomes that very common character, the worshipper of "our enlightened age." Another fixes his attention not upon the value of these advantages, but upon the high price which is paid for them; the relaxation of individual energy and courage; the loss of proud and self-relying independence; the slavery of so large a portion of mankind to artificial wants; their effeminate shrinking from even the shadow of pain; the dull, unexciting monotony of their lives, and the passionless insipidity, and absence of any marked individuality in their characters; the contrast between the narrow mechanical understanding, produced by a life spent in executing by fixed rules a fixed task, and the varied powers of the man of the woods, whose subsistence and safety depend at each instant upon his capacity of extemporarily adapting means to ends; the demoralizing effect of great inequalities in wealth and social rank; and the sufferings of the great mass of the people of civilized countries, whose wants are scarcely better provided for than those of the savage, while they are bound by a thousand fetters in lieu of the freedom and excitement which are his compensations. One who attends to these things, and to these exclusively, will be apt to infer that savage life is preferable to civilized; that the work of civilization should as far as possible be undone; and, from the premises of Rousseau, he will not improbably be led to the practical conclusions of Rousseau's disciple, Robespierre. No two thinkers can be more entirely at variance than the two we have supposed—the worshippers of civilization and of independence, of the present and of the remote past. Yet all that is positive in the opinions of either of them is true; and we see how easy it would be to choose one's path if either half of the truth were the whole of it, and how great may be the difficulty of framing, as it is necessary to do, a set of practical maxims which combine both.

So, again, one person sees in a very strong light the need which the great mass of mankind have of being ruled over by a degree of intelligence and virtue superior to their own. He is deeply impressed with the mischief done to the uneducated and uncultivated by weaning them of all habits of reverence, appealing to them as a competent tribunal to decide the most intricate questions, and making them think themselves capable not only of being a light to themselves, but of giving the law to their superiors in culture. He sees, further, that cultivation, to be carried beyond a certain point, requires leisure; that leisure is the natural attribute of a hereditary aristocracy; that such a body has all the means of acquiring intellectual and moral superiority: and he needs be at no loss to endow them with abundant motives to it. An aristocracy, indeed, being human, are, as he cannot but see, not exempt any more than their inferiors from the common need of being controlled and enlightened by a still greater wisdom and goodness than their own. For this, however, his reliance is upon reverence for a Higher above them, sedulously inculcated and fostered by the course of their education. We thus see brought together all the elements of a conscientious zealot for an aristocratic government, supporting and supported by an established Christian church. There is truth, and important truth, in this thinker's premises. But there is a thinker of a very different description in whose premises there is an equal portion of truth. This is he who says that an average man, even an average member of an aristocracy, if he can postpone the interests of other people to his own calculations or instincts of self-interest, will do so; that all governments in all ages have done so, as far as they were permitted and generally to a ruinous extent; and that the only possible remedy is a pure democracy, in which the people are their own governors and can have no selfish interest in oppressing themselves.

Thus it is in regard to every important partial truth: there are always two conflicting modes of thought—one tending to give to that truth too large, the other to give it too small, a place; and the history of opinion is generally an oscillation between these extremes. From the imperfection of the human faculties, it seldom happens that, even in the minds of eminent thinkers, each partial view of their subject passes for its worth and none for more than its worth. But even if this just balance exist in the mind of the wiser teacher, it will not exist in his disciples, far less in the general mind. He cannot prevent that which is new in his doctrine and on which, being new, he is forced to insist the most strongly, from making a disproportionate impression. The impetus necessary to overcome the obstacles which resist all novelties of opinion seldom fails to carry the public mind almost as far on the contrary side of the perpendicular. Thus every excess in either direction determines a corresponding reaction; improvement consisting only in this—that the oscillation each time departs rather less widely from the centre, and an ever-increasing tendency is manifested to settle finally in it.

Now the Germano-Coleridgian doctrine is, in our view of the matter, the result of such a reaction. It expresses the revolt of the human mind against the philosophy of the eighteenth century. It is ontological, because that was experimental; conservative, because that was innovative; religious, because so much of that was infidel; concrete and historical, because that was abstract and metaphysical; poetical, because that was matter-of-fact and prosaic. In every respect, it flies off in the contrary direction to its predecessor; yet, faithful to the general law of improvement last noticed, it is less extreme in its opposition, it denies less of what is true in the doctrine it wars against, than had been the case in any previous philosophic reaction; and in particular far less than when the philosophy of the eighteenth century triumphed, and so memorably abused its victory, over that which preceded it.

We may begin our consideration of the two systems either at one extreme or the other—with their highest philosophical generalizations, or with their practical conclusions. The former seems preferable, because it is in their highest generalities that the difference between the two systems is most familiarly known.

Every consistent scheme of philosophy requires, as its starting-point, a theory respecting the sources of human knowledge and the objects which the human faculties are capable of taking cognizance of. The prevailing theory in the eighteenth century, on this most comprehensive of questions, was that proclaimed by Locke and commonly attributed to Aristotle—that all knowledge consists of generalizations from experience. Of nature or any thing whatever external to ourselves, we know, according to this theory, nothing except the facts which present themselves to our senses, and such other facts as may by analogy be inferred from these. There is no knowledge *a priori;* no truths cognizable by the mind's inward light and grounded on intuitive evidence. Sensation and the mind's consciousness of its own acts are not only the exclusive sources, but the sole materials, of our knowledge. From this doctrine, Coleridge, with the German philosophers since Kant (not to go farther back) and most of the English since Reid, strongly dissents. He claims for the human mind a capacity, within certain limits, of perceiving the nature and properties of "things in themselves." He distinguishes in the human intellect two faculties, which, in the technical language common to him with the Germans, he calls Understanding and Reason. The former faculty judges of phenomena, or the appearances of things, and forms generalizations from these; to the latter it belongs, by direct intuition, to perceive things, and recognize truths, not cognizable by our senses. These perceptions are not indeed innate, nor could ever have been awakened in us without experience; but they are not copies of it: experience is not their prototype, it is only the occasion by which they are irresistibly suggested. The appearances in nature excite in us, by an inherent law, ideas of those invisible things which

are the causes of the visible appearances, and on whose laws
those appearances depend; and we then perceive that these
things must have pre-existed to render the appearances possible; just as (to use a frequent illustration of Coleridge's) we
see, before we know that we have eyes: but, when once this
is known to us, we perceive that eyes must have pre-existed
to enable us to see. Among the truths which are thus known
a priori, by occasion of experience but not themselves the
subjects of experience, Coleridge includes the fundamental
doctrines of religion and morals, the principles of mathematics, and the ultimate laws even of physical nature—which
he contends cannot be proved by experience, though they
must necessarily be consistent with it, and would, if we knew
them perfectly, enable us to account for all observed facts,
and to predict all those which are as yet unobserved.

It is not necessary to remind any one who concerns himself with such subjects, that between the partisans of these
two opposite doctrines there reigns a *bellum internecinum.*
Neither side is sparing in the imputation of intellectual and
moral obliquity to the perceptions, and of pernicious consequences to the creed, of its antagonists. Sensualism is the
common term of abuse for the one philosophy; mysticism,
for the other. The one doctrine is accused of making men
beasts; the other, lunatics. It is the unaffected belief of numbers on one side of the controversy, that their adversaries
are actuated by a desire to break loose from moral and religious obligation; and of numbers on the other, that their
opponents are either men fit for Bedlam, or who cunningly
pander to the interests of hierarchies and aristocracies by
manufacturing superfine new arguments in favor of old prejudices. It is almost needless to say that those who are freest
with these mutual accusations are seldom those who are most
at home in the real intricacies of the question, or who are
best acquainted with the argumentative strength of the opposite side or even of their own. But without going to these
extreme lengths, even sober men on both sides take no
charitable view of the tendencies of each other's opinions.

It is affirmed that the doctrine of Locke and his followers,
that all knowledge is experience generalized, leads by strict
logical consequence to atheism; that Hume and other sceptics
were right when they contended that it is impossible to prove
a God on grounds of experience; and Coleridge (like Kant)
maintains positively that the ordinary argument for a Deity,
from marks of design in the universe, or in other words from

the resemblance of the order in nature to the effects of human skill and contrivance, is not tenable. It is further said that the same doctrine annihilates moral obligation—reducing morality either to the blind impulses of animal sensibility or to a calculation of prudential consequences, both equally fatal to its essence. Even science, it is affirmed, loses the character of science in this view of it, and becomes empiricism—a mere enumeration and arrangement of facts, not explaining nor accounting for them: since a fact is only then accounted for, when we are made to see in it the manifestation of laws, which, as soon as they are perceived at all, are perceived to be *necessary*. These are the charges brought by the transcendental philosophers against the school of Locke, Hartley, and Bentham. They, in their turn, allege that the transcendentalists make imagination, and not observation, the criterion of truth; that they lay down principles under which a man may enthrone his wildest dreams in the chair of philosophy, and impose them on mankind as intuitions of the pure reason: which has, in fact, been done in all ages by all manner of mystical enthusiasts. And even if, with gross inconsistency, the private revelations of any individual Behmen or Swedenborg be disowned or, in other words, outvoted (the only means of discrimination, which, it is contended, the theory admits of), this is still only substituting, as the test of truth, the dreams of the majority for the dreams of each individual. Whoever form a strong enough party may at any time set up the immediate perceptions of *their* reason, that is to say any reigning prejudice, as a truth independent of experience—a truth not only requiring no proof, but to be believed in opposition to all that appears proof to the mere understanding; nay, the more to be believed, because it cannot be put into words and into the logical form of a proposition without a contradiction in terms: for no less authority than this is claimed by some transcendentalists for their *a priori* truths. And thus a ready mode is provided by which whoever is on the strongest side may dogmatize at his ease, and, instead of proving his propositions, may rail at all who deny them as bereft of "the vision and the faculty divine," or blinded to its plainest revelations by a corrupt heart. . . .

[Although Mill himself agrees with the epistemology of Locke and Bentham, he admits that the doctrines of the school of Locke stood in need of entire renovation, especially since they had led on the Continent to a prevailing philosophy that had destroyed among educated people "any allegiance to the opinions or institutions of ancient times." "To tear away" was all the French *philosophes* aimed at. They forgot that the very reasonableness on which they based their hopes for the future was itself the product of the civilization they despised—that it emerged from the self-discipline learned through *education,* from *loyalty* to some one stable social principle, be it king, God or constitution, and from an active feeling of social *cohesion.*—Ed.]

These essential requisites of civil society the French philosophers of the eighteenth century unfortunately overlooked. They found, indeed, all three—at least the first and second, and most of what nourishes and invigorates the third— already undermined by the vices of the institutions and of the men that were set up as the guardians and bulwarks of them. If innovators, in their theories, disregarded the elementary principles of the social union, conservatives, in their practice, had set the first example. The existing order of things had ceased to realize those first principles; from the force of circumstances, and from the short-sighted selfishness of its administrators, it had ceased to possess the essential conditions of permanent society, and was therefore tottering to its fall. But the philosophers did not see this. Bad as the existing system was in the days of its decrepitude, according to them it was still worse when it actually did what it now only pretended to do. Instead of feeling that the effect of a bad social order, in sapping the necessary foundations of society itself, is one of the worst of its many mischiefs, the philosophers saw only, and saw with joy, that it was sapping its own foundations. In the weakening of all government, they saw only the weakening of bad government, and thought they could not better employ themselves than in finishing the task so well begun—in discrediting all that still remained of restraining discipline, because it rested on the ancient and decayed creeds against which they made war; in unsettling every thing which was still considered settled, making men doubtful of the few things of which they still felt certain; and in uprooting what little remained in the people's minds of reverence for any thing above them, of respect to any of the limits which custom and prescription had set to the indulgence of each man's fancies or inclinations, or of attachment to any of the things which belonged to them as a nation, and which made them feel their unity.

Much of all this was, no doubt, unavoidable and not justly matter of blame. When the vices of all constituted authorities, added to natural causes of decay, have eaten the heart out of old institutions and beliefs, while at the same time the growth of knowledge and the altered circumstances of the age would have required institutions and creeds different from these, even if they had remained uncorrupt, we are far from saying that any degree of wisdom on the part of speculative thinkers could avert the political catastrophes and the subsequent moral anarchy and unsettledness which we have witnessed and are witnessing. Still less do we pretend that those principles and influences which we have spoken of as the conditions of the permanent existence of the social union, once lost, can ever be, or should be attempted to be, revived in connection with the same institutions or the same doctrines as before. When society requires to be rebuilt, there is no use in attempting to rebuild it on the old plan. By the union of the enlarged views and analytic powers of speculative men with the observation and contriving sagacity of men of practice, better institutions and better doctrines must be elaborated; and until this is done, we cannot hope for much improvement in our present condition. The effort to do it in the eighteenth century would have been premature, as the attempts of the Economistes (who, of all persons then living, came nearest to it, and who were the first to form clearly the idea of a social science) sufficiently testify. The time was not ripe for doing effectually any other work than that of destruction. But the work of the day should have been so performed as not to impede that of the morrow. No one can calculate what struggles, which the cause of improvement has yet to undergo, might have been spared if the philosophers of the eighteenth century had done any thing like justice to the past. Their mistake was that they did not acknowledge the historical value of much which had ceased to be useful, nor saw that institutions and creeds, now effete, had rendered essential services to civilization, and still filled a place in the human mind, and in the arrangements of society, which could not without great peril be left vacant. Their mistake was that they did not recognize, in many of the errors which they assailed, corruptions of important truths, and, in many of the institutions most cankered with abuse, necessary elements of civilized society, though in a form and vesture no longer suited to the age; and hence they involved, as far as in them lay, many great truths in a common discredit with the errors which had grown up around them. They threw away the shell without preserving the kernel; and, attempting to new-model society without the binding forces which hold society together, met with such success as might have been anticipated.

Now we claim, in behalf of the philosophers of the reactionary school—of the school to which Coleridge belongs—that exactly what we blame the philosophers of the eighteenth century for not doing, they have done.

Every reaction in opinion, of course, brings into view that portion of the truth which was overlooked before. It was natural that a philosophy which anathematized all that had been going on in Europe from Constantine to Luther, or even to Voltaire, should be succeeded by another, at once a severe critic of the new tendencies of society and an impassioned vindicator of what was good in the past. This is the easy merit of all Tory and Royalist writers. But the peculiarity of the Germano-Coleridgian school is that they saw beyond the immediate controversy to the fundamental principles involved in all such controversies. They were the first (except a solitary thinker here and there) who inquired, with any comprehensiveness or depth, into the inductive laws of the existence and growth of human society. They were the first to bring prominently forward the three requisites which we have enumerated as essential principles of all permanent forms of social existence—as principles, we say, and not as mere accidental advantages inherent in the particular polity or religion which the writer happened to patronize. They were the first who pursued, philosophically and in the spirit of Baconian investigation, not only this inquiry but others ulterior and collateral to it. They thus produced, not a piece of party advocacy, but a philosophy of society in the only form in which it is yet possible—that of a philosophy of history; not a defence of particular ethical or religious doctrines, but a contribution, the largest made by any class of thinkers, towards the philosophy of human culture.

The brilliant light which has been thrown upon history during the last half-century has proceeded almost wholly from this school. The disrespect in which history was held by the *philosophes* is notorious: one of the soberest of them (D'Alembert, we believe) was the author of the wish that all record whatever of past events could be blotted out. And, indeed, the ordinary mode of writing history, and the ordinary mode of drawing lessons from it, were almost sufficient

to excuse this contempt. But the *philosophes* saw as usual
what was not true, not what was. It is no wonder that they,
who looked on the greater part of what had been handed
down from the past as sheer hindrances to man's attaining
a well-being which would otherwise be of easy attainment,
should content themselves with a very superficial study of
history. But the case was otherwise with those who regarded
the maintenance of society at all, and especially its maintenance in a state of progressive advancement, as a very difficult task actually achieved, in however imperfect a manner,
for a number of centuries against the strongest obstacles.
It was natural that they should feel a deep interest in ascertaining how this had been effected; and should be led to
inquire both what were the requisites of the permanent existence of the body politic, and what were the conditions
which had rendered the preservation of these permanent
requisites compatible with perpetual and progressive improvement. And hence that series of great writers and thinkers, from Herder to Michelet, by whom history, which was
till then "a tale told by an idiot, full of sound and fury,
signifying nothing," has been made a science of causes and
effects; who, by making the facts and events of the past have
a meaning, and an intelligible place in the gradual evolution of humanity, have at once given history, even to the
imagination, an interest like romance, and afforded the only
means of predicting and guiding the future, by unfolding
the agencies which have produced and still maintain the
present.[1]

---

[1] There is something at once ridiculous and discouraging in the
signs, which daily meet us, of the Cimmerian darkness still prevailing
in England (wherever recent foreign literature or the speculations of
the Coleridgians have not penetrated) concerning the very existence
of the views of general history, which have been received throughout
the Continent of Europe for the last twenty or thirty years. A writer
in Blackwood's Magazine, certainly not the least able publication
of our day, nor this the least able writer in it, lately announced, with
all the pomp and heraldry of triumphant genius, a discovery which
was to disabuse the world of an universal prejudice and create "the
philosophy of Roman history." This is that the Roman empire perished
not from outward violence, but from inward decay; and that the bar-
barian conquerors were the renovators, not the destroyers, of its civilization. Why, there is not a schoolboy in France or Germany who did
not possess this writer's discovery before him; the contrary opinion has
receded so far into the past that it must be rather a learned Frenchman
or German who remembers that it was ever held. If the writer in Blackwood had read a line of Guizot (to go no further than the most obvious
sources), he would probably have abstained from making himself very
ridiculous, and his country, so far as depends upon him, the laughing-
stock of Europe.

The same causes have naturally led the same class of thinkers to do what their predecessors never could have done for the philosophy of human culture. For the tendency of their speculations compelled them to see, in the character of the national education existing in any political society, at once the principal cause of its permanence as a society and the chief source of its progressiveness; the former by the extent to which that education operated as a system of restraining discipline, the latter by the degree in which it called forth and invigorated the active faculties. Besides, not to have looked upon the culture of the inward man as the problem of problems would have been incompatible with the belief which many of these philosophers entertained in Christianity, and the recognition by all of them of its historical value and the prime part which it has acted in the progress of mankind. But here, too, let us not fail to observe, they rose to principles and did not stick in the particular case. The culture of the human being had been carried to no ordinary height, and human nature had exhibited many of its noblest manifestations, not in Christian countries only but in the ancient world—in Athens, Sparta, Rome: nay, even barbarians, as the Germans, or still more unmitigated savages, the wild Indians, and again the Chinese, the Egyptians, the Arabs, all had their own education, their own culture—a culture which, whatever might be its tendency upon the whole, had been successful in some respect or other. Every form of polity, every condition of society, whatever else it had done, had formed its type of national character. What that type was, and how it had been made what it was, were questions which the metaphysician might overlook; the historical philosopher could not. Accordingly, the views respecting the various elements of human culture and the causes influencing the formation of national character, which pervade the writings of the Germano-Coleridgian school, throw into the shade every thing which had been effected before or which has been attempted simultaneously by any other school. Such views are, more than any thing else, the characteristic feature of the Goethian period of German literature; and are richly diffused through the historical and critical writings of the new French school, as well as of Coleridge and his followers.

In this long though most compressed dissertation on the Continental philosophy preceding the reaction, and on the nature of the reaction so far as directed against that philoso-

phy, we have unavoidably been led to speak rather of the
movement itself than of Coleridge's particular share in it—
which, from his posteriority in date, was necessarily a subordinate one. And it would be useless, even did our limits permit, to bring together, from the scattered writings of a man
who produced no systematic work, any of the fragments
which he may have contributed to an edifice still incomplete,
and even the general character of which we can have rendered very imperfectly intelligible to those who are not acquainted with the theory itself. Our object is to invite to the
study of the original sources, not to supply the place of such
a study. What was peculiar to Coleridge will be better manifested when we now proceed to review the state of popular
philosophy immediately preceding him in our own island—
which was different, in some material respects, from the con-
temporaneous Continental philosophy.

In England, the philosophical speculations of the age had
not, except in a few highly metaphysical minds (whose example rather served to deter than to invite others), taken
so audacious a flight, nor achieved any thing like so complete a victory over the counteracting influences, as on the
Continent. There is in the English mind, both in speculation
and in practice, a highly salutary shrinking from all extremes;
but as this shrinking is rather an instinct of caution than a
result of insight, it is too ready to satisfy itself with any
medium merely because it is a medium, and to acquiesce in
a union of the disadvantages of both extremes instead of
their advantages. The circumstances of the age, too, were
unfavorable to decided opinions. The repose which followed
the great struggles of the Reformation and the Commonwealth; the final victory over Popery and Puritanism, Jacob-
itism and Republicanism, and the lulling of the controversies
which kept speculation and spiritual consciousness alive; the
lethargy which came upon all governors and teachers after
their position in society became fixed; and the growing absorption of all classes in material interests—caused a state
of mind to diffuse itself, with less of deep inward workings,
and less capable of interpreting those it had, than had existed
for centuries. The age seemed smitten with an incapacity
of producing deep or strong feeling, such as at least could
ally itself with meditative habits. There were few poets, and
none of a high order; and philosophy fell mostly into the
hands of men of a dry prosaic nature, who had not enough
of the materials of human feeling in them to be able to

imagine any of its more complex and mysterious manifestations; all of which they either left out of their theories, or introduced them with such explanations as no one who had experienced the feelings could receive as adequate. An age like this, an age without earnestness, was the natural era of compromises and half-convictions.

To make out a case for the feudal and ecclesiastical institutions of modern Europe was by no means impossible: they had a meaning, had existed for honest ends, and an honest theory of them might be made. But the administration of those institutions had long ceased to accord with any honest theory. It was impossible to justify them in principle, except on grounds which condemned them in practice; and grounds of which there was, at any rate, little or no recognition in the philosophy of the eighteenth century. The natural tendency, therefore, of that philosophy, everywhere but in England, was to seek the extinction of those institutions. In England, it would doubtless have done the same, had it been strong enough; but as this was beyond its strength, an adjustment was come to between the rival powers. What neither party cared about, the *ends* of existing institutions, the work that was to be done by teachers and governors, was flung overboard. The wages of that work the teachers and governors did care about; and those wages were secured to them. The existing institutions in Church and State were to be preserved inviolate, in outward semblance at least; but were required to be, practically, as much a nullity as possible. The Church continued to "rear her mitred front in courts and palaces," but not, as in the days of Hildebrand or Becket, as the champion of arts against arms, of the serf against the seigneur, peace against war, or spiritual principles and powers against the domination of animal force; nor even (as in the days of Latimer and John Knox) as a body divinely commissioned to train the nation in a knowledge of God and obedience to his laws, whatever became of temporal principalities and powers, and whether this end might most effectually be compassed by their assistance or by trampling them under foot. No; but the people of England liked old things, and nobody knew how the place might be filled which the doing-away with so conspicuous an institution would leave vacant, and *quieta ne movere* was the favorite doctrine of those times: therefore, on condition of not making too much noise about religion, or taking it too much in earnest, the Church was supported, even by philosophers—as a "bulwark against fanaticism," a sedative to the religious spirit, to prevent it from disturbing the harmony of society or the tranquillity of states. The clergy of the Establishment thought they had a good bargain on these terms, and kept its conditions very faithfully.

The State, again, was no longer considered, according to the old ideal, as a concentration of the force of all the individuals of the nation in the hands of certain of its members, in order to the accomplishment of whatever could be best accomplished by systematic cooperation. It was found that the State was a bad judge of the wants of society; that it in reality cared very little for them, and when it attempted any thing beyond that police against crime and arbitration of disputes, which are indispensable to social existence, the private sinister interest of some class or individual was usually the prompter of its proceedings. The natural inference would have been that the constitution of the State was somehow not suited to the existing wants of society, having indeed descended, with scarcely any modifications that could be avoided, from a time when the most prominent exigencies of society were quite different. This conclusion, however, was shrunk from; and it required the peculiarities of very recent times, and the speculations of the Bentham school, to produce even any considerable tendency that way. The existing Constitution, and all the arrangements of existing society, continued to be applauded as the best possible. The celebrated theory of the three powers was got up, which made the excellence of our Constitution consist in doing less harm than would be done by any other form of government. Government altogether was regarded as a necessary evil, and was required to hide itself—to make itself as little felt as possible. The cry of the people was not, "Help us"; "Guide us"; "Do for us the things we cannot do; and instruct us, that we may do well those which we can" (and truly such requirements from such rulers would have been a bitter jest); the cry was, "Let us alone." Power to decide questions of *meum* and *tuum,* to protect society from open violence, and from some of the most dangerous modes of fraud, could not be withheld; these functions the Government was left in possession of, and to these it became the expectation of the public that it should confine itself.

Such was the prevailing tone of English belief in temporals. What was it in spirituals? Here, too, a similar system of compromise had been at work. Those who pushed their philosophical speculations to the denial of the received religious belief, whether they went to the extent of infidelity or only of heterodoxy, met with little encouragement; neither religion itself, nor the received forms of it, were at all shaken by the few attacks which were made upon them from without. The philosophy, however, of the time made itself felt as effectually in another fashion; it pushed its way *into* religion. The *a priori* arguments for a God were first dismissed. This was indeed inevitable. The internal evidences of Christianity shared nearly the same fate; if not absolutely thrown aside, they fell into the background and were little thought of. The doctrine of Locke that we have no *innate* moral sense, perverted into the doctrine that we have no moral sense at all, made it appear that we had not any capacity of judging, from the doctrine itself, whether it was worthy to have come from a righteous Being. In forgetfulness of the most solemn warnings of the Author of Christianity, as well as of the apostle who was the main diffuser of it through the world, belief in his religion was left to stand upon miracles—a species of evidence which, according to the universal belief of the early Christians themselves, was by no means peculiar to true religion; and it is melancholy to see on what frail reeds able defenders of Christianity preferred to rest, rather than upon that better evidence which alone gave to their so-called evidences any value as a collateral confirmation. In the interpretation of Christianity, the palpablest *bibliolatry* prevailed—if (with Coleridge) we may so term that superstitious worship of particular texts, which persecuted Galileo and, in our own day, anathematized the discoveries of geology. Men whose faith in Christianity rested on the literal infallibility of the sacred volume shrank in terror from the idea that it could have been included in the scheme of Providence, that the human opinions and mental habits of the particular writers should be allowed to mix with and color their mode of conceiving and of narrating the divine transactions. Yet this slavery to the letter has not only raised every difficulty which envelops the most unimportant passage in the Bible into an objection to revelation, but has paralyzed many a well-meant effort to bring Christianity home, as a consistent scheme, to human experience and capacities of apprehension; as if there was much of it which it was more prudent to leave *in nubibus* lest, in the attempt to make the mind seize hold of it as a reality, some text might be found to stand in the way. It might have been expected that this idolatry of the words of Scripture would at least have saved its doctrines from being tampered with by human notions, but the contrary proved to be the effect; for the vague and sophistical mode of interpreting texts, which was necessary in order to reconcile what was manifestly irreconcilable, engendered a habit of playing fast and loose with Scripture and finding in, or leaving out of it, whatever one pleased. Hence, while Christianity was in theory and in intention received and submitted to, with even "prostration of the understanding" before it, much alacrity was in fact displayed in *accommodating* it to the received philosophy and even to the popular notions of the time. To take only one example, but so signal a one as to be *instar omnium*. If there is any one requirement of Christianity less doubtful than another, it is that of being spiritually-minded—of loving and practising good from a pure love, simply because it is good. But one of the crotchets of the philosophy of the age was that all virtue is self-interest; and accordingly, in the text-book adopted by the Church (in one of its universities) for instruction in moral philosophy, the reason for doing good is declared to be that God is stronger than we are and is able to damn us if we do not. This is no exaggeration of the sentiments of Paley, and hardly even of the crudity of his language.

Thus, on the whole, England had neither the benefits, such as they were, of the new ideas, nor of the old. We were just sufficiently under the influences of each to render the other powerless. We had a Government which we respected too much to attempt to change it, but not enough to trust it with any power or look to it for any services that were not compelled. We had a Church which had ceased to fulfil the honest purposes of a church, but which we made a great point of keeping up as the pretence or *simulacrum* of one. We had a highly spiritual religion (which we were instructed to obey from selfish motives), and the most mechanical and worldly notions on every other subject; and we were so much afraid of being wanting in reverence to each particular syllable of the book which contained our religion, that we let its most important meanings slip through our fingers and entertained the most grovelling conceptions of its spirit and general purposes. This was not a state of things which could recommend itself to any earnest mind. It was sure, in no great length of time, to call forth two sorts of men: the one demanding the extinction of the institutions and creeds which had hitherto existed; the other, that they be made a reality: the one pressing the new doctrines to their utmost consequences, the other re-asserting the best meaning and purposes of the old. The first type attained its greatest height in Bentham; the last, in Coleridge.

We hold that these two sorts of men, who seem to be, and believe themselves to be, enemies, are in reality allies. The powers they wield are opposite poles of one great force of progression. What was really hateful and contemptible was the state which preceded them, and which each in its way has been striving now for many years to improve. Each ought to hail with rejoicing the advent of the other. But most of all ought an enlightened Radical or Liberal to rejoice over such a Conservative as Coleridge. For such a Radical must know that the Constitution and Church of England, and the religious opinions and political maxims professed by their supporters, are not mere frauds nor sheer nonsense; have not been got up originally, and all along maintained, for the sole purpose of picking people's pockets, without aiming at, or being found conducive to, any honest end during the whole process. Nothing, of which this is a sufficient account, would have lasted a tithe of five, eight, or ten centuries, in the most improving period and (during much of that period) the most improving nation in the world. These things, we may depend upon it, were not always without much good in them, however little of it may now be left: and reformers ought to hail the man as a brother-reformer who points out what this good is; what it is which we have a right to expect from things established, which they are bound to do for us, as the justification of their being established; so that they may be recalled to it, and compelled to do it, or the impossibility of their any longer doing it may be conclusively manifested. What is any case for reform good for, until it has passed this test? What mode is there of determining whether a thing is fit to exist, without first considering what purposes it exists for, and whether it be still capable of fulfilling them?

We have not room here to consider Coleridge's Conservative philosophy in all its aspects, or in relation to all the quarters from which objections might be raised against it. We shall consider it with relation to Reformers, and especially to Benthamites. We would assist them to determine whether they would have to do with Conservative philosophers or with Conservative dunces; and whether, since there are Tories, it be better that they should learn their Toryism from Lord Eldon, or even Sir Robert Peel, or Coleridge.

Take, for instance, Coleridge's view of the grounds of a Church Establishment. His mode of treating any institution is to investigate what he terms the idea of it, or what in common parlance would be called the principle involved in it. The idea or principle of a national church, and of the Church of England in that character, is, according to him, the reservation of a portion of the land, or of a right to a portion of its produce, as a fund—for what purpose? For the worship of God? For the performance of religious ceremonies? No; for the advancement of knowledge, and the civilization and cultivation of the community. This fund he does not term "church-property," but "the nationalty" or national property. He considers it as destined for "the support and maintenance of a permanent class or order, with the following duties":

A certain smaller number were to remain at the fountain-heads of the humanities, in cultivating and enlarging the knowledge already possessed, and in watching over the interests of physical and moral science; being likewise the instructors of such as constituted, or were to constitute, the remaining more numerous classes of the order. The members of this latter and far more numerous body were to be distributed throughout the country, so as not to leave even the smallest integral part or division without a resident guide, guardian, and instructor; the objects and final intention of the whole order being these—to preserve the stores and to guard the treasures of past civilization, and thus to bind the present with the past; to perfect and add to the same, and thus to connect the present with the future; but especially to diffuse through the whole community, and to every native entitled to its laws and rights, that quantity and quality of knowledge which was indispensable both for the understanding of those rights, and for the performance of the duties correspondent; finally, to secure for the nation, if not a superiority over the neighboring States, yet an equality at least, in that character of general civilization, which, equally with, or rather more than, fleets, armies, and revenue, forms the ground of its defensive and offensive power.

This organized body, set apart and endowed for the cultivation and diffusion of knowledge, is not in Coleridge's view necessarily a religious corporation.

Religion may be an indispensable ally, but is not the essential constitutive end, of that national institute, which is unfortunately, at least improperly, styled the Church; a name which, in its best sense, is exclusively appropriate to the

Church of Christ. . . . The *clerisy* of the nation, or national church in its primary acceptation and original intention, comprehended the learned of all denominations, the sages and professors of the law and jurisprudence, of medicine and physiology, of music, of military and civil architecture, with the mathematical as the common organ of the preceding; in short, all the so-called liberal arts and sciences, the possession and application of which constitute the civilization of a country, as well as the theological. The last was, indeed, placed at the head of all; and of good right did it claim the precedence. But why? Because under the name of theology or divinity were contained the interpretation of languages; the conservation and tradition of past events; the momentous epochs and revolutions of the race and nation; the continuation of the records, logic, ethics, and the determination of ethical science, in application to the rights and duties of men in all their various relations, social and civil; and, lastly, the ground-knowledge, the *prima scientia,* as it was named—philosophy, or the doctrine and discipline of ideas.

Theology formed only a part of the objects, the theologians formed only a portion of the clerks or clergy, of the national church. The theological order had precedency indeed, and deservedly; but not because its members were priests, whose office was to conciliate the invisible powers, and to superintend the interests that survive the grave; nor as being exclusively, or even principally, sacerdotal or templar, which, when it did occur, is to be considered as an accident of the age, a misgrowth of ignorance and oppression, a falsification of the constitutive principle, not a constituent part of the same. No: the theologians took the lead because the science of theology was the root and the trunk of the knowledge of civilized man; because it gave unity and the circulating sap of life to all other sciences, by virtue of which alone they could be contemplated as forming collectively the living tree of knowledge. It had the precedency, because under the name Theology were comprised all the main aids, instruments, and materials of national education, the *nisus formativus* of the body politic, the shaping and informing spirit, which, educing or eliciting the latent man in all the natives of the soil, trains them up to be citizens of the country, free subjects of the realm. And, lastly, because to divinity belong those fundamental truths which are the common groundwork of our civil and our religious duties, not less indispensable to a right view of our temporal concerns than to a rational faith respecting our immortal well-being. Not without celestial observations can even terrestrial charts be accurately constructed. (*Church and State,* Chap. v.)

The nationalty or national property, according to Coleridge, "cannot rightfully be, and without foul wrong to the nation never has been, alienated from its original purposes," from the promotion of "a continuing and progressive civilization," to the benefit of individuals or any public purpose of merely economical or material interest. But the State may withdraw the fund from its actual holders for the better execution of its purposes. There is no sanctity attached to the means, but only to the ends. The fund is not dedicated to any particular scheme of religion, nor even to religion at all; religion has only to do with it in the character of an instrument of civilization, and in common with all the other instruments.

I do not assert that the proceeds from the nationalty cannot be rightfully vested, except in what we now mean by clergymen and the established clergy. I have everywhere implied the contrary. . . . In relation to the national church, Christianity or the Church of Christ is a blessed accident, a providential boon, a grace of God. . . . As the olive-tree is said in its growth to fertilize the surrounding soil, to invigorate the roots of the vines in its immediate neighborhood, and to improve the strength and flavor of the wines; such is the relation of the Christian and the national Church. But as the olive is not the same plant with the vine, or with the elm or poplar (that is, the State) with which the vine is wedded; and as the vine, with its prop, may exist, though in less perfection, without the olive, or previously to its implantation: even so is Christianity, and *a fortiori* any particular scheme of theology derived, and supposed by its partisans to be deduced, from Christianity, no essential part of the being of the national Church, however conducive or even indispensable it may be to its well-being. (Chap. vi.)

What would Sir Robert Inglis, or Sir Robert Peel, or Mr. Spooner say to such a doctrine as this? Will they thank Coleridge for this advocacy of Toryism? What would become of the three-years' debates on the Appropriation Clause, which so disgraced this country before the face of Europe? Will the ends of practical Toryism be much served by a theory under which the Royal Society might claim a part of the church property with as good right as the bench of bishops, if, by endowing that body like the French Institute, science could be better promoted? a theory by which the State, in the conscientious exercise of its judgment, having decided that the Church of England does not fulfil the object for which the nationalty was intended, might transfer its endowments to any other ecclesiastical body, or to any other body not ecclesiastical, which it deemed more competent to fulfill those objects; might establish any other sect, or all sects, or no sect at all, if it should deem that, in the divided condition of religious opinion in this country, the State can no longer with advantage attempt the complete religious instruction of its people, but must for the present content itself with providing secular instruction and such religious teaching, if any, as all can take part in—leaving each sect to apply to its own communion that which they all agree in considering as the keystone of the arch. We believe this to be the true state of affairs in Great Britain at the present time. We are far from thinking it other than a serious evil. We entirely acknowledge that, in any person fit to be a teacher, the view he takes of religion will be intimately connected with the view he will take of all the greatest things which he has to teach. Unless the same teachers who give instruction on those other subjects are at liberty to enter freely on religion, the scheme of education will be to a certain degree fragmentary and incoherent. But the State at present has only the option of such an imperfect scheme, or of intrusting the whole business to perhaps the most unfit body for the exclusive charge of it that could be found among persons of any intellectual attainments: namely, the established clergy as at present trained and composed. Such a body would have no chance of being selected as the exclusive administrators of the nationalty on any foundation but that of divine right; the ground avowedly taken by the only other school of Conservative philosophy which is attempting to raise its head in this country—that of the new Oxford theologians.

Coleridge's merit in this matter consists, as it seems to us, in two things. First, that by setting in a clear light what a national-church establishment ought to be, and what, by the very fact of its existence, it must be held to pretend to be, he has pronounced the severest satire upon what in fact it is. There is some difference, truly, between Coleridge's church, in which the schoolmaster forms the first step in the heirarchy, "who in due time, and under condition of a faithful performance of his arduous duties, should succeed to the pastorate,"[2] and the Church of England such as we now see. But to say the Church, and mean only the clergy, "constituted," according to Coleridge's conviction, "the first and fundamental apostasy."[3] He and the thoughts which have proceeded from him have done more than would have been

[2] *Church and State*, p. 57.
[3] *Literary Remains*, iii, 386.

effected in thrice the time by Dissenters and Radicals to make the Church ashamed of the evil of her ways, and to determine that movement of improvement from within which has begun, where it ought to begin, at the universities and among the younger clergy, and which, if this sect-ridden country is ever to be really taught, must proceed, *pari passu,* with the assault carried on from without.

Secondly, we honor Coleridge for having rescued from the discredit in which the corruptions of the English Church had involved every thing connected with it, and for having vindicated against Bentham and Adam Smith and the whole eighteenth century, the principle of an endowed class for the cultivation of learning and for diffusing its results among the community. That such a class is likely to be behind, instead of before, the progress of knowledge is an induction erroneously drawn from the peculiar circumstances of the last two centuries and in contradiction to all the rest of modern history. If we have seen much of the abuses of endowments, we have not seen what this country might be made by a proper administration of them, as we trust we shall not see what it would be without them. On this subject we are entirely at one with Coleridge and with the other great defender of endowed establishments, Dr. Chalmers; and we consider the definitive establishment of this fundamental principle to be one of the permanent benefits which political science owes to the Conservative philosophers.

Coleridge's theory of the Constitution is not less worthy of notice than his theory of the Church. The Delolme and Blackstone doctrine, the balance of the three powers, he declares he never could elicit one ray of common sense from, no more than from the balance of trade.[4] There is, however, according to him, an Idea of the Constitution of which he says:

Because our whole history, from Alfred onwards, demonstrates the continued influence of such an idea, or ultimate aim, in the minds of our forefathers, in their characters and functions as public men, alike in what they resisted and what they claimed; in the institutions and forms of polity which they established, and with regard to those against which they more or less successfully contended; and because the result has been a progressive, though not always a direct or equable, advance in the gradual realization of the idea; and because it is actually, though (even because it is an idea) not adequately, represented in a correspondent scheme of means

[4] *The Friend,* first collected edition (1818), ii, 75.

really existing—we speak, and have a right to speak, of the idea itself as actually existing; that is, as a principle existing in the only way in which a principle can exist—in the minds and consciences of the persons whose duties it prescribes, and whose rights it determines.[5]

This fundamental idea is at the same time the final criterion by which all particular frames of government must be tried: for here only can we find the great constructive principles of our representative system—those principles in the light of which it can alone be ascertained what are excrescences, symptoms of distemperature, and marks of degeneration, and what are native growths, or changes naturally attendant on the progressive development of the original germ; symptoms of immaturity, perhaps, but not of disease; or, at worst, modifications of the growth by the defective or faulty, but remediless, or only gradually remediable, qualities of the soil and surrounding elements.[6]

Of these principles he gives the following account:

It is the chief of many blessings derived from the insular character and circumstances of our country, that our social institutions have formed themselves out of our proper needs and interests; that long and fierce as the birth-struggle and growing pains have been, the antagonist powers have been of our own system, and have been allowed to work out their final balance with less disturbance from external forces than was possible in the Continental States. . . . Now in every country of civilized men, or acknowledging the rights of property, and by means of determined boundaries and common laws united into one people or nation, the two antagonist powers or opposite interests of the State, under which all other State interests are comprised, are those of *permanence* and of *progression*.

The interest of permanence, or the Conservative interest, he considers to be naturally connected with the land and with landed property. This doctrine, false in our opinion as an universal principle, is true of England and of all countries where landed property is accumulated in large masses.

"On the other hand," he says, "the progression of a State in the arts and comforts of life, in the diffusion of the information and knowledge useful or necessary for all; in short, all advances in civilization and the rights and privileges of citizens are especially connected with, and derived from, the four classes—the mercantile, the manufacturing, the distributive, and the professional." (We must omit the interest-

[5] *Church and State*, p. 18.
[6] *Church and State*, p. 19.

ing historical illustrations of this maxim.) "These four last-mentioned classes I will designate by the name of the Personal Interest, as the exponent of all movable and personal possessions, including skill and acquired knowledge, the moral and intellectual stock in trade of the professional man and the artist, no less than the raw materials, and the means of elaborating, transporting, and distributing them."[7]

The interest of permanence, then, is provided for by a representation of the landed proprietors; that of progression, by a representation of personal property and of intellectual acquirement: and while one branch of the Legislature, the Peerage, is essentially given over to the former, he considers it a part both of the general theory, and of the actual English Constitution, that the representatives of the latter should form "the clear and effectual majority of the Lower House"; or, if not, that at least, by the added influence of public opinion, they should exercise an effective preponderance there. That "the very weight intended for the effectual counterpoise of the great landholders" has, "in the course of events, been shifted into the opposite scale"; that the members for the towns "now constitute a large proportion of the political power and influence of the very class of men whose personal cupidity, and whose partial views of the landed interest at large, they were meant to keep in check"—these things he acknowledges; and only suggests a doubt whether roads, canals, machinery, the press, and other influences favorable to the popular side, do not constitute an equivalent force to supply the deficiency.[8]

How much better a Parliamentary Reformer, then, is Coleridge than Lord John Russell or any Whig who stickles for maintaining this unconstitutional omnipotence of the landed interest! If these became the principles of Tories, we should not wait long for further reform even in our organic institutions. It is true Coleridge disapproved of the Reform Bill, or rather of the principle or the no-principle on which it was supported. He saw in it (as we may surmise) the dangers of a change amounting almost to a revolution, without any real tendency to remove those defects in the machine which alone could justify a change so extensive. And that this is nearly a true view of the matter, all parties seem to be now agreed. The Reform Bill was not calculated materially to improve the general composition of the Legislature. The good it has done, which is considerable, consists chiefly in

[7] *Church and State*, pp. 23-24, 29.
[8] *Church and State*, pp. 31-32.

this, that being so great a change, it has weakened the superstitious feeling against great changes. Any good which is contrary to the selfish interest of the dominant class is still only to be effected by a long and arduous struggle; but improvements which threaten no powerful body in their social importance or in their pecuniary emoluments are no longer resisted as they once were, because of their greatness—because of the very benefit which they promised. Witness the speedy passing of the Poor-law Amendment and the Penny-postage Acts.

Meanwhile, though Coleridge's theory is but a mere commencement not amounting to the first lines of a political philosophy, has the age produced any other theory of government which can stand a comparison with it as to its first principles? Let us take, for example, the Benthamic theory. The principle of this may be said to be that since the general interest is the object of government, a complete control over the government ought to be given to those whose interest is identical with the general interest. The authors and propounders of this theory were men of extraordinary intellectual powers, and the greater part of what they meant by it is true and important. But when considered as the foundation of a science, it would be difficult to find among theories proceeding from philosophers one less like a philosophical theory, or, in the works of analytical minds, any thing more entirely unanalytical. What can a philosopher make of such complex notions as "interest" and "general interest," without breaking them down into the elements of which they are composed? If by men's interest be meant what would appear such to a calculating bystander, judging what would be good for a man during his whole life, and making no account, or but little, of the gratification of his present passions—his pride, his envy, his vanity, his cupidity, his love of pleasure, his love of ease—it may be questioned whether, in this sense, the interest of an aristocracy, and still more that of a monarch, would not be as accordant with the general interest as that of either the middle or the poorer classes; and if men's interest, in this understanding of it, usually governed their conduct, absolute monarchy would probably be the best form of government. But since men usually do what they like, often being perfectly aware that it is not for their ultimate interest, still more often that it is not for the interest of their posterity; and when they do believe that the object they are seeking is permanently good for them, almost always overrating its value—it is necessary to consider, not who are they whose permanent interest, but who are they whose immediate interests and habitual feelings, are likely to be most in accordance with the end we seek to obtain. And as that end (the general good) is a very complex state of things—comprising as its component elements many requisites which are neither of one and the same nature, nor attainable by one and the same means—political philosophy must begin by a classification of these elements, in order to distinguish those of them which go naturally together (so that the provision made for one will suffice for the rest) from those which are ordinarily in a state of antagonism, or at least of separation, and require to be provided for apart. This preliminary classification being supposed, things would in a perfect government be so ordered that, corresponding to each of the great interests of society, there would be some branch or some integral part of the governing body so constituted that it should not be merely deemed by philosophers, but actually and constantly deem itself, to have its strongest interests involved in the maintenance of that one of the ends of society which it is intended to be the guardian of. This, we say, is the thing to be aimed at—the type of perfection in a political constitution. Not that there is a possibility of making more than a limited approach to it in practice: a government must be composed out of the elements already existing in society; and the distribution of power in the constitution cannot vary much or long from the distribution of it in society itself. But wherever the circumstances of society allow any choice, wherever wisdom and contrivance are at all available, this, we conceive, is the principle of guidance; and whatever anywhere exists is imperfect and a failure, just so far as it recedes from this type.

Such a philosophy of government, we need hardly say, is in its infancy; the first step to it, the classification of the exigencies of society, has not been made. Bentham, in his "Principles of Civil Law," has given a specimen, very useful for many other purposes, but not available, nor intended to be so, for founding a theory of representation upon it. For that particular purpose we have seen nothing comparable, as far is it goes, notwithstanding its manifest insufficiency, to Coleridge's division of the interests of society into the two antagonist interests of Permanence and Progression. The Continental philosophers have, by a different path, arrived at the same division; and this is about as far probably as the science of political institutions has yet reached.

In the details of Coleridge's political opinions, there is

much good and much that is questionable or worse. In political economy especially, he writes like an arrant driveller; and it would have been well for his reputation had he never meddled with the subject. But this department of knowledge can now take care of itself. On other points, we meet with far-reaching remarks and a tone of general feeling sufficient to make a Tory's hair stand on end. Thus, in the work from which we have most quoted, he calls the State policy of the last half-century "a Cyclops with one eye, and that in the back of the head"; its measures "either a series of anachronisms, or a truckling to events instead of the science that should command them." He styles the great Commonwealthsmen "the stars of that narrow interspace of blue sky between the black clouds of the First and Second Charles's reigns."[9] The "Literary Remains" are full of disparaging remarks on many of the heroes of Toryism and Church-of-Englandism. He sees, for instance, no difference between Whitgift and Bancroft, and Bonner and Gardiner, except that the last were the most consistent, that the former sinned against better knowledge; and one of the most poignant of his writings is a character of Pitt, the very reverse of panegyrical.[10] As a specimen of his practical views, we have mentioned his recommendation that the parochial clergy should begin by being schoolmasters. He urges "a different division and subdivision of the kingdom," instead of "the present barbarism, which forms an obstacle to the improvement of the country, of much greater magnitude than men are generally aware."[11] But we must confine ourselves to instances in which he has helped to bring forward great principles, either implied in the old English opinions and institutions, or at least opposed to the new tendencies.

For example: he is at issue with the *let-alone* doctrine, or the theory that governments can do no better than to do nothing—a doctrine generated by the manifest selfishness and incompetence of modern European governments, but of which, as a general theory, we may now be permitted to say that one half of it is true and the other half false. All who are on a level with their age now readily admit that government ought not to *interdict* men from publishing their opinions, pursuing their employments, or buying and selling their goods in whatever place or manner they deem the most advantageous. Beyond suppressing force and fraud, govern-

[9] *Church and State,* pp. 69, 102.
[10] Written in the *Morning Post,* and now (as we rejoice to see) reprinted in Mr. Gillman's biographical memoir.
[11] *Literary Remains,* p. 56.

ments can seldom, without doing more harm than good, attempt to chain up the free agency of individuals. But does it follow from this that government cannot exercise a free agency of its own—that it cannot beneficially employ its powers, its means of information, and its pecuniary resources (so far surpassing those of any other association or of any individual), in promoting the public welfare by a thousand means which individuals would never think of, would have no sufficient motives to attempt, or no sufficient powers to accomplish? To confine ourselves to one, and that a limited, view of the subject: a State ought to be considered as a great benefit-society or mutual-insurance company for helping (under the necessary regulations for preventing abuse) that large proportion of its members who cannot help themselves. "Let us suppose," says Coleridge,

the negative ends of a State already attained—namely, its own safety by means of its own strength, and the protection of person and property for all its members; there will then remain its positive ends: 1. To make the means of subsistence more easy to each individual. 2. To secure to each of its members the hope of bettering his own condition or that of his children. 3. The development of those faculties which are essential to his humanity, that is, to his rational and moral being.[12]

In regard to the two former ends, he of course does not mean that they can be accomplished merely by making laws to that effect; or that, according to the wild doctrines now afloat, it is the fault of the government if every one has not enough to eat and drink. But he means that government can do something directly, and very much indirectly, to promote even the physical comfort of the people; and that if, besides making a proper use of its own powers, it would exert itself to teach the people what is in theirs, indigence would soon disappear from the face of the earth.

Perhaps, however, the greatest service which Coleridge has rendered to politics in his capacity of a Conservative philosopher, though its fruits are mostly yet to come, is in reviving the idea of a *trust* inherent in landed property. The land, the gift of nature, the source of subsistence to all, and the foundation of every thing that influences our physical well-being, cannot be considered a subject of *property* in the same absolute sense in which men are deemed proprietors of that in which no one has any interest but themselves—that which they have actually called into existence by their own

[12] *Second Lay Sermon*, p. 414.

bodily exertion. As Coleridge points out, such a notion is altogether of modern growth.

The very idea of individual or private property in our present acceptation of the term, and according to the current notion of the right to it, was originally confined to movable things; and the more movable, the more susceptible of the nature of property.

By the early institutions of Europe, property in land was a public function, created for certain public purposes and held under condition of their fulfilment; and as such, we predict, under the modifications suited to modern society, it will again come to be considered. In this age, when every thing is called in question and when the foundation of private property itself needs to be argumentatively maintained against plausible and persuasive sophisms, one may easily see the danger of mixing up what is not really tenable with what is; and the impossibility of maintaining an absolute right in an individual to an unrestricted control, a *jus utendi et abutendi,* over an unlimited quantity of the mere raw material of the globe to which every other person could originally make out as good a natural title as himself. It will certainly not be much longer tolerated that agriculture should be carried on (as Coleridge expresses it) on the same principles as those of trade; "that a gentleman should regard his estate as a merchant his cargo, or a shopkeeper his stock";[13] that he should be allowed to deal with it as if it only existed to yield rent to him, not food to the numbers whose hands till it; and should have a right, and a right possessing all the sacredness of property, to turn them out by hundreds and make them perish on the high road, as has been done before now by Irish landlords. We believe it will soon be thought that a mode of property in land, which has brought things to this pass, has existed long enough.

We shall not be suspected (we hope) of recommending a general resumption of landed possessions, or the depriving any one without compensation of any thing which the law gives him. But we say that when the State allows any one to exercise ownership over more land than suffices to raise by his own labor his subsistence and that of his family, it confers on him power over other human beings—power affecting them in their most vital interests; and that no notion of private property can bar the right, which the State inherently possesses, to require that the power which it has so given

[13] *Second Lay Sermon,* p. 414.

shall not be abused. We say also that by giving this direct power over so large a portion of the community, indirect power is necessarily conferred over all the remaining portion; and this, too, it is the duty of the State to place under proper control. Further, the tenure of land, the various rights connected with it, and the system on which its cultivation is carried on, are points of the utmost importance both to the economical and to the moral well-being of the whole community. And the State fails in one of its highest obligations, unless it takes these points under its particular superintendence; unless, to the full extent of its power, it takes means of providing that the manner in which land is held, the mode and degree of its division, and every other peculiarity which influences the mode of its cultivation, shall be the most favorable possible for making the best use of the land, for drawing the greatest benefit from its productive resources, for securing the happiest existence to those employed on it, and for setting the greatest number of hands free to employ their labor for the benefit of the community in other ways. We believe that these opinions will become, in no very long period, universal throughout Europe; and we gratefully bear testimony to the fact that the first among us, who has given the sanction of philosophy to so great a reform in the popular and current notions, is a Conservative philosopher.

Of Coleridge as a moral and religious philosopher (the character which he presents most prominently in his principal works), there is neither room, nor would it be expedient for us, to speak more than generally. On both subjects, few men have ever combined so much earnestness with so catholic and unsectarian a spirit. "We have imprisoned," says he, "our own conceptions by the lines which we have drawn in order to exclude the conceptions of others. *J'ai trouvé que la plupart des sectes ont raison dans une bonne partie de ce qu'elles avancent, mais non pas tant en ce qu'elles nient.'*[14] That almost all sects, both in philosophy and religion, are right in the positive part of their tenets, though commonly wrong in the negative is a doctrine which he professes as strongly as the eclectic school in France. Almost all errors he holds to be "truths misunderstood," "half-truths taken as the whole," though not the less, but the more, dangerous on that account.[15] Both the theory and practice of enlightened tolerance, in matters of opinion, might be exhibited in extracts from his writings more copiously than in those of any other

[14] *Biographia Literaria*, ed. 1817, i, 249.
[15] *Literary Remains*, iii, 145.

writer we know; though there are a few (and but a few) exceptions to his own practice of it. In the theory of ethics, he contends against the doctrine of general consequences, and holds that *for man,* "to obey the simple unconditional commandment of eschewing every act that implies a self-contradiction," so to act as to "be able, without involving any contradiction, to will that the maxim of thy conduct should be the law of all intelligent beings—is the one universal and sufficient principle and guide of morality."[16] Yet even a utilitarian can have little complaint to make of a philosopher who lays it down that "the *outward* object of virtue" is "the greatest producible sum of happiness of all men," and that "happiness in its proper sense is but the continuity and sum-total of the pleasure which is allotted or happens to a man."

But his greatest object was to bring into harmony religion and philosophy. He labored incessantly to establish that "the Christian faith—in which," says he, "I include every article of belief and doctrine professed by the first reformers in common"—is not only divine truth, but also "the perfection of human intelligence." [17] All that Christianity has revealed, philosophy, according to him, can prove, though there is much which it could never have discovered; human reason, once strengthened by Christianity, can evolve all the Christian doctrines from its own sources. Moreover, "if infidelity is not to overspread England as well as France," the Scripture, and every passage of Scripture, must be submitted to this test; inasmuch as "the compatibility of a document with the conclusions of self-evident reason, and with the laws of conscience, is a condition *a priori* of any evidence adequate to the proof of its having been revealed by God"; and this, he says, is no philosophical novelty, but a principle "clearly laid down both by Moses and St. Paul." [18] He thus goes quite as far as the Unitarians in making man's reason and moral feelings a test of revelation; but differs *toto cælo* from them in their rejection of its mysteries, which he regards as the highest philosophic truths; and says that "the Christian to whom, after a long profession of Christianity, the mysteries remain as much mysteries as before, is in the same state as a schoolboy, with regard to his arithmetic, to whom the *facit* at the end of the examples in his ciphering-book is the whole ground for his assuming that such and such figures amount to so and so."

[16] *The Friend,* i, 256, 340.
[17] *Aids to Reflection,* pp. 37, 39, Preface.
[18] *Literary Remains,* i, 388; iii, 263, 293.

These opinions are not likely to be popular in the religious world, and Coleridge knew it: "I quite calculate," said he once, "on my being one day or other holden in worse repute by many Christians than the 'Unitarians' and even 'Infidels.' It must be undergone by every one who loves the truth for its own sake, beyond all other things." [19] For our part, we are not bound to defend him; and we must admit that, in his attempt to arrive at theology by way of philosophy, we see much straining and most frequently, as it appears to us, total failure. The question, however, is not whether Coleridge's attempts are successful, but whether it is desirable or not that such attempts should be made. Whatever some religious people may think, philosophy will and must go on, ever seeking to understand whatever can be made understandable; and whatever some philosophers may think, there is little prospect at present that philosophy will take the place of religion, or that any philosophy will be speedily received in this country unless supposed not only to be consistent with, but even to yield collateral support to, Christianity. What is the use, then, of treating with contempt the idea of a religious philosophy? Religious philosophies are among the things to be looked for; and our main hope ought to be that they may be such as fulfil the conditions of a philosophy—the very foremost of which is unrestricted freedom of thought. There is no philosophy possible where fear of consequences is a stronger principle than love of truth; where speculation is paralyzed, either by the belief that conclusions honestly arrived at will be punished by a just and good Being with eternal damnation, or by seeing in every text of Scripture a foregone conclusion with which the results of inquiry must, at any expense of sophistry and self-deception, be made to quadrate.

From both these withering influences, that have so often made the acutest intellects exhibit specimens of obliquity and imbecility in their theological speculations which have made them the pity of subsequent generations, Coleridge's mind was perfectly free. Faith—the faith which is placed among religious duties—was, in his view, a state of the will and of the affections, not of the understanding. Heresy, in "the literal sense and scriptural import of the word," is, according to him, "wilful error, or belief originating in some perversion of the will." He says, therefore, that there may be orthodox heretics, since indifference to truth may as well be shown on the right side of the question as on the wrong; and denounces, in strong language, the contrary doctrine of the "pseudo-Athanasius," who "interprets catholic faith by be-

[19] *Table Talk,* 2d ed. p. 91.

lief," an act of the understanding alone. The "true Lutheran doctrine," he says, is that "neither will truth, as a mere conviction of the understanding, save, nor error condemn. To love truth sincerely is spiritually to have truth; and an error becomes a personal error, not by its aberration from logic or history, but so far as the causes of such error are in the heart, or may be traced back to some antecedent unchristian wish or habit." "The unmistakable passions of a factionary and a schismatic, the ostentatious display, the ambitious and dishonest arts, of a sect-founder, must be superinduced on the false doctrine before the heresy makes the man a heretic."[20]

Against the other terror, so fatal to the unshackled exercise of reason on the greatest questions, the view which Coleridge took of the authority of the Scriptures was a preservative. He drew the strongest distinction between the inspiration which he owned in the various writers, and an express dictation by the Almighty of every word they wrote. "The notion of the absolute truth and divinity of every syllable of the text of the books of the Old and New Testament as we have it," he again and again asserts to be unsupported by the Scripture itself; to be one of those superstitions in which "there is a heart of unbelief;" to be, "if possible, still more extravagant" than the Papal infallibility; and declares that the very same arguments are used for both doctrines.[21] God, he believes, informed the minds of the writers with the truths he meant to reveal, and left the rest to their human faculties. He pleaded most earnestly, says his nephew and editor, for this liberty of criticism with respect to the Scriptures, as "the only middle path of safety and peace between a godless disregard of the unique and transcendent character of the Bible, taken generally, and that scheme of interpretation, scarcely less adverse to the pure spirit of Christian wisdom, which wildly arrays our faith in opposition to our reason, and inculcates the sacrifice of the latter to the former; for he threw up his hands in dismay at the language of some of our modern divinity on this point; as if a faith not founded on insight were aught else than a specious name for wilful positiveness! as if the Father of lights could require, or would accept, from the only one of his creatures whom he had endowed with reason, the sacrifice of fools! . . . Of the aweless doctrine that God might, if he had so pleased, have given to man a religion which to human intelligence should not be rational, and exacted his faith in it, Coleridge's whole middle and later life was one deep and solemn denial. He bewails "bibliolatry" as the pervading error of modern Protestant divinity,

[20] *Literary Remains,* iv, 193; iii, 159, 245.
[21] *Literary Remains,* iii, 229; ii, 385.

and the great stumbling-block of Christianity; and exclaims, "Oh! might I live but to utter all my meditations on this most concerning point, . . . in what sense the Bible may be called the word of God, and how and under what conditions the unity of the Spirit is translucent through the letter which, read as the letter merely, is the word of this and that pious but fallible and imperfect man."[22] It is known that he did live to write down these meditations; and speculations so important will one day, it is devoutly to be hoped, be given to the world.[23]

Theological discussion is beyond our province, and it is not for us, in this place, to judge these sentiments of Coleridge; but it is clear enough that they are not the sentiments of a bigot, or of one who is to be dreaded by Liberals lest he should illiberalize the minds of the rising generation of Tories and High-Churchmen. We think the danger is, rather, lest they should find him vastly too liberal. And yet now, when the most orthodox divines, both in the Church and out of it, find it necessary to explain away the obvious sense of the whole first chapter of Genesis, or, failing to do that, consent to disbelieve it provisionally, on the speculation that there may hereafter be discovered a sense in which it can be believed, one would think the time gone by for expecting to learn from the Bible what it never could have been intended to communicate, and to find in all its statements a literal truth neither necessary nor conducive to what the volume itself declares to be the ends of revelation. Such, at least, was Coleridge's opinion; and whatever influence such an opinion may have over Conservatives, it cannot do other than make them less bigots and better philosophers.

But we must close this long essay—long in itself, though short in its relation to its subject and to the multitude of topics involved in it. We do not pretend to have given any sufficient account of Coleridge; but we hope we may have proved to some, not previously aware of it, that there is something, both in him and in the school to which he belongs, not unworthy of their better knowledge. We may have done something to show that a Tory philosopher cannot be wholly a Tory, but must often be a better Liberal than Liberals themselves; while he is the natural means of rescuing from oblivion truth which Tories have forgotten and which the prevailing schools of Liberalism never knew.

[22] *Literary Remains,* iii, Preface; iv, 6.
[23] (This wish has, to a certain extent, been fulfilled by the publication of the series of letters on the Inspiration of the Scriptures, which bears the not very appropriate name of "Confessions of an Inquiring Spirit.")

And even if a Conservative philosophy were an absurdity, it is well calculated to drive out a hundred absurdities worse than itself. Let no one think that it is nothing to accustom people to give a reason for their opinion, be the opinion ever so untenable, the reason ever so insufficient. A person accustomed to submit his fundamental tenets to the test of reason will be more open to the dictates of reason on every other point. Not from him shall we have to apprehend the owl-like dread of light, the drudge-like aversion to change, which were the characteristics of the old unreasoning race of bigots. A man accustomed to contemplate the fair side of Toryism (the side that every attempt at a philosophy of it must bring to view), and to defend the existing system by the display of its capabilities as an engine of public good— such a man, when he comes to administer the system, will be more anxious than another person to realize those capabilities, to bring the fact a little nearer to the specious theory. "Lord, enlighten thou our enemies," should be the prayer of every true reformer; sharpen their wits, give acuteness to their perceptions, and consecutiveness and clearness to their reasoning powers. We are in danger from their folly, not from their wisdom; their weakness is what fills us with apprehension, not their strength.

For ourselves, we are not so blinded by our particular opinions as to be ignorant that in this and in every other country of Europe, the great mass of the owners of large property and of all the classes intimately connected with the owners of large property, are, and must be expected to be, in the main Conservative. To suppose that so mighty a body can be without immense influence in the commonwealth, or to lay plans for effecting great changes, either spiritual or temporal, in which they are left out of the question, would be the height of absurdity. Let those who desire such changes ask themselves if they are content that these classes should be, and remain, to a man banded against them; and what progress they expect to make, or by what means, unless a process of preparation shall be going on in the minds of these very classes, not by the impracticable method of converting them from Conservatives to Liberals, but by their being led to adopt one liberal opinion after another as a part of Conservatism itself. The first step to this is to inspire them with the desire to systematize and rationalize their own actual creed, and the feeblest attempt to do this has an intrinsic value; far more, then, one which has so much in it, both of moral goodness and true insight, as the philosophy of Coleridge.

Son of a Clapham Evangelical, Macaulay was a Whig who believed like the Benthamites in progress and laissez-faire, but was more genial, literary, conventional and far less philosophical than they. He was thus closer to popular thinking, and is the most eloquent spokesman of that early-Victorian liberal, middle-class opinion against which most Victorian literary men were reacting. In this 1830 *Edinburgh Review* attack on the romantic Toryism of the Poet Laureate Southey, Macaulay raises most of the issues of the age. He argues for the severe limitation of governmental power—questioning whether any class can be trusted to rule in any but its own interest. Most important, Macaulay thinks English life has improved under industrialism and will continue to improve; whereas Southey sees only decline.

Macaulay's defense of political liberty is still resoundingly valid; but we are likely to sympathize with Southey's worry over the declining *quality* of life under industrialism, and with his suggestion that taxation and government spending might bring more relief to society than governmental economy. Here again we see how in the nineteenth century a reactionary political program is often coupled to an economic program that with hindsight seems progressive. Macaulay's rather smug optimism, based always on numerical increase in population and wealth, is the sort of attitude Arnold was to stigmatize as "Philistine." A. L. Rowse, the contemporary British historian, calls Macaulay "a Philistine of genius."

THOMAS BABINGTON MACAULAY

Southey's Colloquies on Society

Sir Thomas More; or, Colloquies on the Progress and Prospects of Society. By ROBERT SOUTHEY, Esq. LL.D., Poet Laureate. 2 vols. 8vo. London: 1829.

It would be scarcely possible for a man of Mr. Southey's talents and acquirements to write two volumes so large as those before us, which should be wholly destitute of information and amusement. Yet we do not remember to have read with so little satisfaction any equal quantity of matter, written by any man of real abilities. We have for some time past observed with great regret the strange infatuation which leads the Poet Laureate to abandon those departments of literature in which he might excel, and to lecture the public on sciences of which he has still the very alphabet to learn. He has now, we think, done his worst. The subject which he has at last undertaken to treat is one which demands all the highest intellectual and moral qualities of a philosophical statesman, an understanding at once comprehensive and acute, a heart at once upright and charitable. Mr. Southey brings to the task two faculties which were never, we believe, vouchsafed in measure so copious to any human being, the faculty of believing without a reason, and the faculty of hating without a provocation.

It is, indeed, most extraordinary that a mind like Mr. Southey's, a mind richly endowed in many respects by nature and highly cultivated by study, a mind which has exercised considerable influence on the most enlightened generation of the most enlightened people that ever existed, should be utterly destitute of the power of discerning truth from falsehood. Yet such is the fact. Government is to Mr. Southey one of the fine arts. He judges of a theory, of a public measure, of a religion or a political party, of a peace or a war, as men judge of a picture or a statue, by the effect produced on his imagination. A chain of associations is to him what a chain of reasoning is to other men; and what he calls his opinions are in fact merely his tastes. . . .

THE WORKS OF LORD MACAULAY, edited by his sister Lady Trevelyan, 8 vols. (London: Longmans, Green, 1875), V, 330, 339-42, 346-47, 349-55, 358-62, 363-68.

We now come to the conversations which pass between Mr. Southey and Sir Thomas More, or rather between two Southeys, equally eloquent, equally angry, equally unreasonable, and equally given to talking about what they do not understand. Perhaps we could not select a better instance of the spirit which pervades the whole book than the passages in which Mr. Southey gives his opinion of the manufacturing system. There is nothing which he hates so bitterly. It is, according to him, a system more tyrannical than that of the feudal ages, a system of actual servitude, a system which destroys the bodies and degrades the minds of those who are engaged in it. He expresses a hope that the competition of other nations may drive us out of the field; that our foreign trade may decline; and that we may thus enjoy a restoration of national sanity and strength. But he seems to think that the extermination of the whole manufacturing population would be a blessing, if the evil could be removed in no other way.

Mr. Southey does not bring forward a single fact in support of these views; and, as it seems to us, there are facts which lead to a very different conclusion. In the first place, the poor-rate is very decidedly lower in the manufacturing than in the agricultural districts. If Mr. Southey will look over the Parliamentary returns on this subject, he will find that the amount of parochial relief required by the labourers in the different counties of England is almost exactly in inverse proportion to the degree in which the manufacturing system has been introduced into those counties. The returns for the years ending in March 1825, and in March 1828, are now before us. In the former year we find the poor-rate highest in Sussex, about twenty shillings to every inhabitant. Then come Buckinghamshire, Essex, Suffolk, Bedfordshire, Huntingdonshire, Kent, and Norfolk. In all these the rate is above fifteen shillings a head. We will not go through the whole. Even in Westmoreland and the North Riding of Yorkshire, the rate is at more than eight shillings. In Cumberland and Monmouthshire, the most fortunate of all the agricultural districts, it is at six shillings. But in the West Riding of Yorkshire, it is as low as five shillings; and when we come to Lancashire, we find it at four shillings, one fifth of what it is in Sussex. The returns of the year ending in March 1828 are a little, and but a little, more unfavourable to the manufacturing districts. Lancashire, even in that season of distress, required a smaller poor-rate than any other district, and little more than one fourth of the poor-rate raised in Sussex. Cumberland alone, of the agricultural districts, was as well off as the West Riding of Yorkshire. These facts seem to indicate that the manufacturer is both in a more comfortable and in a less dependent situation than the agricultural labourer.

As to the effect of the manufacturing system on the bodily health, we must beg leave to estimate it by a standard far too low and vulgar for a mind so imaginative as that of Mr. Southey, the proportion of births and deaths. We know that, during the growth of this atrocious system, this new misery, to use the phrases of Mr. Southey, this new enormity, this birth of a portentous age, this pest which no man can approve whose heart is not seared or whose understanding has not been darkened, there has been a great diminution of mortality, and that this diminution has been greater in the manufacturing towns than any where else. The mortality still is, as it always was, greater in towns than in the country. But the difference has diminished in an extraordinary degree. There is the best reason to believe that the annual mortality of Manchester, about the middle of the last century, was one in twenty-eight. It is now reckoned at one in forty-five. In Glasgow and Leeds a similar improvement has taken place. Nay, the rate of mortality in these three great capitals of the manufacturing districts is now considerably less than it was, fifty years ago, over England and Wales taken together, open country and all. We might with some plausibility maintain that the people live longer because they are better fed, better lodged, better clothed, and better attended in sickness, and that these improvements are owing to that increase of national wealth which the manufacturing system has produced.

Much more might be said on this subject. But to what end? It is not from bills of mortality and statistical tables that Mr. Southey has learned his political creed. He cannot stoop to study the history of the system which he abuses, to strike the balance between the good and evil which it has produced, to compare district with district, or generation with generation. We will give his own reason for his opinion, the only reason which he gives for it, in his own words:

We remained awhile in silence looking upon the assemblage of dwellings below. Here, and in the adjoining hamlet of Millbeck, the effects of manufactures and of agriculture may be seen and compared. The old cottages are such as the poet and the painter equally delight in beholding. Substantially built of the native stone without mortar, dirtied with no white lime, and their long low roofs covered with slate; if they had been raised by the magic of some indigenous Amphion's music, the materials could not have adjusted themselves more beautifully in accord with the surrounding scene: and time has still further harmonized them with weatherstains, lichens, and moss, short grasses, and short fern, and stoneplants of various kinds. The ornamented chimneys, round or square, less adorned than those which, like little turrets, crest the houses of the Portuguese peasantry; and yet not less happily suited to their place, the edge of clipt box beneath the windows, the rose-bushes beside the door, the little patch of flower-ground, with its tall hollyhocks in front; the garden beside, the bee-hives, and the orchard with its bank of daffodils and snow-drops, the earliest and the profusest in these parts, indicate in the owners some portion of ease and leisure, some regard to neatness and comfort, some sense of natural, and innocent, and healthful enjoyment. The new cottages of the manufacturers are upon the manufacturing pattern—naked and in a row.

"How is it," said I, "that every thing which is connected with manufactures presents such features of unqualified deformity? From the largest of Mammon's temples down to the poorest hovel in which his helotry are stalled, these edifices have all one character. Time will not mellow them; nature will neither clothe nor conceal them; and they will remain always as offensive to the eye as to the mind."

Here is wisdom. Here are the principles on which nations are to be governed. Rose-bushes and poor-rates, rather than steam-engines and independence. Mortality and cottages with weather-stains, rather than health and long life with edifices which time cannot mellow. We are told that our age has invented atrocities beyond the imagination of our fathers, that society has been brought into a state compared with which extermination would be a blessing; and all because the dwellings of cotton-spinners are naked and rectangular. Mr. Southey has found out a way, he tells us, in which the effects of manufactures and agriculture may be compared. And what is this way? To stand on a hill, to look at a cottage and a factory, and to see which is the prettier. Does Mr. Southey think that the body of the English peasantry live, or ever lived, in substantial or ornamented cottages with box-hedges, flower-gardens, beehives, and orchards? If not, what is his parallel worth? We despise those mock philosophers, who think that they serve the cause of science by depreciating literature and the fine arts. But if any thing could excuse their narrowness of mind, it would be such a book as this. It is not strange that, when one enthusiast makes the picturesque the test of political good, another should feel inclined to proscribe altogether the pleasures of taste and imagination. . . .

In every season of distress which we can remember, Mr. Southey has been proclaiming that it is not from economy, but from increased taxation, that the country must expect relief; and he still, we find, places the undoubting faith of a political Diafoirus, in his

> Resaignare, repurgare, et reclysterizare.

"A people," he tells us, "may be too rich, but a government cannot be so."

"A state," says he, "cannot have more wealth at its command than may be employed for the general good, a liberal expenditure in national works being one of the surest means of promoting national prosperity; and the benefit being still more obvious, of an expenditure directed to the purposes of national improvement. But a people may be too rich."

We fully admit that a state cannot have at its command more wealth than may be employed for the general good. But neither can individuals, or bodies of individuals, have at their command more wealth than may be employed for the general good. If there be no limit to the sum which may be usefully laid out in public works and national improvement, then wealth, whether in the hands of private men or of the government, may always, if the possessors choose to spend it usefully, be usefully spent. The only ground, therefore, on which Mr. Southey can possibly maintain that a government cannot be too rich, but that a people may be too rich, must be this, that governments are more likely to spend their money on good objects than private individuals. But what is useful expenditure? "A liberal expenditure in national work," says Mr. Southey, "is one of the surest means of promoting national prosperity." What does he mean by national prosperity? Does he mean the wealth of the state? If so, his reasoning runs thus: The more wealth a state has the better; for the more wealth a state has the more wealth it will have. This is surely something like that fallacy which is ungallantly termed a lady's reason. If by national prosperity he means the wealth of the people, of how gross a contradiction is Mr. Southey guilty. A people, he tells us, may be too rich, a government cannot; for a government can employ its riches in making the people richer. The wealth of the people is to be taken from them, because they have too much, and laid out in works which will yield them more.

We are really at a loss to determine whether Mr. Southey's reason for recommending large taxation is that it will make the people rich, or that it will make them poor. But we are sure that if his object is to make them rich, he takes the wrong course. There are two or three principles respecting public works which, as an experience of vast extent proves, may be trusted in almost every case.

It scarcely ever happens that any private man or body of men will invest property in a canal, a tunnel or a bridge, but from an expectation that the outlay will be profitable to them. No work of this sort can be profitable to private speculators, unless the public be willing to pay for the use of it. The public will not pay of their own accord for what yields no profit or convenience to them. There is thus a direct and obvious connexion between the motive which induces individuals to undertake such a work and the utility of the work.

Can we find any such connexion in the case of a public work executed by a government? If it is useful, are the individuals who rule the country richer? If it is useless, are they poorer? A public man may be solicitous for his credit. But is not he likely to gain more credit by an useless display of ostentatious architecture in a great town than by the best road or the best canal in some remote province? The fame of public works is a much less certain test of their utility than the amount of toll collected at them. In a corrupt age, there will be direct embezzlement. In the purest age, there will be abundance of jobbing. Never were the statesmen of any country more sensitive to public opinion, and more spotless in pecuniary transactions, than those who have of late governed England. Yet we have only to look at the buildings recently erected in London for a proof of our rule. In a bad age, the fate of the public is to be robbed outright. In a good age, it is merely to have the dearest and the worst of everything.

Buildings for state purposes the state must erect. And here we think that, in general, the state ought to stop. We firmly believe that five-hundred-thousand pounds subscribed by individuals for railroads or canals would produce more advantage to the public than five millions voted by Parliament for the same purpose. There are certain old saws about the master's eye and about everybody's business, in which we place very great faith. . . .

What does Mr. Southey mean by saying that religion is demonstrably the basis of civil government? He cannot surely mean that men have no motives except those derived from religion for establishing and supporting civil government, that no temporal advantage is derived from civil government, that men would experience no temporal inconvenience from living in a state of anarchy? If he allows, as we think he must allow, that it is for the good of mankind in this world to have civil government, and that the great majority of mankind have always thought it for their good in this world to have civil government, we then have a basis for government quite distinct from religion. It is true that the Christian religion sanctions government, as it sanctions every thing which promotes the happiness and virtue of our species. But we are at a loss to conceive in what sense religion can be said to be the basis of government, in which religion is not also the basis of the practices of eating, drinking and lighting fires in cold weather. Nothing in history is more certain than that government has existed, has received some obedience and has given some protection, in times in which it derived no support from religion, in times in which there was no religion that influenced the hearts and lives of men. It was not from dread of Tartarus, or from belief in the Elysian fields, that an Athenian wished to have some institutions which might keep Orestes from filching his cloak, or Midias from breaking his head. "It is from religion," says Mr. Southey, "that power derives its authority and laws their efficacy." From what religion does our power over the Hindoos derive its authority, or the law in virtue of which we hang Brahmins its efficacy? For thousands of years civil government has existed in almost every corner of the world, in ages of priestcraft, in ages of fanaticism, in ages of Epicurean indifference, in ages of enlightened piety. However pure or impure the faith of the people might be, whether they adored a beneficent or a malignant power, whether they thought the soul mortal or immortal, they have, as soon as they ceased to be absolute savages, found out their need of civil government and instituted it accordingly. It is as universal as the practice of cookery. Yet it is as certain, says Mr. Southey, as any thing in abstract science, that government is founded on religion. We should like to know what notion Mr. Southey has of the demonstrations of abstract science. A very vague one, we suspect.

The proof proceeds. As religion is the basis of government, and as the state is secure in proportion as the people are attached to public institutions, it is therefore, says Mr. Southey, the first rule of policy that the government should train the people in the way they should go; and it is plain that those who train them in any other way are undermining the state.

Now it does not appear to us to be the first object that people should always believe in the established religion and be attached to the established government. A religion may be false. A government may be oppressive. And whatever support government gives to false religions, or religion to oppressive governments, we consider as a clear evil.

The maxim, that governments ought to train the people in the way in which they should go, sounds well. But is there any reason for believing that a government is more likely to lead the people in the right way than the people to fall into the right way of themselves? Have there not been governments which were blind leaders of the blind? Are there not still such governments? Can it be laid down as a general rule that the movement of political and religious truth is rather downwards from the government to the people than upwards from the people to the government? These are questions which it is of importance to have clearly resolved. Mr. Southey declaims against public opinion, which is now, he tells us, usurping supreme power. Formerly, according to him, the laws governed; now public opinion governs. What are laws but expressions of the opinion of some class which has power over the rest of the community? By what was the world ever governed but by the opinion of some person or persons? By what else can it ever be governed? What are all systems, religious, political, or scientific, but opinions resting on evidence more or less satisfactory? The question is not between human opinion and some higher and more certain mode of arriving at truth, but between opinion and opinion, between the opinions of one man and another, or of one class and another, or of one generation and another. Public opinion is not infallible; but can Mr. Southey construct any institutions which shall secure to us the guidance of an infallible opinion? Can Mr. Southey select any family, any profession, any class, in short, distinguished by any plain badge from the rest of the community, whose opinion is more likely to be just than this much abused public opinion? Would he choose the peers, for example? Or the two hundred tallest men in the country? Or the poor Knights of Windsor? Or children who are born with cauls? Or the seventh sons of seventh sons? We cannot suppose that he would recommend popular election; for that is merely an appeal to public opinion. And to say that society ought to be governed by the opinion of the wisest and best, though true, is useless. Whose opinion is to decide who are the wisest and best. . . .

The duties of government would be, as Mr. Southey says that they are, paternal, if a government were necessarily as much superior in wisdom to a people as the most foolish father, for a time, is to the most intelligent child, and if a government loved a people as fathers generally love their children. But there is no reason to believe that a government will have either the paternal warmth of affection or the paternal superiority of intellect. Mr. Southey might as well say that the duties of the shoemaker are paternal, and that it is an usurpation in any man not of the craft to say that his shoes are bad and to insist on having better. The division of labour would be no blessing, if those by whom a thing is done were to pay no attention to the opinion of those for whom it is done. The shoemaker in *The Relapse* tells Lord Foppington that his lordship is mistaken in supposing that his shoe pinches. "It does not pinch; it cannot pinch; I know my business; and I never made a better shoe." This is the way in which Mr. Southey would have a government treat a people who usurp the privilege of thinking. Nay, the shoemaker of Vanbrugh has the advantage in the comparison. He contented himself with regulating his customer's shoes, about which he had peculiar means of information, and did not presume to dictate about the coat and hat. But Mr. Southey would have the rulers of a country prescribe opinions to the people, not only about politics, but about matters concerning which a government has no peculiar sources of information, and concerning which any man in the streets may know as much and think as justly as the King, namely religion and morals.

Men are never so likely to settle a question rightly as when they discuss it freely. A government can interfere in discussion only by making it less free than it would otherwise be. Men are most likely to form just opinions when they have no other wish than to know the truth, and are exempt from all influence either of hope or fear. Government, as government, can bring nothing but the influence of hopes and fears to support its doctrines. It carries on controversy, not with reasons, but with threats and bribes. If it employs reasons, it does so not in virtue of any powers which belong to it as a government. Thus, instead of a contest between argument and argument, we have a contest between argument and force. Instead of a contest in which truth, from the natural constitution of the human mind, has a decided advantage over falsehood, we have a contest in which truth can be victorious only by accident.

And what, after all, is the security which this training gives to governments? Mr. Southey would scarcely propose that discussion should be more effectually shackled, that public opinion should be more strictly disciplined into conformity with established institutions, than in Spain and Italy. Yet we know that the restraints which exist in Spain and Italy have not prevented atheism from spreading among the educated classes, and especially among those whose office it is to minister at the altars of God. All our readers know how, at the time of the French Revolution, priest after priest came forward to declare that his doctrine, his ministry, his whole life, had been a lie, a mummery during which he could scarcely compose his countenance sufficiently to carry on the imposture. This was the case of a false, or at least of a grossly corrupted religion. Let us take then the case of all others most favourable to Mr. Southey's argument. Let us take that form of religion which he holds to be the purest, the system of the Arminian part of the Church of England. Let us take the form of government which he most admires and regrets, the government of England in the time of Charles the First. Would he wish to see a closer connexion between church and state than then existed? Would he wish for more powerful ecclesiastical tribunals; for a more zealous king; for a more active primate? Would he wish to see a more complete monopoly of public instruction given to the Established Church? Could any government do more to train the people in the way in which he would have them go? And in what did all this training end? The Report of the state of the Province of Canterbury, delivered by Laud to his master at the close of 1639, represents the Church of England as in the highest and most palmy state. So effectually had the government pursued that policy which Mr. Southey wishes to see revived that there was scarcely the least appearance of dissent. Most of the bishops stated that all was well among their flocks. Seven or eight persons in the diocese of Peterborough had seemed refractory to the church, but had made ample submission. In Norfolk and Suffolk all whom there had been reason to suspect had made profession of conformity, and appeared to observe it strictly. It is confessed that there was a little difficulty in bringing some of the vulgar in Suffolk to take the sacrament at the rails in the chancel. This was the only open instance of nonconformity which the vigilant eye of Laud could detect in all the dioceses of his twenty-one suffragans, on the very eve of a revolution in which primate and church and monarch and monarchy were to perish together.

At which time would Mr. Southey pronounce the constitution more secure; in 1639, when Laud presented this report to Charles; or now, when thousands of meetings openly collect millions of dissenters, when designs against the tithes are openly avowed, when books attacking not only the Establishment, but the first principles of Christianity, are openly sold in the streets? The signs of discontent, he tells us, are stronger in England now than in France when the States-General met; and hence he would have us infer that a revolution like that of France may be at hand. Does he not know that the danger of states is to be estimated, not by what breaks out of the public mind, but by what stays in it? Can he conceive anything more terrible than the situation of a government which rules without apprehension over a people of hypocrites, which is flattered by the press and cursed in the inner chambers, which exults in the attachment and obedience of its subjects, and knows not that those subjects are leagued against it in a freemasonry of hatred, the sign of which is every day conveyed in the glance of ten-thousand eyes, the pressure of ten-thousand hands, and the tone of ten-thousand voices? Profound and ingenious policy! Instead of curing the disease, to remove those symptoms by which alone its nature can be known! To leave the serpent his deadly sting, and deprive him only of his warning rattle! . . .

The signs of the times, Mr. Southey tells us, are very threatening. His fears for the country would decidedly preponderate over his hopes, but for his firm reliance on the mercy of God. Now as we know that God has once suffered the civilised world to be overrun by savages and the Christian religion to be corrupted by doctrines which made it for some ages almost as bad as Paganism, we cannot think it inconsistent with his attributes that similar calamities should again befall mankind.

We look, however, on the state of the world, and of this kingdom in particular, with much greater satisfaction and with better hopes. Mr. Southey speaks with contempt of those who think the savage state happier than the social. On this subject, he says, Rousseau never imposed on him even in his youth. But he conceives that a community which has advanced a little way in civilisation is happier than one which has made greater progress. The Britons in the time of Cæsar were happier, he suspects, than the English of the nineteenth century. On the whole, he selects the generation which preceded the Reformation as that in which the people of this country were better off than at any time before or since.

This opinion rests on nothing, as far as we can see, except his own individual associations. He is a man of letters; and a life destitute of literary pleasures seems insipid to him. He abhors the spirit of the present generation, the severity of its studies, the boldness of its enquiries, and the disdain with which it regards some old prejudices by which his own mind is held in bondage. He dislikes an utterly unenlightened age; he dislikes an investigating and reforming age. The first twenty years of the sixteenth century would have exactly suited him. They furnished just the quantity of intellectual excitement which he requires. The learned few read and wrote largely. A scholar was held in high estimation. But the rabble did not presume to think; and even the most inquiring and independent of the educated classes paid more reverence to authority, and less to reason, than is usual in our time. This is a state of things in which Mr. Southey would have found himself quite comfortable; and, accordingly, he pronounces it the happiest state of things ever known in the world.

The savages were wretched, says Mr. Southey; but the people in the time of Sir Thomas More were happier than either they or we. Now we think it quite certain that we have the advantage over the contemporaries of Sir Thomas More, in every point in which they had any advantage over savages.

Mr. Southey does not even pretend to maintain that the people in the sixteenth century were better lodged or clothed than at present. He seems to admit that in these respects there has been some little improvement. It is indeed a matter about which scarcely any doubt can exist in the most perverse mind that the improvements of machinery have lowered the price of manufactured articles, and have brought within the reach of the poorest some conveniences which Sir Thomas More or his master could not have obtained at any price.

The labouring classes, however, were, according to Mr. Southey, better fed three hundred years ago than at present. We believe that he is completely in error on this point. The condition of servants in noble and worthy families, and of scholars at the Universities, must surely have been better in those times than that of day labourers; and we are sure that it was not better than that of our workhouse paupers. From the household book of the Northumberland family, we find that in one of the greatest establishments of the kingdom the servants lived very much as common sailors live now. In the reign of Edward the Sixth the state of the students at Cambridge is described to us, on the very best authority, as most wretched. Many of them dined on pottage made of a farthing's worth of beef with a little salt and oatmeal, and literally nothing else. This account we have from a contemporary master of St. John's. Our parish poor now eat wheaten bread. In the sixteenth century the labourer was glad to get barley, and was often forced to content himself with poorer fare. In Harrison's introduction to Holinshed we have an account of the state of our working population in the "golden days," as Mr. Southey calls them, "of good Queen Bess." "The gentilitie," says he, "commonly provide themselves sufficiently of wheat for their own tables, whylest their household and poore neighbours in some shires are inforced to content themselves with rye or barleie; yea, and in time of dearth, many with bread made eyther of beanes, peason, or otes, or of altogether, and some acornes among. I will not say that this extremity is oft so well to be seen in time of plentie as of dearth; but if I should I could easily bring my trial: for albeit there be much more grounde eared nowe almost in everye place than hathe beene of late yeares, yet such a price of corne continueth in eache towne and markete, without any just cause, that the artificer and poore labouring man is not able to reach unto it, but is driven to content himself with horse-corne." We should like to see what the effect would be of putting any parish in England now on allowance of "horse-corne." The helotry of Mammon are not, in our day, so easily enforced to content themselves as the peasantry of that happy period, as Mr. Southey considers it, which elapsed between the fall of the feudal and the rise of the commercial tyranny. . . .

The advice and medicine which the poorest labourer can now obtain, in disease or after an accident, is far superior to what Henry the Eighth could have commanded. Scarcely any part of the country is out of the reach of practitioners who are probably not so far inferior to Sir Henry Halford as they are superior to Dr. Butts. That there has been a great improvement in this respect, Mr. Southey allows. Indeed he could not well have denied it. "But," says he, "the evils for which these sciences are the palliative have increased, since the time of the Druids, in a proportion that heavily overweighs the benefit of improved therapeutics." We know nothing either of the diseases or the remedies of the Druids. But we are quite sure that the improvement of medicine has far more than kept pace with the increase of disease during the last three centuries. This is proved by the best possible evidence. The term of human life is decidedly longer in England than in any former age, respecting which we possess any information on which we can rely. All the rants in the world about picturesque cottages and temples of Mammon will not shake this argument. No test of the physical well-being of society can be named so decisive as that which is furnished by bills of mortality. That the lives of the people of this country have been gradually lengthening during the course of several generations, is as certain as any fact in statistics; and that the lives of men should become longer and longer, while their bodily condition during life is becoming worse and worse, is utterly incredible.

Let our readers think over these circumstances. Let them take into the account the sweating sickness and the plague. Let them take into the account that fearful disease which first made its appearance in the generation to which Mr. Southey assigns the palm of felicity, and raged through Europe with a fury at which the physician stood aghast, and before which the people were swept away by myriads. Let them consider the state of the northern counties, constantly the scene of robberies, rapes, massacres and conflagrations. Let them add to all this the fact that seventy-two thousand persons suffered death by the hands of the executioner during the reign of Henry the Eighth, and judge between the nineteenth and the sixteenth century.

We do not say that the lower orders in England do not suffer severe hardships. But, in spite of Mr. Southey's assertions, and in spite of the assertions of a class of politicians who, differing from Mr. Southey in every other point, agree with him in this, we are inclined to doubt whether the labouring classes here really suffer greater physical distress than the labouring classes of the most flourishing countries of the Continent. . . .

There are countries in which the people quietly endure distress that here would shake the foundations of the state, countries in which the inhabitants of a whole province turn out to eat grass with less clamour than one Spitalfields weaver would make here if the overseers were to put him on barley-bread. In those new commonwealths in which a civilised population has at its command a boundless extent of the richest soil, the condition of the labourer is probably happier than in any society which has lasted for many centuries. But in the old world we must confess ourselves unable to find any satisfactory record of any great nation, past or present, in which the working classes have been in a more comfortable situation than in England during the last thirty years. When this island was thinly peopled, it was barbarous; there was little capital, and that little was insecure. It is now the richest and the most highly civilised spot in the world; but the population is dense. Thus we have never known that golden age which the lower orders in the United States are now enjoying. We have never known an age of liberty, of order, and of education, an age in which the mechanical sciences were carried to a great height, yet in which the people were not sufficiently numerous to cultivate even the most fertile valleys. But when we compare our own condition with that of our ancestors, we think it clear that the advantages arising from the progress of civilisation have far more than counterbalanced the disadvantages arising from the progress of population. While our numbers have increased tenfold, our wealth has increased a hundredfold. Though there are so many more people to share the wealth now existing in the country than there were in the sixteenth century, it seems certain that a greater share falls to almost every individual than fell to the share of any of the corresponding class in the sixteenth century. The King keeps a more splendid court. The establishments of the nobles are more magnificent. The esquires are richer; the merchants are richer; the shopkeepers are richer. The servingman, the artisan, and the husbandman have a more copious and palatable supply of food, better clothing and better furniture. This is no reason for tolerating abuses, or for neglecting any means of ameliorating the condition of our poorer countrymen. But it is a reason against telling them, as some of our philosophers are constantly telling them, that they are the most wretched people who ever existed on the face of the earth.

We have already adverted to Mr. Southey's amusing doctrine about national wealth. A state, says he, cannot be too rich; but a people may be too rich. His reason for thinking this is extremely curious.

A people may be too rich, because it is the tendency of the commercial, and more especially of the manufacturing system, to collect wealth rather than to diffuse it. Where wealth is necessarily employed in any of the speculations of trade, its increase is in proportion to its amount. Great capitalists become like pikes in a fish pond, who devour the weaker fish; and it is but too certain that the poverty of one part of the people seems to increase in the same ratio as the riches of another. There are examples of this in history. . . .

The fact is that Mr. Southey's proposition is opposed to all history and to the phenomena which surround us on every side. England is the richest country in Europe, the most commercial country, and the country in which manufactures flourish most. Russia and Poland are the poorest countries in Europe. They have scarcely any trade and none but the rudest manufactures. Is wealth more diffused in Russia and Poland than in England? There are individuals in Russia and Poland whose incomes are probably equal to those of our richest countrymen. It may be doubted whether there are not in those countries as many fortunes of eighty thousand a year as here. But are there as many fortunes of two thousand a year or of one thousand a year? There are parishes in England which contain more people of between three hundred and three thousand pounds a year than could be found in all the dominions of the Emperor Nicholas. The neat and commodious houses which have been built in London and its vicinity for people of this class, within the last thirty years, would of themselves form a city larger than the capitals of some European kingdoms. And this is the state of society in which the great proprietors have devoured a smaller!

The cure which Mr. Southey thinks that he has discovered is worthy of the sagacity which he has shown in detecting the evil. The calamities arising from the collection of wealth in the hands of a few capitalists are to be remedied by collecting it in the hands of one great capitalist, who has no conceivable motive to use it better than other capitalists, the all-devouring state.

It is not strange that, differing so widely from Mr. Southey as to the past progress of society, we should differ from him also as to its probable destiny. He thinks, that to all outward appearance, the country is hastening to destruction; but he relies firmly on the goodness of God. We do not see either the piety or the rationality of thus confidently expecting that the Supreme Being will interfere to disturb the common succession of causes and effects. We, too, rely on his goodness, on his goodness as manifested, not in extraordinary interpositions, but in those general laws which it has pleased him to establish in the physical and in the moral world. We rely on the natural tendency of the human intellect to truth, and on the natural tendency of society to improvement. We know no well authenticated instance of a people which has decidedly retrograded in civilisation and prosperity except from the influence of violent and terrible calamities, such as those which laid the Roman empire in ruins or those which, about the beginning of the sixteenth century, desolated Italy. We know of no country which, at the end of fifty years of peace and tolerably good government, has been less prosperous than at the beginning of that period. The political importance of a state may decline as the balance of power is disturbed by the introduction of new forces. Thus the influence of Holland and of Spain is much diminished. But are Holland and Spain poorer than formerly? We doubt it. Other countries have outrun them. But we suspect that they have been positively, though not relatively, advancing. We suspect that Holland is richer than when she sent her navies up the Thames, that Spain is richer than when a French king was brought captive to the footstool of Charles the Fifth.

History is full of the signs of this natural progress of society. We see in almost every part of the annals of mankind how the industry of individuals, struggling up against wars, taxes, famines, conflagrations, mischievous prohibitions, and more mischievous protections, creates faster than governments can squander and repairs whatever invaders can destroy. We see the wealth of nations increasing and all the arts of life approaching nearer and nearer to perfection, in spite of the grossest corruption and the wildest profusion on the part of rulers.

The present moment is one of great distress. But how small will that distress appear when we think over the history of the last forty years; a war compared with which all other wars sink into insignificance; taxation such as the most heavily taxed people of former times could not have conceived; a debt larger than all the public debts that ever existed in the world added together; the food of the people studiously rendered dear; the currency imprudently debased and imprudently restored. Yet is the country poorer than in 1790? We firmly believe that, in spite of all the misgovernment of her rulers, she has been almost constantly becoming richer and richer. Now and then there has been a stoppage, now and then a short retrogression; but as to the general tendency, there can be no doubt. A single breaker may recede; but the tide is evidently coming in.

If we were to prophesy that in the year 1930 a population of fifty millions, better fed, clad and lodged than the English of our time, will cover these islands, that Sussex and Huntingdonshire will be wealthier than the wealthiest parts of the West Riding of Yorkshire now are, that cultivation, rich as that of a flower garden, will be carried up to the very tops of Ben Nevis and Helvellyn, that machines constructed on principles yet undiscovered will be in every house, that there will be no highways but railroads, no travelling but by steam, that our debt, vast as it seems to us, will appear to our great-grandchildren a trifling encumbrance which might easily be paid off in a year or two—many people would think us insane. We prophesy nothing, but this we say: If any person had told the Parliament which met in perplexity and terror after the crash in 1720 that in 1830 the wealth of England would surpass all their wildest dreams, that the annual revenue would equal the principal of that debt which they considered as an intolerable burden, that for one man of ten-thousand pounds then living there would be five men of fifty-thousand pounds, that London would be twice as large and twice as populous, and that nevertheless the rate of mortality would have diminished to one-half of what it then was, that the post-office would bring more into the exchequer than the excise and customs had brought in together under Charles the Second, that stage-coaches would run from London to York in twenty-four hours, that men would be in the habit of sailing without wind and would be beginning to ride without horses, our ancestors would have given as much credit to the prediction as they gave to *Gulliver's Travels.* Yet the prediction would have been true; and they would have perceived that it was not altogether absurd, if they had considered that the country was then raising every year a sum which would have purchased the fee-simple of the revenue of the Plantagenets, ten times what supported the government of Elizabeth, three times what, in the time of Oliver Cromwell, had been thought intolerably oppressive. To almost all men the state of things under which they have been used to live seems to be the necessary state of things. We have heard it said that five per cent is the natural interest of money, that twelve is the natural number of a jury, that forty shillings is the natural qualification of a county voter. Hence it is that, though in every age everybody knows that up to his own time progressive improvement has been taking place, nobody seems to reckon on any improvement during the next generation. We cannot absolutely prove that those are in error who tell us that society has reached a turning point, that we have seen our best days. But so said all who came before us, and with just as much apparent reason. "A million a year will beggar us," said the patriots of 1640. "Two millions a year will grind the country to powder," was the cry in 1660. "Six millions a year and a debt of fifty millions!" exclaimed Swift; "the high allies have been the ruin of us." "A hundred and forty millions of debt!" said Junius; "well may we say that we owe Lord Chatham more than we shall ever pay, if we owe him such a load as this." "Two hundred and forty millions of debt!" cried all the statesmen of 1783 in chorus; "what abilities, or what economy on the part of a minister, can save a country so burdened?" We know that if, since 1783, no fresh debt had been incurred, the increased resources of the country would have enabled us to defray that debt at which Pitt, Fox, and Burke stood aghast, nay to defray it over and over again and that with much lighter taxation than what we have actually borne. On what principle is it that, when we see nothing but improvement behind us, we are to expect nothing but deterioration before us?

It is not by the intermeddling of Mr. Southey's idol, the omniscient and omnipotent State, but by the prudence and energy of the people that England has hitherto been carried forward in civilisation; and it is to the same prudence and the same energy that we now look with comfort and good hope. Our rulers will best promote the improvement of the nation by strictly confining themselves to their own legitimate duties, by leaving capital to find its most lucrative course, commodities their fair price, industry and intelligence their natural reward, idleness and folly their natural punishment, by maintaining peace, by defending property, by diminishing the price of law, and by observing strict economy in every department of the state. Let the Government do this; the People will assuredly do the rest.

The first of the Victorian "prophets" or "sages," Carlyle follows Coleridge in emphasizing the principles that bind society together, and in suggesting that institutions be changed or renewed so that society can go on satisfying the same needs it always has satisfied. Writing in response to depression and Chartism, Carlyle, in *Past and Present* (1843), compares feudalism and industrialism in order to show that it is not mainly poverty that disaffects the modern laboring classes; it is mainly their sense of alienation from a society in which the only link among men is the cash nexus. In this respect, Gurth, the medieval serf in Scott's *Ivanhoe*, was better off than the modern industrial worker; for Gurth had economic and social security, even if at the lowest level.

Political liberty is not enough if it offers us only "Liberty to die by starvation." The problem is "How, in conjuction with inevitable Democracy, indispensable Sovereignty is to exist." Carlyle, who even proposes a guaranteed annual wage, might be called a social democrat, if he didn't place so much reliance on great men and "hero worship." In *Past and Present*, the young, radical Carlyle wants a new aristocracy of talent to replace the landed aristocracy, whose only occupation is hunting and whose sponsorship of the Corn Laws, the tariff on imported wheat, damages the market for manufactured exports. He wants modern captains of industry to become, through responsibility for their workers, the equivalent of feudal lords. The older, reactionary Carlyle lost faith in the industrialists and looked to the landed artistocracy for leadership. But it was never really a class, it was the exceptional individual, the genius, that Carlyle had in mind when he spoke of the importance to society of great men.

Thomas Carlyle

PAST AND PRESENT

May it please your Serene Highnesses, your Majesties, Lordships and Law-wardships, the proper Epic of this world is not now "Arms and the Man"; how much less, "Shirt-frills and the Man": no, it is now "Tools and the Man": that, henceforth to all time, is now our Epic—and you, first of all others, I think, were wise to take note of that!

If the Serene Highnesses and Majesties do not take note of that, then as I perceive, *that* will take note of itself! The time for levity, insincerity, and idle babble and play-acting, in all kinds, is gone by; it is a serious, grave time. Old long-vexed questions, not yet solved in logical words or parliamentary laws, are fast solving themselves in facts, somewhat unblessed to behold! This largest of questions, this question of Work and Wages, which ought, had we heeded Heaven's voice, to have begun two generations ago or more, cannot be delayed longer without hearing Earth's voice. "Labor" will verily need to be somewhat "organized," as they say—God knows with what difficulty. Man will actually need to have his debts and earnings a little better paid by man; which, let Parliament speak of them or be silent of them, are eternally his due from man and cannot, without penalty and at length not without death-penalty, be withheld. How much ought to cease among us straightway; how much ought to begin straightway, while the hours yet are!

Truly they are strange results to which this of leaving all to "Cash," of quietly shutting up the God's Temple, and gradually opening wide open the Mammon's Temple, with "Laissez-faire, and Every man for himself"—have led us in these days! We have Upper, speaking Classes, who indeed do "speak" as never man spake before; the withered flimsiness, the godless baseness and barrenness of whose Speech might of itself indicate what kind of Doing and practical Governing went on under it! For Speech is the gaseous element out of which most kinds of Practice and Performance, especially

THE WORKS OF THOMAS CARLYLE, Centenary Edition, 30 vols. (London: Chapman and Hall, 1897), X, 209-20, 250-51. PAST AND PRESENT, mainly from Book III, Chap. XIII, "Democracy." See also Emery Neff, *Carlyle and Mill* (New York, 1926).

all kinds of moral Performance, condense themselves and take shape; as the one is, so will the other be. Descending, accordingly, into the Dumb Class in its Stockport Cellars and Poor-Law Bastilles,[1] have we not to announce that they also are hitherto unexampled in the History of Adam's Posterity.

Life was never a May-game for men: in all times the lot of the dumb millions born to toil was defaced with manifold sufferings, injustices, heavy burdens, avoidable and unavoidable; not play at all, but hard work that made the sinews sore and the heart sore. As bond-slaves, *villani, bordarii, sochemanni,* nay indeed as dukes, earls and kings, men were oftentimes made weary of their life; and had to say, in the sweat of their brow and of their soul, Behold, it is not sport, it is grim earnest, and our back can bear no more! Who knows not what massacrings and harryings there have been; grinding, long-continuing, unbearable injustices—till the heart had to rise in madness, and some *"Eu Sachsen, nimith euer saches,* You Saxons, out with your gully-knives, then!" You Saxons, some "arrestment," partial "arrestment of the Knaves and Dastards" to become indispensable! The page of Dryasdust[2] is heavy with such details.

And yet I will venture to believe that in no time, since the beginnings of Society, was the lot of those same dumb millions of toilers so entirely unbearable as it is even in the days now passing over us. It is not to die, or even to die of hunger, that makes a man wretched; many men have died; all men must die—the last exit of us all is in a Fire-Chariot of Pain. But it is to live miserable we know not why; to work sore and yet gain nothing; to be heart-worn, weary, yet isolated, unrelated, girt in with a cold universal Laissez-faire: it is to die slowly all our life long, imprisoned in a deaf, dead, Infinite Injustice, as in the accursed iron belly of a Phalaris' Bull! This is and remains forever intolerable to all men whom God has made. Do we wonder at French Revolutions, Chartisms, Revolts of Three Days? The times, if we will consider them, are really unexampled.

Never before did I hear of an Irish Widow reduced to "prove her sisterhood by dying of typhus-fever and infecting seventeen persons"—saying in such undeniable way, "You *see* I was your sister!" Sisterhood, brotherhood was often forgotten; but not till the rise of these ultimate Mammon and Shot-belt Gospels did I ever see it so expressly denied. If no

---

[1] [A cellar where three children were poisoned by their starving parents for the insurance benefits; workhouses for the unemployed.—Ed.]

[2] [Carlyle's name for pedantic Whig historians.—Ed.]

pious Lord or *Law-ward* would remember it, always some-pious Lady (*"Hlaf-dig,"* Benefactress, *"Loaf-giveress,"* they say she is—blessings on her beautiful heart!) was there, with mild mother-voice and hand, to remember it; some pious thoughtful *Elder,* what we now call "Prester," *Presbyter* or "Priest," was there to put all men in mind of it in the name of the God who had made all.

Not even in Black Dahomey was it ever, I think, forgotten to the typhus-fever length. Mungo Park, resourceless, had sunk down to die under the Negro Village-Tree, a horrible White object in the eyes of all. But in the poor Black Woman, and her daughter who stood aghast at him, whose earthly wealth and funded capital consisted of one small calabash of rice, there lived a heart richer than *Laissez-faire:* they, with a royal munificence, boiled their rice for him; they sang all night to him, spinning assiduous on their cotton distaffs as he lay to sleep: "Let us pity the poor white man; no mother has he to fetch him milk, no sister to grind him corn!" Thou poor black Noble One—thou *Lady* too: did not a God make thee too; was there not in thee too something of a God!

Gurth, born thrall of Cedric the Saxon, has been greatly pitied by Dryasdust and others. Gurth, with the brass collar round his neck, tending Cedric's pigs in the glades of the wood, is not what I call an exemplar of human felicity: but Gurth, with the sky above him, with the free air and tinted boscage and umbrage round him, and in him at least the certainty of supper and social lodging when he came home; Gurth to me seems happy in comparison with many a Lanca-shire and Buckinghamshire man of these days, not born thrall of anybody! Gurth's brass collar did not gall him; Cedric *deserved* to be his master. The pigs were Cedric's, but Gurth too would get his parings of them. Gurth had the inexpres-sible satisfaction of feeling himself related indissolubly, though in a rude brass-collar way, to his fellow-mortals in this Earth. He had superiors, inferiors, equals. Gurth is now "emancipated" long since; has what we call "Liberty." Liberty, I am told, is a divine thing. Liberty, when it becomes the "Liberty to die by starvation," is not so divine!

Liberty? The true liberty of a man, you would say, con-sisted in his finding out, or being forced to find out the right path, and to walk thereon. To learn, or to be taught, what work he actually was able for; and then by permission, per-suasion, and even compulsion, to set about doing of the same! That is his true blessedness, honor, "liberty" and maximum of well-being; if liberty be not that, I for one have small care about liberty. You do not allow a palpable madman to leap over precipices; you violate his liberty, you that are wise; and keep him, were it in strait-waistcoats, away from the precipices! Every stupid, every cowardly and foolish man is but a less palpable madman; his true liberty were that a wiser man, that any and every wiser man could, by brass collars or in whatever milder or sharper way, lay hold of him, when he was going wrong, and order and compel him to go a little righter. Oh, if thou really art my *Senior,* Seigneur, my *Elder,* Presbyter or Priest—if thou art in very deed my *Wiser,* may a beneficent instinct lead and impel thee to "conquer" me, to command me! If thou do know better than I what is good and right, I conjure thee in the name of God, force me to do it; were it by never such brass collars, whips and handcuffs, leave me not to walk over precipices! That I have been called, by all the Newspapers, a "free man" will avail me little, if my pilgrimage have ended in death and wreck. Oh that the Newspapers had called me slave, coward, fool, or what it pleased their sweet voices to name me, and I had attained not death, but life! Liberty requires new definitions.

A conscious abhorrence and intolerance of Folly, of Baseness, Stupidity, Poltroonery and all that brood of things, dwells deep in some men: still deeper in others an *un*conscious abhorrence and intolerance, clothed moreover by the beneficent Supreme Powers in what stout appetites, energies, egoisms so called, are suitable to it; these latter are your Conquerors, Romans, Normans, Russians, Indo-English— Founders of what we call Aristocracies. Which indeed have they not the most "divine right" to found—being themselves very truly "Αριστοι, BRAVEST, BEST; and conquering generally a confused rabble of WORST, or at lowest, clearly enough, of WORSE? I think their divine right, tried, with affirmatory verdict, in the greatest Law-Court known to me, was good! A class of men who are dreadfully exclaimed against by Dryasdust; of whom nevertheless beneficent Nature has oftentimes had need; and may, alas, again have need.

When across the hundredfold poor scepticisms, trivialisms, and constitutional cobwebberies of Dryasdust, you catch any glimpse of a William the Conqueror, a Tancred of Hauteville or such like—do you not discern veritably some rude outline of a true God-made King; whom not the Champion of England cased in tin, but all Nature and the Universe were calling to the throne? It is absolutely necessary that he get thither. Nature does not mean her poor Saxon children to perish of obesity, stupor or other malady, as yet: a stern Ruler and Line of Rulers therefore is called in—a stern but most beneficent *perpetual House-Surgeon* is by Nature herself called in, and even the appropriate *fees* are provided for him. Dryasdust talks lamentably about Hereward and the Fen Counties; fate of Earl Waltheof; Yorkshire and the North reduced to ashes: all which is undoubtedly lamentable. But even Dryasdust apprises me of one fact: "A child, in this William's reign, might have carried a purse of gold from end to end of England." My erudite friend, it is a fact which outweighs a thousand! Sweep away thy constitutional, sentimental and other cobwebberies; look eye to eye, if thou still have any eye, in the face of this big burly William Bastard: thou wilt see a fellow of most flashing discernment, of most strong lion-heart—in whom, as it were, within a frame of oak and iron, the gods have planted the soul of "a man of genius"! Dost thou call that nothing? I call it an immense thing! Rage enough was in this Willelmus Conquæstor, rage enough for his occasions; and yet the essential element of him, as of all such men, is not scorching *fire* but shining illuminative *light*. Fire and light are strangely interchangeable; nay, at bottom, I have found them different forms of the same most godlike "elementary substance" in our world: a thing worth stating in these days. The essential element of this Conquæstor is, first of all, the most sun-eyed perception of what *is* really what on this God's-Earth—which, thou wilt find, does mean at bottom "Justice" and "Virtues" not a few: *Conformity* to what the Maker has seen good to make; that, I suppose, will mean Justice and a Virtue or two?

Dost thou think Willelmus Conquæstor would have tolerated ten years' jargon, one hour's jargon, on the propriety of killing Cotton-manufacturers by partridge Corn-Laws? I fancy, this was not the man to knock out of his night's rest with nothing but a noisy bedlamism in your mouth! "Assist us still better to bush the partridges; strangle Plugson who spins the shirts?" *"Par la Splendeur de Dieu!"* Dost thou think Willelmus Conquæstor, in this new time, with Steam-engine Captains of Industry on one hand of him, and Joe-Manton[3] Captains of Idleness on the other, would have

[3] [The London gunsmith from whom the aristocrats bought their hunting pieces.—Ed.]

doubted which *was* really the BEST; which did deserve strangling and which not?

I have a certain indestructible regard for Willelmus Conquæstor. A resident House-Surgeon, provided by nature for her beloved English People, and even furnished with the requisite fees, as I said; for he by no means felt himself doing Nature's work, this Willelmus, but his own work exclusively! And his own work withal it was; informed *"par la Splendeur de Dieu."* I say, it is necessary to get the work out of such a man, however harsh that be! When a world, not yet doomed for death, is rushing down to ever-deeper Baseness and Confusion, it is a dire necessity of Nature's to bring in her ARISTOCRACIES, her BEST, even by forcible methods. When their descendants or representatives cease entirely to *be* the Best, Nature's poor world will very soon rush down again to Baseness; and it becomes a dire necessity of Nature's to cast them out. Hence French Revolutions, Five-point Charters, Democracies, and a mournful list of *Etceteras,* in these our afflicted times.

To what extent Democracy has now reached, how it advances irresistible with ominous, ever-increasing speed, he that will open his eyes on any province of human affairs may discern. Democracy is everywhere the inexorable demand of these ages, swift fulfilling itself. From the thunder of Napoleon battles, to the jabbering of Open-vestry in St. Mary Axe, all things announce Democracy. A distinguished man, whom some of my readers will hear again with pleasure, thus writes to me what in these days he notes from the Wahngasse of Weissnichtwo, where our London fashions seem to be in full vogue. Let us hear the Herr Teufelsdröckh[4] again, were it but the smallest word!

"Democracy, which means despair of finding any Heroes to govern you, and contented putting up with the want of them—alas, thou too, *mein Lieber,* seest well how close it is of kin to *Atheism* and other sad *Isms;* he who discovers no God whatever, how shall he discover Heroes, the visible Temples of God? Strange enough meanwhile it is to observe with what thoughtlessness, here in our rigidly Conservative Country, men rush into Democracy with full cry. Beyond doubt, his Excellenz the Titular-Herr Ritter Kauderwälsch von Pferdefuss-Quacksalber, he our distinguished Conserva-

---

[4] [The fictitious German philosopher who, as hero of *Sartor Resartus* (1833), is spokesman for Carlyle's clothes philosophy.—Ed.]

tive Premier[5] himself, and all but the thicker-headed of his Party, discern Democracy to be inevitable as death, and are even desperate of delaying it much!

"You cannot walk the streets without beholding Democracy announce itself; the very Tailor has become, if not properly Sansculottic,[6] which to him would be ruinous, yet a Tailor unconsciously symbolizing and prophesying with his scissors, the reign of Equality. What now is our fashionable coat? A thing of superfinest texture, of deeply meditated cut; with Malines-lace cuffs; quilted with gold; so that a man can carry without difficulty an estate of land on his back? *Keineswegs,* by no manner of means! The Sumptuary Laws have fallen into such a state of desuetude as was never before seen. Our fashionable coat is an amphibium between barn-sack and drayman's doublet. The cloth of it is studiously coarse; the color a speckled soot-black or rust-brown gray; the nearest approach to a Peasant's. And for shape—thou shouldst see it! The last consummation of the year now passing over us is definable as Three Bags; a big bag for the body, two small bags for the arms, and by way of collar a hem! The first Antique Cheruscan who, of felt-cloth or bear's-hide, with bone or metal needle, set about making himself a coat, before Tailors had yet awakened out of Nothing —did not he make it even so? A loose wide poke for body, with two holes to let out the arms; this was his original coat: to which holes it was soon visible that two small loose pokes, or sleeves, easily appended, would be an improvement.

"Thus has the Tailor-art, so to speak, overset itself, like most other things; changed its centre-of-gravity; whirled suddenly over from zenith to nadir. Your Stulz, with huge somerset, vaults from his high shopboard down to the depths of primal savagery—carrying much along with him! For I will invite thee to reflect that the Tailor, as topmost ultimate froth of Human Society, is indeed swift-passing, evanescent, slippery to decipher; yet significant of much, nay of all. Topmost evanescent froth, he is churned up from the very lees, and from all intermediate regions of the liquor. The general outcome he, visible to the eye, of what men aimed to do, and were obliged and enabled to do, in this one public department of symbolizing themselves to each other by covering of their skins. A smack of all Human Life lies in the

---

[5] [Peel, who was then working toward repeal of the Corn Laws.—Ed.]
[6] [Favorable to the cause of the people who do not wear knee breeches— i.e. clothes that signify rank.—Ed.]

Tailor; its wild struggles towards beauty, dignity, freedom, victory; and how, hemmed in by Sedan and Huddersfield, by Nescience, Dulness, Prurience, and other sad necessities and laws of Nature, it has attained just to this: Gray savagery of Three Sacks with a hem!

"When the very Tailor verges towards Sansculottism, is it not ominous? The last Divinity of poor mankind dethroning himself; sinking *his* taper too, flame downmost, like the Genius of Sleep or of Death; admonitory that Tailor time shall be no more! For, little as one could advise Sumptuary Laws at the present epoch, yet nothing is clearer than that where ranks do actually exist, strict division of costumes will also be enforced; that if we ever have a new Hierarchy and Aristocracy, acknowledged veritably as such, for which I daily pray Heaven, the Tailor will reawaken; and be, by volunteering and appointment, consciously and unconsciously, a safeguard of that same." Certain farther observations, from the same invaluable pen, on our never-ending changes of mode, our "perpetual nomadic and even ape-like appetite for change and mere 'change' in all the equipments of our existence, and the fatal revolutionary character" thereby manifested, we suppress for the present. It may be admitted that Democracy, in all meanings of the word, is in full career; irresistible by any Ritter Kauderwälsch or other Son of Adam, as times go. "Liberty" is a thing men are determined to have.

But truly, as I had to remark in the meanwhile, "the liberty of not being oppressed by your fellow man" is an indispensable, yet one of the most insignificant fractional parts of Human Liberty. No man oppresses thee, can bid thee fetch or carry, come or go, without reason shown. True, from all men thou art emancipated; but from Thyself and from the Devil? No man, wiser, unwiser, can make thee come or go; but thy own futilities, bewilderments, thy false appetites for Money, Windsor Georges and such like? No man oppresses thee, O free and independent Franchiser; but does not this stupid Porter-pot oppress thee? No Son of Adam can bid thee come or go; but this absurd Pot of Heavy-wet, this can and does! Thou art the thrall not of Cedric the Saxon, but of thy own brutal appetites and this scoured dish of liquor. And thou pratest of thy "liberty"? Thou entire blockhead!

Heavy-wet and gin; alas, these are not the only kinds of thraldom. Thou who walkest in a vain show, looking out with ornamental dilettante sniff and serene supremacy at all Life and all Death; and amblest jauntily; perking up thy poor talk into crotchets, thy poor conduct into fatuous somnambulisms—and *art* as an "enchanted Ape" under God's sky, where thou mightest have been a man, had proper Schoolmasters and Conquerors, and Constables with cat-o'-nine tails, been vouchsafed thee; dost thou call that "liberty"? Or your unreposing Mammon-worshipper again, driven as if by Galvanisms, by Devils and Fixed-Ideas, who rises early and sits late, chasing the impossible; straining every faculty to "fill himself with the east-wind"—how merciful were it, could you, by mild persuasion, or by the severest tyranny so called, check him in his mad path, and turn him into a wiser one! All painful tyranny, in that case again, were but mild "surgery"; the pain of it cheap, as health and life instead of galvanism and fixed-idea, are cheap at any price.

Sure enough, of all paths a man could strike into, there *is* at any given moment a *best path* for every man; a thing which here and now it were of all things *wisest* for him to do—which could he be but led or driven to do, he were then doing "like a man," as we phrase it; all men and gods agreeing with him, the whole Universe virtually exclaiming Well-done to him! His success, in such case, were complete; his felicity a maximum. This path, to find this path and walk in it, is the one thing needful for him. Whatsoever forwards him in that, let it come to him even in the shape of blows and spurnings, is liberty; whatsoever hinders him, were it wardmotes, open-vestries, poll-booths, tremendous cheers, rivers of heavy-wet, is slavery.

The notion that a man's liberty consists in giving his vote at election-hustings, and saying, "Behold, now I too have my twenty-thousandth part of a Talker in our National Palaver; will not all the gods be good to me?"—is one of the pleasantest! Nature nevertheless is kind at present; and puts it into the heads of many, almost of all. The liberty especially which has to purchase itself by social isolation, and each man standing separate from the other, having "no business with him" but a cash-account: this is such a liberty as the Earth seldom saw—as the Earth will not long put up with, recommend it how you may. This liberty turns out, before it have long continued in action, with all men flinging up their caps round it, to be, for the Working Millions a liberty to die by want of

food; for the Idle Thousands and Units, alas, a still more
fatal liberty to live in want of work; to have no earnest duty
to do in this God's-World any more. What becomes of a man
in such predicament? Earth's Laws are silent; and Heaven's
speak in a voice which is not heard. No work, and the
ineradicable need of work, give rise to new very wondrous
life-philosophies, new very wondrous life-practices! Dilettantism, Pococurantism, Beau-Brummelism, with perhaps an occasional, half-mad, protesting burst of Byronism, establish
themselves; at the end of a certain period—if you go back
to "the Dead Sea," there is, say our Moslem friends, a very
strange "Sabbath-day" transacting itself there! Brethren, we
know but imperfectly yet, after ages of Constitutional Government, what Liberty and Slavery are.

Democracy, the chase of Liberty in that direction, shall
go its full course; unrestrainable by him of Pferdefuss-
Quacksalber or any of *his* household. The Toiling Millions
of Mankind, in most vital need and passionate instinctive
desire of Guidance, shall cast away False-Guidance, and hope
for an hour, that No-Guidance will suffice them; but it can be
for an hour only. The smallest item of human Slavery is the
oppression of man by his Mock-Superiors; the palpablest, but
I say at bottom the smallest. Let him shake off such oppression, trample it indignantly under his feet; I blame him
not, I pity and commend him. But oppression by your Mock-
Superiors well shaken off, the grand problem yet remains to
solve: that of finding government by your Real-Superiors!
Alas, how shall we ever learn the solution of that—benighted,
bewildered, sniffing, sneering, God-forgetting unfortunates as
we are? It is a work for centuries; to be taught us by tribu-
lations, confusions, insurrections, obstructions; who knows if
not by conflagration and despair! It is a lesson inclusive of
all other lessons; the hardest of all lessons to learn. . . .

One wide and widest "outline" ought really, in all ways,
to be becoming clear to us; this namely: that a "Splendour of
God," in one form or other, will have to unfold itself from the
heart of these our Industrial Ages too; or they will never get
themselves "organized," but continue chaotic, distressed, distracted evermore, and have to perish in frantic suicidal dissolution. A second "outline" or prophecy, narrowed, but also
wide enough, seems not less certain: that there will again
be a King in Israel; a system of Order and Government; and
every man shall, in some measure, see himself constrained to
do that which is right in the King's eyes. This too we may

call a sure element of the Future; for this too is of the Eternal—this too is of the Present, though hidden from most; and without it no fibre of the Past ever was. An actual new Sovereignty, Industrial Aristocracy, real not imaginary Aristocracy, is indispensable and indubitable for us.

But what an Aristocracy; on what new, far more complex and cunningly devised conditions than that old Feudal fighting one! For we are to bethink us that the Epic verily is not *Arms and the Man,* but *Tools and the Man*—an infinitely wider kind of Epic. And again we are to bethink us that men cannot now be bound to men by *brass-collars*—not at all: that this brass-collar method, in all figures of it, has vanished out of Europe forevermore! Huge Democracy, walking the streets everywhere in its Sack Coat, has asserted so much; irrevocably, brooking no reply! True enough, man *is* forever the "born thrall" of certain men, born master of certain other men, born equal of certain others, let him acknowledge the fact or not. It is unblessed for him when he cannot acknowledge this fact; he is in the chaotic state, ready to perish, till he do get the fact acknowledged. But no man is, or can henceforth be, the brass-collar thrall of any man; you will have to bind him by other, far nobler and cunninger methods. Once for all, he is to be loose of the brass-collar, to have a scope *as* wide as his faculties now are—will he not be all the usefuler to you in that new state? Let him go abroad as a trusted one, as a free one; and return home to you with rich earnings at night! Gurth could only tend pigs; this one will build cities, conquer waste worlds. How, in conjunction with inevitable Democracy, indispensable Sovereignty is to exist: certainly it is the hugest question ever heretofore propounded to Mankind! The solution of which is work for long years and centuries. Years and centuries, of one knows not what complexion—blessed or unblessed, according as they shall with earnest valiant effort make progress therein, or, in slothful unveracity and dilettantism, only talk of making progress. For either progress therein, or swift and ever swifter progress towards dissolution, is henceforth a necessity.

In this chapter from *Culture and Anarchy* (1869), the argument again is for government as a positive good and not merely a necessary evil. Again the issue is laissez-faire, treated here just after the second Reform Bill of 1867 has opened the way to political power for still a new class, the workers. Writing after the so-called Hyde Park riots of 1866—which occurred when working-class demonstrators, denied entrance into Hyde Park, pulled down the railings, burst in and trampled the flowerbeds—Arnold warns in *Culture and Anarchy* of what will happen when the working class starts looking after its own interests, according to the principle taught them by the middle class. The result will be class war, anarchy.

It is because Englishmen assume that any class in power will merely look after its own interests that they protect themselves by making government as weak as possible. But such safety "cannot save us from anarchy." We must cultivate, says Arnold, the idea "familiar on the Continent and to antiquity, *of the State.*" And we can only do so through culture; for culture develops in us a *"best self"* that is capable of rising above self-interest to think and act according to rational and moral principles. Only the best self can adequately conceive of the State. Culture, as Arnold defines it in the chapter preceding this one, is the opposite of what we nowadays call ideology, for culture "seeks to do away with classes; to make the best that has been thought and known in the world current everywhere; to make all men live in an atmosphere of sweetness and light, where they may use ideas, as it uses them itself, freely—nourished and not bound by them. This is the *social idea*; and the men of culture are the true apostles of equality." Only if we can arrive through culture, says Arnold in concluding this chapter, at an idea of *the State,* can we carry forward our "revolution by due course of law"—can we have, to paraphrase Carlyle, "great changes" with indispensable "order."

154

MATTHEW ARNOLD

CULTURE AND ANARCHY

Doing as One Likes

When I began to speak of culture, I insisted on our bondage to machinery, on our proneness to value machinery as an end in itself, without looking beyond it to the end for which alone, in truth, it is valuable. Freedom, I said, was one of those things which we thus worshipped in itself, without enough regarding the ends for which freedom is to be desired. In our common notions and talk about freedom, we eminently show our idolatry of machinery. Our prevalent notion is—and I quoted a number of instances to prove it— that it is a most happy and important thing for a man merely to be able to do as he likes. On what he is to do when he is thus free to do as he likes, we do not lay so much stress. Our familiar praise of the British Constitution under which we live, is that it is a system of checks—a system which stops and paralyses any power in interfering with the free action of individuals. To this effect Mr. Bright, who loves to walk in the old ways of the Constitution, said forcibly in one of his great speeches what many other people are every day saying less forcibly, that the central idea of English life and politics is *the assertion of personal liberty*. Evidently this is so; but evidently, also, as feudalism, which with its ideas and habits of subordination was for many centuries silently behind the British Constitution, dies out, and we are left with nothing but our system of checks, and our notion of its being the great right and happiness of an Englishman to do as far as possible what he likes, we are in danger of drifting towards anarchy. We have not the notion, so familiar on the Continent and to antiquity, of *the State*—the nation in its collective and corporate character, entrusted with stringent powers for the general advantage, and controlling in-

Matthew Arnold, CULTURE AND ANARCHY: AN ESSAY IN POLITICAL AND SOCIAL CRITICISM, Second Edition (New York, 1875), pp. 50-83. See also Lionel Trilling, *Matthew Arnold* (New York, 1949); Edward Alexander, *Matthew Arnold and John Stuart Mill* (New York and London, 1965); David J. DeLaura, "Arnold and Carlyle," PMLA, LXXIX (March 1964), 104-29.

dividual wills in the name of an interest wider than that of individuals. We say, what is very true, that this notion is often made instrumental to tyranny; we say that a State is in reality made up of the individuals who compose it, and that every individual is the best judge of his own interests. Our leading class is an aristocracy, and no aristocracy likes the notion of a State-authority greater than itself, with a stringent administrative machinery superseding the decorative inutilities of lord-lieutenancy, deputy-lieutenancy and the *posse comitatus,* which are all in its own hands. Our middle class, the great representative of trade and Dissent, with its maxims of every man for himself in business, every man for himself in religion, dreads a powerful administration which might somehow interfere with it; and besides, it has its own decorative inutilities of vestrymanship and guardianship, which are to this class what lord-lieutenancy and the county magistracy are to the aristocratic class, and a stringent administration might either take these functions out of its hands, or prevent its exercising them in its own comfortable, independent manner as at present.

Then as to our working class. This class, pressed constantly by the hard daily compulsion of material wants, is naturally the very centre and stronghold of our national idea, that it is man's ideal right and felicity to do as he likes. I think I have somewhere related how M. Michelet said to me of the people of France, that it was "a nation of barbarians civilised by the conscription." He meant that through their military service the idea of public duty and of discipline was brought to the mind of these masses, in other respects so raw and uncultivated. Our masses are quite as raw and uncultivated as the French; and so far from their having the idea of public duty and of discipline, superior to the individual's self-will, brought to their mind by a universal obligation of military service, such as that of the conscription—so far from their having this, the very idea of a conscription is so at variance with our English notion of the prime right and blessedness of doing as one likes, that I remember the manager of the Clay Cross works in Derbyshire told me during the Crimean war, when our want of soldiers was much felt and some people were talking of a conscription, that sooner than submit to a conscription the population of that district would flee to the mines and lead a sort of Robin Hood life under ground.

For a long time, as I have said, the strong feudal habits of subordination and deference continued to tell upon the working class. The modern spirit has now almost entirely dissolved those habits, and the anarchical tendency of our worship of freedom in and for itself, of our superstitious faith, as I say, in machinery, is becoming very manifest. More and more, because of this our blind faith in machinery, because of our want of light to enable us to look beyond machinery to the end for which machinery is valuable, this and that man and this and that body of men, all over the country, are beginning to assert and put in practice an Englishman's right to do what he likes; his right to march where he likes, meet where he likes, enter where he likes, hoot as he likes, threaten as he likes, smash as he likes. All this, I say, tends to anarchy; and though a number of excellent people, and particularly my friends of the Liberal or progressive party, as they call themselves, are kind enough to reassure us by saying that these are trifles, that a few transient outbreaks of rowdyism signify nothing, that our system of liberty is one which itself cures all the evils which it works, that the educated and intelligent classes stand in overwhelming strength and majestic repose, ready, like our military force in riots, to act at a moment's notice—yet one finds that one's Liberal friends generally say this because they have such faith in themselves and their nostrums when they shall return, as the public welfare requires, to place and power. But this faith of theirs one cannot exactly share, when one has so long had them and their nostrums at work and sees that they have not prevented our coming to our present embarrassed condition. And one finds also that the outbreaks of rowdyism tend to become less and less of trifles, to become more frequent rather than less frequent; and that meanwhile our educated and intelligent classes remain in their majestic repose, and somehow or other, whatever happens, their overwhelming strength, like our military force in riots, never does act.

How, indeed, *should* their overwhelming strength act, when the man who gives an inflammatory lecture, or breaks down the park railings, or invades a Secretary of State's office, is only following an Englishman's impulse to do as he likes; and our own conscience tells us that we ourselves have always regarded this impulse as something primary and sacred? Mr. Murphy lectures at Birmingham and showers on the Catholic population of that town "words," says the Home Secretary, "only fit to be addressed to thieves or murderers."

What then? Mr. Murphy has his own reasons of several kinds. He suspects the Roman Catholic Church of designs upon Mrs. Murphy; and he says if mayors and magistrates do not care for their wives and daughters, he does. But, above all, he is doing as he likes; or, in worthier language, asserting his personal liberty. "I will carry out my lectures if they walk over my body as a dead corpse; and I say to the Mayor of Birmingham that he is my servant while I am in Birmingham, and as my servant he must do his duty and protect me." Touching and beautiful words, which find a sympathetic chord in every British bosom! The moment it is plainly put before us that a man is asserting his personal liberty, we are half disarmed; because we are believers in freedom, and not in some dream of a right reason to which the assertion of our freedom is to be subordinated. Accordingly, the Secretary of State had to say that although the lecturer's language was "only fit to be addressed to thieves or murderers," yet, "I do not think he is to be deprived, I do not think that anything I have said could justify the inference that he is to be deprived, of the right of protection in a place built by him for the purpose of these lectures; because the language was not language which afforded grounds for a criminal prosecution." No, nor to be silenced by Mayor or Home Secretary or any administrative authority on earth, simply on their notion of what is discreet and reasonable! This is in perfect consonance with our public opinion, and with our national love for the assertion of personal liberty.

In quite another department of affairs, an experienced and distinguished Chancery Judge relates an incident which is just to the same effect as this of Mr. Murphy. A testator bequeathed £300 a year, to be for ever applied as a pension to some person who had been unsuccessful in literature and whose duty should be to support and diffuse, by his writings, the testator's own views, as enforced in the testator's publications. The views were not worth a straw, and the bequest was appealed against in the Court of Chancery on the ground of its absurdity; but being only absurd, it was upheld and the so-called charity was established. Having, I say, at the bottom of our English hearts a very strong belief in freedom and a very weak belief in right reason, we are soon silenced when a man pleads the prime right to do as he likes, because this is the prime right for ourselves too; and even if we attempt now and then to mumble something about reason, yet we have ourselves thought so little about this and so much about liberty, that we are in conscience forced, when our brother Philistine with whom we are meddling turns boldly round upon us and asks: *Have you any light?*—to shake our heads ruefully, and to let him go his own way after all.

There are many things to be said on behalf of this exclusive attention of ours to liberty, and of the relaxed habits of government which it has engendered. It is very easy to mistake or to exaggerate the sort of anarchy from which we are in danger through them. We are not in danger from Fenianism, fierce and turbulent as it may show itself; for against this our conscience is free enough to let us act resolutely and put forth our overwhelming strength the moment there is any real need for it. In the first place, it never was any part of our creed that the great right and blessedness of an Irishman, or, indeed, of anybody on earth except an Englishman, is to do as he likes; and we can have no scruple at all about abridging, if necessary, a non-Englishman's assertion of personal liberty. The British Constitution, its checks and its prime virtues, are for Englishmen. We may extend them to others out of love and kindness; but we find no real divine law written on our hearts constraining us so to extend them. And then the difference between an Irish Fenian and an English rough is so immense, and the case, in dealing with the Fenian, so much more clear! He is so evidently desperate and dangerous, a man of a conquered race, a Papist, with centuries of ill-usage to inflame him against us, with an alien religion established in his country by us at his expense, with no admiration of our institutions, no love of our virtues, no talents for our business, no turn for our comfort! Show him our symbolical Truss Manufactory on the finest site in Europe, and tell him that British industrialism and individualism can bring a man to that, and he remains cold! Evidently, if we deal tenderly with a sentimentalist like this, it is out of pure philanthropy.

But with the Hyde Park rioter how different! He is our own flesh and blood; he is a Protestant; he is framed by nature to do as we do, hate what we hate, love what we love; he is capable of feeling the symbolical force of the Truss Manufactory; the question of questions, for him, is a wages question. That beautiful sentence Sir Daniel Gooch quoted to the Swindon workmen, and which I treasure as Mrs. Gooch's Golden Rule, or the Divine Injunction "Be ye Perfect" done into British—the sentence Sir Daniel Gooch's mother repeated to him every morning when he was a boy going to work: *"Ever remember, my dear Dan, that you should look forward to being some day manager of that concern!"*—this truthful maxim is perfectly fitted to shine forth in the heart of the Hyde Park rough also, and to be his guiding-star through life. He has no visionary schemes of revolution and transformation, though of course he would like his class to rule, as the aristocratic class like their class to rule, and the middle class theirs. But meanwhile our social machine is a little out of order; there are a good many people in our paradisiacal centres of industrialism and individualism taking the bread out of one another's mouths. The rough has not yet quite found his groove and settled down to his work, and so he is just asserting his personal liberty a little, going where he likes, assembling where he likes, bawling as he likes, hustling as he likes. Just as the rest of us—as the country squires in the aristocratic class, as the political dissenters in the middle class—he has no idea of a *State,* of the nation in its collective and corporate character controlling, as government, the free swing of this or that one of its members in the name of the higher reason of all of them, his own as well as that of others. He sees the rich, the aristocratic class, in occupation of the executive government, and so if he is stopped from making Hyde Park a bear-garden or the streets impassable, he says he is being butchered by the aristocracy.

His apparition is somewhat embarrassing, because too many cooks spoil the broth; because, while the aristocratic and middle classes have long been doing as they like with great vigour, he has been too undeveloped and submissive hitherto to join in the game; and now, when he does come, he comes in immense numbers and is rather raw and rough. But he does not break many laws, or not many at one time; and as our laws were made for very different circumstances from our present (but always with an eye to Englishmen doing as they like), and as the clear letter of the law must be against our Englishman who does as he likes and not only the spirit of the law and public policy, and as Government must neither have any discretionary power nor act resolutely on its own interpretation of the law if any one disputes it, it is evident our laws give our playful giant, in doing as he likes, considerable advantage. Besides, even if he can be clearly proved to commit an illegality in doing as he likes, there is always the resource of not putting the law in force or of abolishing it. So he has his way, and if he has his way he is soon satisfied for the time. However, he falls into the habit of taking it oftener and oftener, and at last begins to create by his operations a confusion of which mischievous people can take advantage, and which, at any rate, by troubling the common course of business throughout the country, tends to cause distress and so to increase the sort of anarchy and social disintegration which had previously commenced. And thus that profound sense of settled order and security, without which a society like ours cannot live and grow at all, sometimes seems to be beginning to threaten us with taking its departure.

Now if culture, which simply means trying to perfect oneself and one's mind as part of oneself, brings us light, and if light shows us that there is nothing so very blessed in merely doing as one likes, that the worship of the mere freedom to do as one likes is worship of machinery, that the really blessed thing is to like what right reason ordains and to follow her authority, then we have got a practical benefit out of culture. We have got a much wanted principle, a principle of authority, to counteract the tendency to anarchy which seems to be threatening us.

But how to organise this authority, or to what hands to entrust the wielding of it? How to get your *State* summing up the right reason of the community and giving effect to it, as circumstances may require, with vigour? And here I think I see my enemies waiting for me with a hungry joy in their eyes. But I shall elude them.

The *State,* the power most representing the right reason of the nation and most worthy, therefore, of ruling—of exercising, when circumstances require it, authority over us all— is for Mr. Carlyle the aristocracy. For Mr. Lowe, it is the middle class with its incomparable Parliament. For the Reform League, it is the working class, the class with "the brightest powers of sympathy and readiest powers of action." Now culture, with its disinterested pursuit of perfection, culture, simply trying to see things as they are in order to seize on the best and to make it prevail, is surely well fitted to help us to judge rightly, by all the aids of observing, reading, and thinking, the qualifications and titles to our confidence of these three candidates for authority, and can thus render us a practical service of no mean value.

So when Mr. Carlyle, a man of genius to whom we have all at one time or other been indebted for refreshment and stimulus, says we should give rule to the aristocracy, mainly because of its dignity and politeness, surely culture is useful in reminding us that in our idea of perfection the characters of beauty and intelligence are both of them present, and sweetness and light, the two noblest of things, are united. Allowing, therefore, with Mr. Carlyle, the aristocratic class to possess sweetness, culture insists on the necessity of light also, and shows us that aristocracies, being by the very nature of things inaccessible to ideas, unapt to see how the world is going, must be somewhat wanting in light, and must therefore be, at a moment when light is our great requisite, inadequate to our needs. Aristocracies, those children of the established fact, are for epochs of concentration. In epochs of expansion, epochs such as that in which we now live, epochs when always the warning voice is again heard: *Now is the judgment of this world*—in such epochs aristocracies with their natural clinging to the established fact, their want of sense for the flux of things, for the inevitable transitoriness of all human institutions, are bewildered and helpless. Their serenity, their high spirit, their power of haughty resistance— the great qualities of an aristocracy and the secret of its distinguished manners and dignity—these very qualities, in an epoch of expansion, turn against their possessors. Again and again I have said how the refinement of an aristocracy may be precious and educative to a raw nation as a kind of shadow of true refinement; how its serenity and dignified freedom from petty cares may serve as a useful foil to set off the vulgarity and hideousness of that type of life which a hard middle class tends to establish, and to help people to see this vulgarity and hideousness in their true colours. But the true grace and serenity is that of which Greece and Greek art suggest the admirable ideals of perfection—a serenity which comes from having made order among ideas and harmonised them; whereas the serenity of aristocracies, at least the peculiar serenity of aristocracies of Teutonic origin, appears to come from their never having had any ideas to trouble them. And so, in a time of expansion like the present, a time for ideas, one gets perhaps, in regarding an aristocracy, even more than the idea of serenity, the idea of futility and sterility.

One has often wondered whether upon the whole earth there is anything so unintelligent, so unapt to perceive how the world is really going, as an ordinary young Englishman of our upper class. Ideas he has not, and neither has he that seriousness of our middle class which is, as I have often said, the great strength of this class and may become its salvation. Why, a man may hear a young Dives of the aristocratic class, when the whim takes him to sing the praises of wealth and material comfort, sing with a cynicism from which the conscience of the veriest Philistine of our industrial middle class would recoil in affright. And when, with the natural sympathy of aristocracies for firm dealing with the multitude and his uneasiness at our feeble dealing with it at home, an unvarnished young Englishman of our aristocratic class applauds the absolute rulers on the Continent, he in general manages completely to miss the grounds of reason and intelligence which alone can give any colour of justification, any possibility of existence, to those rulers, and applauds them on grounds which it would make their own hair stand on end to listen to.

And all this time we are in an epoch of expansion; and the essence of an epoch of expansion is a movement of ideas, and the one salvation of an epoch of expansion is a harmony of ideas. The very principle of the authority which we are seeking as a defence against anarchy is right reason, ideas, light. The more, therefore, an aristocracy calls to its aid its innate forces—its impenetrability, its high spirit, its power of haughty resistance—to deal with an epoch of expansion, the graver is the danger, the greater the certainty of explosion, the surer the aristocracy's defeat; for it is trying to do violence to nature instead of working along with it. The best powers shown by the best men of an aristocracy at such an epoch are, it will be observed, non-aristocratical powers, powers of industry, powers of intelligence; and these powers, thus exhibited, tend really not to strengthen the aristocracy but to take their owners out of it, to expose them to the dissolving agencies of thought and change, to make them men of the modern spirit and of the future. If, as sometimes happens, they add to their non-aristocratical qualities of labour and thought, a strong dose of aristocratical qualities also —of pride, defiance, turn for resistance—this truly aristocratical side of them, so far from adding any strength to them, really neutralises their force and makes them impracticable and ineffective.

Knowing myself to be indeed sadly to seek, as one of my many critics says, in "a philosophy with coherent, interdependent, subordinate, and derivative principles," I continually have recourse to a plain man's expedient of trying to make what few simple notions I have, clearer and more intelligible to myself by means of example and illustration. And having been brought up at Oxford in the bad old times, when we were stuffed with Greek and Aristotle and thought nothing of preparing ourselves by the study of modern languages— as after Mr. Lowe's great speech at Edinburgh we shall do— to fight the battle of life with the waiters in foreign hotels, my head is still full of a lumber of phrases we learnt at Oxford from Aristotle, about virtue being in a mean, and about excess and defect, and so on. Once when I had had the advantage of listening to the Reform debates in the House of Commons, having heard a number of interesting speakers and among them a well-known lord and a well-known baronet, I remember it struck me, applying Aristotle's machinery of the mean to my ideas about our aristocracy, that the lord was exactly the perfection, or happy mean, or virtue, of aristocracy, and the baronet the excess. And I fancied that by observing these two we might see both the inadequacy of aristocracy to supply the principle of authority needful for our present wants, and the danger of its trying to supply it when it was not really competent for the business. On the one hand, in the brilliant lord, showing plenty of high spirit, but remarkable far above and beyond his gift of high spirit for the fine tempering of his high spirit, for ease, serenity, politeness—the great virtues, as Mr. Carlyle says, of aristocracy—in this beautiful and virtuous mean, there seemed evidently some insufficiency of light; while, on the other hand, the worthy baronet, in whom the high spirit of aristocracy, its impenetrability, defiant courage, and pride of resistance, were developed even in excess, was manifestly capable, if he had his way given him, of causing us greater danger and, indeed, of throwing the whole commonwealth into confusion. Then I reverted to that old fundamental notion of mine about the grand merit of our race being really our honesty. And the very helplessness of our aristocratic or governing class in dealing with our perturbed social condition, their jealousy of entrusting too much power to the State as it now actually exists—that is to themselves—gave me a sort of pride and satisfaction; because I saw they were as a whole too honest to try and manage a business for which they did not feel themselves capable.

Surely, now, it is no inconsiderable boon which culture confers upon us, if in embarrassed times like the present it enables us to look at the ins and the outs of things in this way, without hatred and without partiality, and with a disposition to see the good in everybody all round. And I try to follow just the same course with our middle class as with our aristocracy. Mr. Lowe talks to us of this strong middle part of the nation, of the unrivalled deeds of our Liberal middle-class Parliament, of the noble, the heroic work it has performed in the last thirty years; and I begin to ask myself if we shall not, then, find in our middle class the principle of authority we want, and if we had not better take administration as well as legislation away from the weak extreme which now administers for us, and commit both to the strong middle part. I observe, too, that the heroes of middle-class liberalism, such as we have hitherto known it, speak with a kind of prophetic anticipation of the great destiny which awaits them, and as if the future was clearly theirs. The advanced party, the progressive party, the party in alliance with the future, are the names they like to give themselves. "The principles which will obtain recognition in the future," says Mr. Miall, a personage of deserved eminence among the political Dissenters, as they are called, who have been the backbone of middle-class liberalism—"the principles which will obtain recognition in the future are the principles for which I have long and zealously laboured. I qualified myself for joining in the work of harvest by doing to the best of my ability the duties of seedtime." These duties, if one is to gather them from the works of the great Liberal party in the last thirty years, are, as I have elsewhere summed them up, the advocacy of free trade, of Parliamentary reform, of abolition of church-rates, of voluntaryism in religion and education, of non-interference of the State between employers and employed, and of marriage with one's deceased wife's sister.

Now I know, when I object that all this is machinery, the great Liberal middle class has by this time grown cunning enough to answer that it always meant more by these things than meets the eye; that it has had that within which passes show, and that we are soon going to see, in a Free Church and all manner of good things, what it was. But I have learned from Bishop Wilson (if Mr. Frederic Harrison will forgive my again quoting that poor old hierophant of a decayed superstition): "If we would really know our heart let us impartially view our actions"; and I cannot help thinking that if our Liberals had had so much sweetness and light in their inner minds as they allege, more of it must have come out in their sayings and doings.

An American friend of the English Liberals says, indeed,

that their Dissidence of Dissent has been a mere instrument
of the political Dissenters for making reason and the will of
God prevail (and no doubt he would say the same of marriage with one's deceased wife's sister); and that the abolition of a State Church is merely the Dissenter's means to this
end, just as culture is mine. Another American defender of
theirs says just the same of their industrialism and free
trade; indeed, this gentleman, taking the bull by the horns,
proposes that we should for the future call industrialism
culture, and the industrialists the men of culture, and then
of course there can be no longer any misapprehension about
their true character; and besides the pleasure of being wealthy
and comfortable, they will have authentic recognition as
vessels of sweetness and light.

All this is undoubtedly specious; but I must remark that
the culture of which I talked was an endeavour to come at
reason and the will of God by means of reading, observing,
and thinking; and that whoever calls anything else culture,
may, indeed, call it so if he likes, but then he talks of something quite different from what I talked of. And again, as
culture's way of working for reason and the will of God is
by directly trying to know more about them, while the Dissidence of Dissent is evidently in itself no effort of this kind,
nor is its Free Church, in fact, a church with worthier conceptions of God and the ordering of the world than the State
Church professes, but with mainly the same conceptions of
these as the State Church has, only that every man is to com-
port himself as he likes in professing them—this being so,
I cannot at once accept the Nonconformity any more than
the industrialism and the other great works of our Liberal
middle class as proof positive that this class is in possession
of light, and that here is the true seat of authority for which
we are in search; but I must try a little further, and seek for
other indications which may enable me to make up my mind.

Why should we not do with the middle class as we have
done with the aristocratic class—find in it some representative men who may stand for the virtuous mean of this class,
for the perfection of its present qualities and mode of being,
and also for the excess of them. Such men must clearly not
be men of genius like Mr. Bright; for, as I have formerly
said, so far as a man has genius he tends to take himself out
of the category of class altogether and to become simply a
man. Some more ordinary man would be more to the purpose
—would sum up better in himself, without disturbing influ-

ences, the general liberal force of the middle class, the force by which it has done its great works of free trade, Parliamentary reform, voluntaryism, and so on, and the spirit in which it has done them. Now it happens that a typical middle-class man, the member for one of our chief industrial cities, has given us a famous sentence which bears directly on the resolution of our present question: whether there is light enough in our middle class to make it the proper seat of the authority we wish to establish. When there was a talk some little while ago about the state of middle-class education, our friend, as the representative of that class, spoke some memorable words: "There had been a cry that middle-class education ought to receive more attention. He confessed himself very much surprised by the clamour that was raised. He did not think that class need excite the sympathy either of the legislature or the public." Now this satisfaction of our middle-class member of Parliament with the mental state of the middle class was truly representative, and makes good his claim to stand as the beautiful and virtuous mean of that class. But it is obviously at variance with our definition of culture, or the pursuit of light and perfection, which made light and perfection consist, not in resting and being, but in growing and becoming, in a perpetual advance in beauty and wisdom. So the middle class is by its essence, as one may say, by its incomparable self-satisfaction decisively expressed through its beautiful and virtuous mean, self-excluded from wielding an authority of which light is to be the very soul.

Clear as this is, it will be made clearer still if we take some representative man as the excess of the middle class, and remember that the middle class, in general, is to be conceived as a body swaying between the qualities of its mean and of its excess, and on the whole, of course, as human nature is constituted, including rather towards the excess than the mean. Of its excess no better representative can possibly be imagined than a Dissenting minister from Walsall, who came before the public in connection with the proceedings at Birmingham of Mr. Murphy, already mentioned. Speaking in the midst of an irritated population of Catholics, this Walsall gentleman exclaimed: "I say, then, away with the Mass! It is from the bottomless pit; and in the bottomless pit shall all liars have their part, in the lake that burneth with fire and brimstone." And again: "When all the praties [potatoes—Ed.] were black in Ireland, why didn't the priests say the hocus-pocus over them and make them all good again?" He shared, too, Mr. Murphy's fears of some invasion of his domestic happiness: "What I wish to say to you as Protestant husbands is, *Take care of your wives!*" And finally, in the true vein of an Englishman doing as he likes, a vein of which I have at some length pointed out the present dangers, he recommended for imitation the example of some church-wardens at Dublin, among whom, said he, "there was a Luther and also a Melanchthon" who had made very short work with some ritualist or other, hauled him down from his pulpit and kicked him out of church. Now it is manifest, as I said in the case of our aristocratical baronet, that if we let this excess of the sturdy English middle class, this conscientious Protestant Dissenter, so strong, so self-reliant, so fully persuaded in his own mind, have his way, he would be capable, with his want of light—or, to use the language of the religious world, with his zeal without knowledge—of stirring up strife which neither he nor any one else could easily compose.

And then comes in, as it did also with the aristocracy, the honesty of our race, and by the voice of another middle-class man, Alderman of the City of London and Colonel of the City of London Militia, proclaims that it has twinges of conscience, and that it will not attempt to cope with our social disorders and to deal with a business which it feels to be too high for it. Every one remembers how this virtuous Alderman-Colonel, or Colonel-Alderman, led his militia through the London streets; how the bystanders gathered to see him pass; how the London roughs, asserting an Englishman's best and most blissful right of doing what he likes, robbed and beat the bystanders; and how the blameless warrior-magistrate refused to let his troops interfere. "The crowd," he touchingly said afterwards, "was mostly composed of fine healthy strong men, bent on mischief; if he had allowed his soldiers to interfere they might have been overpowered, their rifles taken from them and used against them by the mob; a riot, in fact, might have ensued and been attended with bloodshed, compared with which the assaults and loss of property that actually occurred would have been as nothing." Honest and affecting testimony of the English middle class to its own inadequacy for the authoritative part one's admiration would sometimes incline one to assign to it! "Who are we," they say by the voice of their Alderman-Colonel, "that we should not be overpowered if we attempt to cope with social anarchy, our rifles taken from us

and used against us by the mob, and we, perhaps, robbed
and beaten ourselves? Or what light have we, beyond a free-
born Englishman's impulse to do as he likes, which could
justify us in preventing, at the cost of bloodshed, other free-
born Englishmen from doing as they like, and robbing and
beating us as much as they please?"

This distrust of themselves as an adequate centre of authority does not mark the working class, as was shown by
their readiness the other day in Hyde Park to take upon themselves all the functions of government. But this comes from
the working class being, as I have often said, still an embryo,
of which no one can yet quite foresee the final development;
and from its not having the same experience and self-knowl-
edge as the aristocratic and middle classes. Honesty it no
doubt has, just like the other classes of Englishmen, but
honesty in an inchoate and untrained state; and meanwhile
its powers of action, which are, as Mr. Frederic Harrison
says, exceedingly ready, easily run away with it. That it cannot at present have a sufficiency of light which comes by
culture—that is, by reading, observing, and thinking—is clear
from the very nature of its condition; and, indeed, we saw
that Mr. Frederic Harrison, in seeking to make a free stage
for its bright powers of sympathy and ready powers of action, had to begin by throwing overboard culture and flouting
it as only fit for a professor of *belles-lettres*. Still, to make
it perfectly manifest that no more in the working class than
in the aristocratic and middle classes can one find an adequate centre of authority—that is, as culture teaches us to
conceive our required authority, of light—let us again follow
with this class the method we have followed with the aristocratic and middle classes, and try to bring before our minds
representative men who may figure to us its virtue and its
excess.

We must not take, of course, men like the chiefs of the
Hyde Park demonstration, Colonel Dickson or Mr. Beales;
because Colonel Dickson, by his martial profession and
dashing exterior, seems to belong properly, like Julius Cæsar
and Mirabeau and other great popular leaders, to the aristocratic class, and to be carried into the popular ranks only by
his ambition or his genius; while Mr. Beales belongs to our
solid middle class, and, perhaps, if he had not been a great
popular leader, would have been a Philistine. But Mr. Odger,
whose speeches we have all read, and of whom his friends
relate, besides, much that is favourable, may very well stand

for the beautiful and virtuous mean of our present work-ing class; and I think everybody will admit that in Mr. Odger there is manifestly, with all his good points, some insuffi-ciency of light. The excess of the working class, in its present state of development, is perhaps best shown in Mr. Brad-laugh, the iconoclast, who seems to be almost for baptizing us all in blood and fire into his new social dispensation, and to whose reflections, now that I have once been set going on Bishop Wilson's track, I cannot forbear commending this maxim of the good old man: "Intemperance in talk makes a dreadful havoc in the heart." Mr. Bradlaugh, like our types of excess in the aristocratic and middle classes, is evidently capable, if he had his head given him, of running us all into great dangers and confusion. I conclude, therefore—what indeed, few of those who do me the honour to read this dis-quisition are likely to dispute—that we can as little find in the working class as in the aristocratic or in the middle class our much-wanted source of authority, as culture suggests it to us.

Well, then, what if we tried to rise above the idea of class to the idea of the whole community, *the State,* and to find our centre of light and authority there? Every one of us has the idea of country, as a sentiment; hardly any one of us has the idea of *the State,* as a working power. And why? Be-cause we habitually live in our ordinary selves, which do not carry us beyond the ideas and wishes of the class to which we happen to belong. And we are all afraid of giving to the State too much power, because we only conceive of the State as something equivalent to the class in occupation of the executive government, and are afraid of that class abusing power to its own purposes. If we strengthen the State with the aristocratic class in occupation of the executive government, we imagine we are delivering ourselves up captive to the ideas and wishes of our fierce aristocratical baronet; if with the middle class in occupation of the executive government, to those of our truculent middle-class Dissenting minister; if with the working class, to those of its notorious tribune, Mr. Bradlaugh. And with much justice; owing to the exag-gerated notion which we English, as I have said, entertain of the right and blessedness of the mere doing as one likes, of the affirming oneself, and oneself just as it is. People of the aristocratic class want to affirm their ordinary selves, their likings and dislikings; people of the middle class the same, people of the working class the same. By our everyday selves, however, we are separate, personal, at war; we are only safe from one another's tyranny when no one has any power; and this safety, in its turn, cannot save us from anarchy. And when, therefore, anarchy presents itself as a danger to us, we know not where to turn.

But by our *best self* we are united, impersonal, at harmony. We are in no peril from giving authority to this, because it is the truest friend we all of us can have; and when anarchy is a danger to us, to this authority we may turn with sure trust. Well, and this is the very self which culture, or the study of perfection, seeks to develop in us; at the expense of our old untransformed self, taking pleasure only in doing what it likes or is used to do, and exposing us to the risk of clashing with every one else who is doing the same! So that our poor culture, which is flouted as so unpractical, leads us to the very ideas capable of meeting the great want of our present embarrassed times! We want an authority, and we find nothing but jealous classes, checks, and a deadlock; culture suggests the idea of *the State*. We find no basis for a firm State-power in our ordinary selves; culture suggests one to us in our *best self*.

It cannot but acutely try a tender conscience to be accused, in a practical country like ours, of keeping aloof from the work and hope of a multitude of earnest-hearted men, and of merely toying with poetry and æsthetics. So it is with no little sense of relief that I find myself thus in the position of one who makes a contribution in aid of the practical necessities of our times. The great thing, it will be observed, is to find our *best* self and to seek to affirm nothing but that; not—as we English with our over-value for merely being free and busy have been so accustomed to do—resting satisfied with a self which comes uppermost long before our best self, and affirming that with blind energy. In short—to go back yet once more to Bishop Wilson—of these two excellent rules of Bishop Wilson's for a man's guidance: "Firstly, never go against the best light you have; secondly, take care that your light be not darkness," we English have followed with praiseworthy zeal the first rule, but we have not given so much heed to the second. We have gone manfully according to the best light we have; but we have not taken enough care that this should be really the best light possible for us, that it should not be darkness. And, our honesty being very great, conscience has whispered to us that the light we were following, our ordinary self, was, indeed, perhaps, only an inferior self, only darkness; and that it would not do to impose this seriously on all the world.

But our best self inspires faith, and is capable of affording a serious principle of authority. For example. We are on our way to what the late Duke of Wellington, with his strong sagacity, foresaw and admirably described as "a revolution by due course of law." This is undoubtedly—if we are still to live and grow, and this famous nation is not to stagnate and dwindle away on the one hand or, on the other, to perish miserably in mere anarchy and confusion—what we are on the way to. Great changes there must be, for a revolution cannot accomplish itself without great changes; yet order there must be, for without order a revolution cannot accomplish itself by due course of law. So whatever brings risk of tumult and disorder, multitudinous processions in the streets of our crowded towns, multitudinous meetings in their public places and parks—demonstrations perfectly unnecessary in the present course of our affairs—our best self, or right reason, plainly enjoins us to set our faces against. It enjoins us to encourage and uphold the occupants of the executive power, whoever they may be, in firmly prohibiting them. But it does this clearly and resolutely, and is thus a real principle of authority, because it does it with a free conscience; because in thus provisionally strengthening the executive power, it knows that it is not doing this merely to enable our aristocratical baronet to affirm himself as against our working-men's tribune, or our middle-class Dissenter to affirm himself as against both. It knows that it is establishing *the State*, or organ of our collective best self, of our national right reason. And it has the testimony of conscience that it is stablishing the State on behalf of whatever great changes are needed, just as much as on behalf of order; stablishing it to deal just as stringently, when the time comes, with our baronet's aristocratical prejudices, or with the fanaticism of our middle-class Dissenter, as it deals with Mr. Bradlaugh's street processions.

Ruskin's ostensible purpose in the four volumes of *Modern Painters* (1843-1856) was to argue for the greatness of Turner's landscape painting. But to do so, he had to talk about art, literature, morals, society and history. This chapter from Volume III (1856) is an acute study in cultural history; for Ruskin shows that the appropriately nineteenth-century subject is landscape, because man and man-made things are no longer beautiful or significant enough to make a subject for art. We use not only nature but the past, too, as an escape from modern civilization. Unlike all peoples before us, we think we know better than our ancestors; we regard them "as foolish and wicked, but yet find our chief artistic pleasure in descriptions of their ways of life." With us, Ruskin implies, thoughts of political, economic and scientific progress are mixed with thoughts of cultural decline.

The cause of all this is the decline of religion—as evidenced by our preference in landscape painting for *cloudiness,* for nebulous and shifting rather than definite and stable forms. We locate spirituality, in other words, in the irrational and unknown rather than in the rational and the known. Hence our love of mountains and the wildest possible nature. Hence our love of dark colors in our paintings and our clothes; for "these are much *sadder* ages than the early ones." The Godless Renaissance has in the end lost us the very Beauty for which it was ready to sacrifice all other values, including that of Truth. Like Carlyle, Ruskin draws significance from the marked change in clothing in the nineteenth century. A self-declared disciple of Carlyle, Ruskin differs from him in that he uses aesthetic quality as an important criterion for judging a civilization. In this Ruskin resembles Arnold. Both announced a criterion of judgment that was to increase steadily in importance during the latter half of the century.

John Ruskin

MODERN PAINTERS

Of Modern Landscape

We turn our eyes, therefore, as boldly and as quickly as may be, from these serene fields and skies of medieval art, to the most characteristic examples of modern landscape. And, I believe, the first thing that will strike us, or that ought to strike us, is their *cloudiness*.

Out of perfect light and motionless air, we find ourselves on a sudden brought under sombre skies, and into drifting wind; and, with fickle sunbeams flashing in our face, or utterly drenched with sweep of rain, we are reduced to track the changes of the shadows on the grass, or watch the rents of twilight through angry cloud. And we find that whereas all the pleasure of the medieval was in *stability*, *definiteness*, and *luminousness*, we are expected to rejoice in darkness and triumph in mutability; to lay the foundation of happiness in things which momentarily change or fade; and to expect the utmost satisfaction and instruction from what it is impossible to arrest and difficult to comprehend.

We find, however, together with this general delight in breeze and darkness, much attention to the real form of clouds, and careful drawing of effects of mist; so that the appearance of objects, as seen through it, becomes a subject of science with us; and the faithful representation of that appearance is made of primal importance, under the name of aerial perspective. The aspects of sunset and sunrise, with all their attendant phenomena of cloud and mist, are watchfully delineated; and in ordinary daylight landscape, the sky is considered of so much importance that a principal mass of foliage, or a whole foreground, is unhesitatingly thrown into shade merely to bring out the form of a white cloud. So that, if a general and characteristic name were needed for modern landscape art, none better could be invented than "the service of clouds."

THE WORKS OF JOHN RUSKIN, ed. E. T. Cook and Alexander Wedderburn, Library Edition, 39 vols. (London: George Allen; New York: Longmans, Green, 1903-12), V, 317-33. See also John D. Rosenberg, *The Darkening Glass: A Portrait of Ruskin's Genius* (New York and London, 1961).

And this name would, unfortunately, be characteristic of our art in more ways than one. In the last chapter, I said that all the Greeks spoke kindly about the clouds, except Aristophanes; and he, I am sorry to say (since his report is so unfavourable), is the only Greek who had studied them attentively. He tells us, first, that they are "great goddesses to idle men"; then, that they are "mistresses of disputings and logic and monstrosities and noisy chattering"; declares that whoso believe in their divinity must first disbelieve in Jupiter and place supreme power in the hands of an unknown god "Whirlwind"; and finally he displays their influence over the mind of one of their disciples, in his sudden desire "to speak ingeniously concerning smoke."

There is, I fear, an infinite truth in this Aristophanic judgment applied to our modern cloud-worship. Assuredly, much of the love of mystery in our romances, our poetry, our art, and above all in our metaphysics, must come under that definition so long ago given by the great Greek, "speaking ingeniously concerning smoke." And much of the instinct which, partially developed in painting, may be now seen throughout every mode of exertion of mind—the easily encouraged doubt, easily excited curiosity, habitual agitation, and delight in the changing and the marvellous, as opposed to the old quiet serenity of social custom and religious faith—is again deeply defined in those few words, the "dethroning of Jupiter," the "coronation of the whirlwind."

Nor of whirlwind merely, but also of darkness or ignorance respecting all stable facts. That darkening of the foreground to bring out the white cloud is, in one aspect of it, a type of the subjection of all plain and positive fact to what is uncertain and unintelligble. And, as we examine farther into the matter, we shall be struck by another great difference between the old and modern landscape, namely, that in the old no one ever thought of drawing anything but as well *as he could*. That might not be *well*, as we have seen in the case of rocks; but it was as well as he *could,* and always distinctly. Leaf or stone or animal or man, it was equally drawn with care and clearness, and its essential characters shown. If it was an oak tree, the acorns were drawn; if a flint pebble, its veins were drawn; if an arm of the sea, its fish were drawn; if a group of figures, their faces and dresses were drawn—to the very last subtlety of expression and end of thread that could be got into the space, far off or near. But now our ingenuity is all "concerning smoke." Nothing is truly drawn but that; all else is vague, slight, imperfect; got with as little pains as possible. You examine your closest foreground, and find no leaves; your largest oak, and find no acorns; your human figure, and find a spot of red paint instead of a face; and in all this, again and again, the Aristophanic words come true, and the clouds seem to be "great goddesses to idle men."

The next thing that will strike us, after this love of clouds, is the love of liberty. Whereas the medieval was always shutting himself into castles and behind fosses, and drawing brickwork neatly and beds of flowers primly, our painters delight in getting to the open fields and moors, abhor all hedges and moats; never paint anything but free-growing trees and rivers gliding "at their own sweet will"; eschew formality down to the smallest detail; break and displace the brickwork which the medieval would have carefully cemented; leave unpruned the thickets he would have delicately trimmed; and, carrying the love of liberty even to license and the love of wildness even to ruin, take pleasure at last in every aspect of age and desolation which emancipates the objects of nature from the government of men—on the castle wall displacing its tapestry with ivy, and spreading through the garden the bramble for the rose.

Connected with this love of liberty we find a singular manifestation of love of mountains, and see our painters traversing the wildest places of the globe in order to obtain subjects with craggy foregrounds and purple distances. Some few of them remain content with pollards and flat land; but these are always men of third-rate order, and the leading masters, while they do not reject the beauty of the low grounds, reserve their highest powers to paint Alpine peaks or Italian promontories. And it is eminently noticeable, also, that this pleasure in the mountains is never mingled with fear, or tempered by a spirit of meditation as with the medieval; but is always free and fearless, brightly exhilarating, and wholly unreflective; so that the painter feels that his mountain foreground may be more consistently animated by a sportsman than a hermit; and our modern society in general goes to the mountains not to fast, but to feast, and leaves their glaciers covered with chicken-bones and egg-shells.

Connected with this want of any sense of solemnity in mountain scenery, is a general profanity of temper in regarding all the rest of nature; that is to say, a total absence of faith in the presence of any deity therein. Whereas the medieval never painted a cloud but with the purpose of placing an angel in it, and a Greek never entered a wood without expecting to meet a god in it; *we* should think the appearance of an angel in the cloud wholly unnatural, and should be seriously surprised by meeting a god anywhere. Our chief ideas about the wood are connected with poaching. We have no belief that the clouds contain more than so many inches of rain or hail, and from our ponds and ditches expect nothing more divine than ducks and watercresses.

Finally, connected with this profanity of temper is a strong tendency to deny the sacred element of colour, and make our boast in blackness. For though occasionally glaring or violent, modern colour is on the whole eminently sombre, tending continually to grey or brown, and by many of our best painters consistently falsified with a confessed pride in what they call chaste or subdued tints; so that, whereas a medieval paints his sky bright blue and his foreground bright green, gilds the towers of his castles and clothes his figures with purple and white, we paint our sky grey, our foreground black, and our foliage brown, and think that enough is sacrificed to the sun in admitting the dangerous brightness of a scarlet cloak or a blue jacket.

These, I believe, are the principal points which would strike us instantly, if we were to be brought suddenly into an exhibition of modern landscapes out of a room filled with medieval work. It is evident that there are both evil and good in this change; but how much evil or how much good, we can only estimate by considering, as in the former divisions of our inquiry, what are the real roots of the habits of mind which have caused them.

At first, it is evident that the title "Dark Ages," given to the medieval centuries, is, respecting art, wholly inapplicable. They were, on the contrary, the bright ages; ours are the dark ones. I do not mean metaphysically, but literally. They were the ages of gold; ours are the ages of umber.

This is partly mere mistake in us; we build brown brick walls and wear brown coats, because we have been blunderingly taught to do so and go on doing so mechanically. There is, however, also some cause for the change in our own tempers. On the whole, these are much *sadder* ages than the early ones; not sadder in a noble and deep way, but in a dim wearied way—the way of ennui, and jaded intellect, and uncomfortableness of soul and body. The Middle Ages had their wars and agonies, but also intense delights. Their gold was dashed with blood; but ours is sprinkled with dust. Their life was inwoven with white and purple; ours is one seamless stuff of brown. Not that we are without apparent festivity, but festivity more or less forced, mistaken, embittered, incomplete—not of the heart. How wonderfully, since Shakspere's time, have we lost the power of laughing at bad jests! The very finish of our wit belies our gaiety.

The profoundest reason of this darkness of heart is, I believe, our want of faith. There never yet was a generation of men (savage or civilized) who, taken as a body, so wofully fulfilled the [Biblical—Ed.] words "having no hope, and without God in the world," as the present civilized European race. A Red Indian or Otaheitan savage has more sense of a divine existence round him, or government over him, than the plurality of refined Londoners and Parisians: and those among us who may in some sense be said to believe, are divided almost without exception into two broad classes, Romanist and Puritan; who, but for the interference of the unbelieving portions of society, would, either of them, reduce the other sect as speedily as possible to ashes; the Romanist having always done so whenever he could, from the beginning of their separation, and the Puritan at this time holding himself in complacent expectation of the destruction of Rome by volcanic fire. Such division as this between persons nominally of one religion, that is to say, believing in the same God and the same Revelation, cannot but become a stumbling block of the gravest kind to all thoughtful and far-sighted men—a stumbling-block which they can only surmount under the most favourable circumstances of early education. Hence, nearly all our powerful men in this age of the world are unbelievers; the best of them in doubt and misery; the worst in reckless defiance; the plurality, in plodding hesitation, doing as well as they can what practical work lies ready to their hands. Most of our scientific men are in this last class; our popular authors either set themselves definitely against all religious form, pleading for simple truth and benevolence (Thackeray, Dickens), or give themselves up to bitter and fruitless statement of facts (De Balzac), or surface-painting (Scott), or careless blasphemy, sad or smiling (Byron, Béranger). Our earnest poets and deepest thinkers are doubtful and indignant (Tennyson, Carlyle); one or two, anchored, indeed, but anxious or weeping (Wordsworth, Mrs. Browning); and of these two, the first is not so sure of his anchor but that now and then it drags with him, even to make him cry out,

> Great God! I'd rather be
> A Pagan suckled in a creed outworn;
> So might I, standing on this pleasant lea,
> Have glimpses that would make me less forlorn.[1]

In politics, religion is now a name; in art, a hypocrisy or affectation. Over German religious pictures the inscription, "See how Pious I am," can be read at a glance by any clear-sighted person. Over French and English religious pictures the inscription, "See how Impious I am," is equally legible. All sincere and modest art is, among us, profane.[2]

This faithlessness operates among us according to our tempers, producing either sadness or levity, and being the ultimate root alike of our discontents and of our wantonnesses. It is marvellous how full of contradiction it makes us: we are first dull, and seek for wild and lonely places because we have no heart for the garden; presently we recover our spirits, and build an assembly-room among the mountains because we have no reverence for the desert. I do not know if there be game on Sinai, but I am always expecting to hear of some one's shooting over it.

There is, however, another and a more innocent root of our delight in wild scenery.

All the Renaissance principles of art tended, as I have before often explained, to the setting Beauty above Truth and seeking for it always at the expense of truth. And the proper punishment of such pursuit—the punishment which all the laws of the universe rendered inevitable—was that those who thus pursued beauty should wholly lose sight of beauty. All the thinkers of the age, as we saw previously, declared that it did not exist. The age seconded their efforts and banished beauty, so far as human effort could succeed in doing so, from the face of the earth and the form of man. To powder the hair, to patch the cheek, to hoop the body, to buckle the foot, were all part and parcel of the same system which reduced streets to brick walls and pictures to brown stains. One desert of Ugliness was extended before the eyes of mankind; and their pursuit of the beautiful, so recklessly continued, received unexpected consummation in high-heeled shoes and periwigs —Gower Street and Gaspar Poussin.

---

[1][Wordsworth's sonnet, "The World Is Too Much with Us."—Ed.]

[2] Pre-Raphaelitism, of course, excepted, which is a new phase of art, in no wise considered in this chapter. Blake was sincere, but full of wild creeds and somewhat diseased in brain.

Reaction from this state was inevitable, if any true life was left in the races of mankind; and accordingly, though still forced by rule and fashion to the producing and wearing all that is ugly, men steal out, half-ashamed of themselves for doing so, to the fields and mountains; and finding among these the colour and liberty and variety and power which are for ever grateful to them, delight in these to an extent never before known; rejoice in all the wildest shattering of the mountain side as an opposition to Gower Street, gaze in a rapt manner at sunsets and sunrises to see there the blue and gold and purple which glow for them no longer on knight's armour or temple porch; and gather with care out of the fields, into their blotted herbaria, the flowers which the five orders of architecture have banished from their doors and casements.

The absence of care for personal beauty, which is another great characteristic of the age, adds to this feeling in a two-fold way: first, by turning all reverent thoughts away from human nature; and making us think of men as ridiculous or ugly creatures, getting through the world as well as they can and spoiling it in doing so—not ruling it in a kingly way and crowning all its loveliness. In the Middle Ages hardly anything but vice could be caricatured, because virtue was always visibly and personally noble: now virtue itself is apt to inhabit such poor human bodies that no aspect of it is invulnerable to jest; and for all fairness we have to seek to the flowers, for all sublimity, to the hills.

The same want of care operates, in another way, by lowering the standard of health, increasing the susceptibility to nervous or sentimental impressions, and thus adding to the other powers of nature over us whatever charm may be felt in her fostering the melancholy fancies of brooding idleness.

It is not, however, only to existing inanimate nature that our want of beauty in person and dress has driven us. The imagination of it, as it was seen in our ancestors, haunts us continually; and while we yield to the present fashions, or act in accordance with the dullest modern principles of economy and utility, we look fondly back to the manners of the ages of chivalry, and delight in painting to the fancy the fashions we pretend to despise and the splendours we think it wise to abandon. The furniture and personages of our romance are sought, when the writer desires to please most easily, in the centuries which we profess to have surpassed in everything; the art which takes us into the present times is considered as both daring and degraded, and while the weakest words please us and are regarded as poetry, which recall the manners of our forefathers or of strangers, it is only as familiar and vulgar that we accept the description of our own.

In this we are wholly different from all the races that preceded us. All other nations have regarded their ancestors with reverence as saints or heroes; but have nevertheless thought their own deeds and ways of life the fitting subjects for their arts of painting or of verse. We, on the contrary, regard our ancestors as foolish and wicked, but yet find our chief artistic pleasure in descriptions of their ways of life.

The Greeks and medievals honoured, but did not imitate their forefathers; we imitate, but do not honour.

With this romantic love of beauty, forced to seek in history and in external nature the satisfaction it cannot find in ordinary life, we mingle a more rational passion, the due and just result of newly awakened powers of attention. Whatever may first lead us to the scrutiny of natural objects, that scrutiny never fails of its reward. Unquestionably they are intended to be regarded by us with both reverence and delight; and every hour we give to them renders their beauty more apparent and their interest more engrossing. Natural science—which can hardly be considered to have existed before modern times—rendering our knowledge fruitful in accumulation and exquisite in accuracy, has acted for good or evil according to the temper of the mind which received it; and though it has hardened the faithfulness of the dull and proud, has shown new grounds for reverence to hearts which were thoughtful and humble. The neglect of the art of war, while it has somewhat weakened and deformed the body, has given us leisure and opportunity for studies to which, before, time and space were equally wanting; lives which once were early wasted on the battlefield are now passed usefully in the study; nations which exhausted themselves in annual warfare now dispute with each other the discovery of new planets; and the serene philosopher dissects the plants and analyses the dust of lands which were of old only traversed by the knight in hasty march, or by the borderer in heedless rapine.

The elements of progress and decline being thus strangely mingled in the modern mind, we might beforehand anticipate that one of the notable characters of our art would be its inconsistency; that efforts would be made in every direction, and arrested by every conceivable cause and manner of failure; that in all we did, it would become next to impossible to distinguish accurately the grounds for praise or for regret; that all previous canons of practice and methods of thought would be gradually overthrown, and criticism continually defied by successes which no one had expected and sentiments which no one could define.

Accordingly, while in our inquiries into Greek and medieval art I was able to describe in general terms what all men did or felt, I find now many characters in many men; some, it seems to me, founded on the inferior and evanescent principles of modernism, on its recklessness, impatience, or faithlessness; others founded on its science, its new affection for nature, its love of openness and liberty. And among all these characters, good or evil, I see that some, remaining to us from old or transitional periods, do not properly belong to us and will soon fade away, and others, though not yet distinctly developed, are yet properly our own and likely to grow forward into greater strength.

For instance, our reprobation of bright colour is, I think, for the most part mere affectation and must soon be done away with. Vulgarity, dulness, or impiety will indeed always express themselves through art in brown and grey, as in Rembrandt, Caravaggio, and Salvator; but we are not wholly vulgar, dull, or impious; nor, as moderns, are we necessarily obliged to continue so in anywise. Our greatest men, whether sad or gay, still delight, like the great men of all ages, in brilliant hues. The colouring of Scott and Byron is full and pure; that of Keats and Tennyson rich even to excess. Our practical failures in colouring are merely the necessary consequences of our prolonged want of practice during the periods of Renaissance affectation and ignorance; and the only durable difference between old and modern colouring is the acceptance of certain hues by the modern, which please him by expressing that melancholy peculiar to his more reflective or sentimental character, and the greater variety of them necessary to express his greater science.

Again, if we ever become wise enough to dress consistently and gracefully, to make health a principal object in education, and to render our streets beautiful with art, the external charm of past history will in great measure disappear. There is no essential reason, because we live after the fatal seventeenth century, that we should never again be able to confess interest in sculpture, or see brightness in embroidery;

nor, because now we choose to make the night deadly with our pleasures and the day with our labours, prolonging the dance till dawn and the toil to twilight, that we should never again learn how rightly to employ the sacred trusts of strength, beauty, and time. Whatever external charm attaches itself to the past, would then be seen in proper subordination to the brightness of present life; and the elements of romance would exist, in the earlier ages, only in the attraction which must generally belong to whatever is unfamiliar; in the reverence which a noble nation always pays to its ancestors; and in the enchanted light which races, like individuals, must perceive in looking back to the days of their childhood.

Again, the peculiar levity with which natural scenery is regarded by a large number of modern minds cannot be considered as entirely characteristic of the age, inasmuch as it never can belong to its greatest intellects. Men of any high mental power must be serious, whether in ancient or modern days; a certain degree of reverence for fair scenery is found in all our great writers without exception—even the one who has made us laugh oftenest, taking us to the valley of Chamouni and to the sea beach, there to give peace after suffering and change revenge into pity.[3] It is only the dull, the uneducated, or the worldly whom it is painful to meet on the hill sides; and levity, as a ruling character, cannot be ascribed to the whole nation, but only to its holiday-making apprentices and its House of Commons.

We need not, therefore, expect to find any single poet or painter representing the entire group of powers, weaknesses, and inconsistent instincts which govern or confuse our modern life. But we may expect that in the man who seems to be given by Providence as the type of the age (as Homer and Dante were given as the types of classical and medieval mind), we shall find whatever is fruitful and substantial to be completely present, together with those of our weaknesses which are indeed nationally characteristic and compatible with general greatness of mind, just as the weak love of fences and dislike of mountains were found compatible with Dante's greatness in other respects.

Farther, as the admiration of mankind is found in our times to have in great part passed from men to mountains, and from human emotion to natural phenomena, we may anticipate that the great strength of art will also be warped

<hr>

[3] See *David Copperfield*, Chap. lv. and lviii.

in this direction; with this notable result for us, that whereas
the greatest painters or painter of classical and medieval
periods, being wholly devoted to the representation of humanity, furnished us with but little to examine in landscape,
the greatest painters or painter of modern times will in all
probability be devoted to the landscape principally; and
farther, because in representing human emotion words surpass painting, but in representing natural scenery painting
surpasses words, we may anticipate also that the painter and
poet (for convenience' sake I here use the words in opposition) will somewhat change their relations of rank in illustrating the mind of the age; that the painter will become of
more importance, the poet of less; and that the relations
between the men who are the types and first-fruits of the age
in word and work—namely, Scott and Turner—will be, in
many curious respects, different from those between Homer
and Phidias, or Dante and Giotto.

Part Three

THE MODERN LITERARY VIEW

There is no question that the great literary form of the Victorian age is the novel, and most critics nowadays would agree that the greatest Victorian novelists are Dickens and George Eliot. In the 1850's, highbrow readers began to desert Dickens, first for Thackeray, then for George Eliot, and finally for Meredith and Hardy—and for the Russian novelists, especially Dostoevsky, who were themselves passionate admirers of Dickens. From this development, George Ford charts the changing interests of Victorian readers and writers. The Victorians became increasingly interested in the internal life (in the analysis of character and motives), in ideas, and, to the extent that they admired George Eliot, in a notion of realism as, in her words, "an unsensational record of everyday life" that ruled out "theatrical exaggeration." The key word that occurs as each successive novelist is preferred over Dickens is "adult"; for it was held against Dickens that he could be read with pleasure by children.

For a similar combination of reasons, highbrow readers began in the sixties to desert Tennyson for Browning. The words that best describe the direction of Victorian literary development are the words Ford uses as epigraph to this chapter—words from Browning's 1863 preface to *Sordello,* which Hardy, significantly, copied into his notebook.

GEORGE H. FORD

The Discovery of the Soul
[Changing Tastes in Fiction]

" 'Incidents in the development of a soul!
little else is worth study.'—Browning."—
From the notebooks of Thomas Hardy, 1889.

I

IN "The Soul of Man under Socialism" (1891), Oscar
Wilde paid tribute to the "incomparable" genius of George
Meredith as a novelist. There were better artists in France,
he admitted, but artists whose view of life was more restricted.
And in Russia there were writers with "a more vivid sense
of what pain in fiction may be." But to Meredith "belongs
philosophy in fiction." "His people not merely live, but they
live in thought. . . . There is soul in them and around them.
. . . And he who made them . . . has never asked the public
what they wanted." Without mentioning Dickens, this passage
tells a great deal about his status among many cultivated
readers. It has already been demonstrated that such readers
were abandoning Dickens in the fifties, a process that was
accelerated by the publication of novels by Thackeray and
the Brontës, and later, more markedly, by those of George
Eliot and George Meredith, for the gradual undermining of
Dickens' reputation owed a great deal to his critics' being able
to compare his books unfavorably with the writings of other
major novelists whose aims differed from his. That is, the
process of dethroning (which was to be most in evidence
about 1900) really depended upon a combination of interdependent factors. There was a shift of taste; there was a
development of new theories of the novel, and there was a
recognition by English readers of fresh talents among the
novelists of England, France, America, and Russia, a recogni-

George H. Ford, DICKENS AND HIS READERS (Princeton, N. J.: Princeton
University Press, 1955), pp. 180-91. Reprinted by permission of the publisher, copyright 1955 by Princeton University Press. See also Richard D.
Altick, *The English Common Reader: A Social History of the Mass Reading Public, 1800-1900* (Chicago, 1957); Kathleen Tillotson, *Novels of
the Eighteen-Forties* (London, 1956).

tion stimulated partly because these talents were in accord
with the shift of taste. . . .

In 1854, Thackeray was wondering how soon it would be
before "some young fellow" would arrive to knock Dickens
and himself "both off the stage." He did not have to wait long,
but the young fellow turned out to be a woman of almost
forty years of age. Just as *Vanity Fair* had made many readers
dissatisfied with the vulgarity of Dickens' novels, so *Adam
Bede* made readers dissatisfied with Thackeray as well as
with Dickens. Beside the prodigious erudition of George Eliot,
Thackeray's learning seemed almost schoolboy-like, and beside the warm-hearted earnestness of her tone, his half-cynical
airs (Thackeray's most glaring fault, in Victorian eyes)
seemed meretricious.

Even though the expression has been sanctioned by Thackeray as well as by Ernest Hemingway, to speak of one novelist
knocking another off the stage is an obvious historical sim-
plification. Many readers were content to enjoy all three
novelists equally. In general, however, *Adam Bede* was as
timely a publication as *Pickwick* had been earlier, and as
damaging to other novelists. It seemed to satisfy the demands
being made of the novel by cultivated critics, demands which
Dickens and Thackeray had failed to satisfy. A few years
later, William Cory, an admirer of the French Academy, was
looking back upon the decline of taste since the time of
Wordsworth. "I think it is Dickens that has brought us down,"
he wrote, and added that it was "wonderful" how George
Eliot had risen "so very far above him and his dominant set."
Here is the note of the representative Victorian admirer of
George Eliot—a sense of having successfully taken flight
into higher realms. When a reviewer praised *Adam Bede* as
"one of the best novels we have read for a long time," G. H.
Lewes was indignant. "The nincompoop couldn't see the difference between *Adam* and the mass of novels he had been
reading."

Aside from the effect of her novels upon other readers,
George Eliot is of interest as a critical reader of fiction. Like
many of her contemporaries, her literary diet in childhood
included a feast of Scott's novels, which was later followed by
a period of revulsion from fiction during which she looked
upon novel-reading as a sinful waste of time. "Have I, then,
any time to spend on things that never existed?" The Evangelical phase was soon outgrown but left its mark on her
mature attitude towards fiction. Some writers such as Rous-

seau and George Sand she was prepared to accept because they swept her away with their cascade of emotions, but, as a general rule, she argued that the novelist's special forte ought to be an unsensational record of everyday life. Observation ought to be colored by sentiment but by nothing else. The happiness of her union with Lewes must have been augmented by their mutual love of Jane Austen's novels. As a reviewer in the fifties, she used Austen as a standard by which to measure "silly novels by lady novelists," and her sarcasm fell most heavily upon theatrical exaggeration. "Only cultivated minds fairly appreciate the exquisite art of Miss Austen. Those who demand the stimulus of 'effects,' those who can only see by strong lights and shadows, will find her tame and uninteresting." Even Mrs. Gaskell, she said, "seems to me to be constantly misled by a love of sharp contrasts—of 'dramatic' effects. She is not contented with the subdued coloring, the half-tints, of real life.

Although in Eliot's own novels there are some lapses into sensationalism in the endings of *Adam Bede* and *The Mill on the Floss,* and in the Raffles incident in *Middlemarch,* she usually achieved the plain, unvarnished tale which she had recommended as a critic. Her realism was, however, of a much more revolutionary turn than has so far been indicated. "You see, it was really George Eliot who started it all," so the young D. H. Lawrence said to a friend. "And how wild they all were with her for doing it. It was she who started putting all the action inside. Before, you know, with Fielding and the others, it had been outside. Now I wonder which is right?" [1] Lawrence was perceptive to include Fielding with "all the others." Eliot's admiration for Fielding has misled some of her critics. The general direction of her novels is Richardsonian. As H. D. Traill said in 1897, Fielding's triumph had made readers forget how Richardson ("that great but exasperating artist") had displayed human nature by "working away . . . at 'how he felt,' 'how she felt,' 'what he thought' . . . until he has traced . . . a human soul." George Eliot and Henry James thus restored a balance.

It is not surprising that Eliot seldom refers to Dickens' novels in her letters, novels, or criticism, and her most important comment upon them (published a year before *Scenes from Clerical Life*) is a manifesto for her own fictional revolution:

[1] E. T., *D. H. Lawrence: A Personal Record* (London, 1935), p. 105.

We have one great novelist who is gifted with the utmost power of rendering the external traits of our town population; and if he could give us their psychological character—their conception of life, and their emotions—with the same truth as their idiom and manners, his books would be the greatest contribution Art has ever made to the awakening of social sympathies. But . . . he scarcely ever passes from the humorous and external to the emotional and tragic, without becoming . . . transcendent in his unreality.[2]

Eliot's criticism here is parallel to George Brimley's review of *Bleak House* in which he had pointed out Dickens' concentration upon the "purely outward" aspects of character and his failure (with Tulkinghorn for example) to deal with motives. Such were the readers who were more than ready to welcome Eliot's novels. Parenthetically, it should be noted that one of the warmest welcomes came from an unexpected source, from Dickens himself. Eliot had looked for encouragement from Thackeray, thinking him "as I suppose the majority of people with any intellect do, on the whole the most powerful of living novelists." It was Dickens, however, who characteristically overwhelmed her with his enthusiasm for her first two novels.

With the possible exception of Thomas Hardy, George Eliot was the last English novelist to succeed fully in the same way as Dickens, with his early novels, had succeeded. She gained the highest acclaim from critical readers, and she satisfied the tastes of a large public. R. E. Francillon reports that in 1859, the *annus mirabilis* of English publishing, *Adam Bede* "threw the whole nation into excitement." As *The Times* indicated, George Eliot could challenge Dickens successfully on his own ground. Mrs. Poyser, "the gem of the novel," is "likely to outvie all the characters of recent fiction" with the single exception, according to *The Times,* of Mr. Samuel Weller. In addition, with such characters as Arthur Donnithorne, there was a painstaking exploration of motives which was quite beyond Dickens' methods. In the eighties, one reviewer looked back with satisfaction upon Eliot's accomplishment in changing the direction of the novel away from Dickens and Collins: "Within the past twenty-five or thirty years English fiction has taken on itself an introspective hue, and the taste of readers of fiction is all for analysis of character and motive, while the taste of the period immedi-

[2] "The Natural History of German Life," in George Eliot's *Works* (New York, n.d.), vi. 161-62.

ately preceding was entirely for the display of character and motive in action."

The reception by the reviewers of some of her later novels was not always so triumphant. Fatuous attacks on the immorality of *The Mill on the Floss* (to which she was painfully vulnerable) are said to have affected her artistic development by accentuating her concern with the exposition of a moral system. The sale of her novels nevertheless continued, and the eight thousand pounds she received from the *Cornhill* for *Romola* caused Meredith (who lacked a popular audience) to gasp with astonishment.[3]

It is interesting that one of Meredith's most ardent admirers, the poet James Thomson, complimented the novel-reading public of the seventies upon their choice of George Eliot as a popular favorite. Popularity did not, as in Dickens' case, cost her the following of the cultivated. John Addington Symonds, a very discriminating reader, said that if Balzac had been less fantastic and less sceptical, he "would certainly be one of the two greatest novelists of the world, Miss Evans the other. For the most extravagant praise, however, one should turn to the American poet, Sidney Lanier, whose lectures on the history of the English novel were delivered in 1881. An expert upon prosody, Lanier was virtually an ignoramus concerning the art of fiction. His book being one of the most inept studies of the novel, the kind of book which gives the false impression that no one in the nineteenth century knew how to read, it is embarrassing to find that George Eliot was its heroine. For Lanier, as for others during the seventies and eighties, when her fame was at its apex, George Eliot was not a novelist but a high priestess whose pronouncements solved the religious dilemmas of a troubled age. In "Daniel Deronda: A Conversation," Henry James gives a delightful portrait of another such devotee and pits her against a lively reader who finds *Daniel Deronda* dull.

In time the sibyl-phase exhausted itself. By 1897, Clement Shorter had the impression that unlike Dickens and Thackeray, George Eliot had failed to maintain her hold upon readers. "Of the idolatry which almost made her a prophetess of a new cult we hear nothing now." Some of the Victorian poets such as Hopkins, Fitzgerald, Swinburne, and

---

[3] *Letters of George Meredith* (New York, 1912), I, 74. See also *The Autobiography of Mrs. Oliphant* (New York 1899), p. 326. Mrs. Oliphant considered George Eliot to have been the most highly paid author of the age.

Rossetti had detected a prosy dullness in her novels which they compared unfavorably with the liveliness of Dickens. Their verdict came to be more and more accepted after the turn of the century. Although her own reputation became temporarily dimmed by this development, Eliot's achievement in revolutionizing the English novel left its mark. It was her method of analyzing Bulstrode's hypocrisy rather than Dickens' method of presenting Pecksniff which became the norm not only for major novelists but for critical readers. When Matthew Arnold was recommending Tolstoy's *Anna Karenina* to English readers in 1887, he used virtually the same terms which Eliot had used in her manifesto against Dickens: "The Russian novelist is thus master of a spell to which the secrets of human nature—both what is external and what is internal, gesture and manner no less than thought and feeling—willingly make themselves known." [4]

II

In their own special way, George Meredith's novels reflect the same development. To expose the inner lives of his characters, to present a minute analysis of human motives, to impart an air of philosophical discussion into the novel were certainly among Meredith's objectives. He is, however, so many-sided a figure that he keeps breaking out of the brown paper wrapping in which literary historians have attempted to package him.

In 1887, the poet Gerard Manley Hopkins observed to Robert Bridges that "the abundance of genius in English romance in this age appears to me comparable with its abundance in drama in the Elizabethan." [5] This fictional renaissance, which still continues despite annual predictions to the contrary, has had a marked effect on writers of what booksellers call *non-fiction*. As a contemporary poet complained: "Your novel is a great thief." The progressive pressure of a predominant literary form has driven poets such as Hardy and essayists such as Aldous Huxley into attempting a form not altogether congenial. Meredith is an early example of the somewhat reluctant novelist. One might say that he was a promising poet who could have been a major essayist but

[4] ["Count Leo Tolstoi," *Essays in Criticism: Second Series* (London, 1891), p. 257—Ed.]

[5] *Letters of Hopkins to Bridges,* ed. C. C. Abbott (London, 1935), p. 262.

chose, instead, to make his name as a novelist. Under the circumstances, it was inevitable that he would set about making changes in the traditional form which had come down through Smollett to Dickens. It saddened him that Thackeray, who was "Titan enough" to make animated his puppets "with positive brainstuff," had failed to make the changes required. Had he done so, "he would . . . have raised the art in dignity on a level with history."[6] In Dickens he had no comparable confidence. "Dickens gone!" he wrote in a letter of 1870. "The 'Spectator' says he beat Shakespeare at his best, and instances Mrs. Gamp as superior to Juliet's nurse. This in a critical newspaper!"[7] His dislike of Dickens was not qualified with any of George Eliot's indulgent benevolence:

Not much of Dickens will live, because it has so little correspondence to life. He was the incarnation of cockneydom, a caricaturist who aped the moralist; he should have kept to short stories. If his novels are read at all in the future, people will wonder what we saw in them. . . . The world will never let Mr. Pickwick, who to me is full of the lumber of imbecility, share honours with Don Quixote.[8]

In 1899, Meredith was obliged to reconsider his verdict when his friend Alice Meynell published an excellent essay "in defence of a slumbering popular favourite." By means of well-chosen quotations (Meredith called them "plums") Miss Meynell set about proving that Dickens had been "very much a craftsman," a great literary artist, a stylist of the first magnitude. "Portia is not to be withstood," wrote Meredith gallantly and added that he had been won over by the "very handsome pleading" to restore "his Homer to the Cockney."[9]

In this last phrase, rather than in his comments on realism, we seem to have the principal reason for Meredith's dislike. His own novels are not realistic in the sense that Trollope's and Eliot's are realistic. As his fugue-like dialogues illustrate, he is an even more stylized novelist than Dickens, and, in his early work, he sometimes imitated Dickens' manner. What he disliked was the lack of intellectual challenge. As

[6] Quoted by Siegfried Sassoon, *Meredith* (New York, 1948) p. 80.

[7] *Letters of George Meredith* (New York, 1912), I, 206.

[8] Edward Clodd, "George Meredith: Some Recollections," *Fortnightly Review*, n.s., LXXXVI (1909), 27.

[9] *Letters from George Meredith to Alice Meynell* (London, 1923), p. 63.

Dr. Alvan says in *The Tragic Comedians* (1880), vulgar readers demand "to have pleasures in their own likeness" instead of learning about life from "noble fiction," in which the positive brainstuff, rather than mere narrative, engages the reader's attention. An early reviewer commented: "No man we know of has more resolutely gone into literature with a total disregard of popularity. . . . His novels are not amusing; they require thought." Meredith replied bluntly that reviewers and critics had become so slavishly obsessed with whether or not a writer was popular that they were mere "umpires" recording failures or success. "Now the pig supplies the most popular of dishes, but it is not accounted the most honoured of animals, unless it be by the cottager. Our public might surely be led to try other, perhaps finer, meat." [10]

After baffling and astonishing the reviewers with his independent style, philosophical virtuosity, and dazzling experiments, Meredith's novels finally won a considerable recognition. In summary, the detailed studies which have been made of his reception indicate that Meredith exaggerated the unkindness of his early critics. Although they did not become popular, his early novels gained him a small but enthusiastic following among the elite. Accoding to René Galland: "the seventies mark the turning of the tide"; the reviews of *Beauchamp's Career* (1876) were extremely friendly. In the eighties he became fashionable, and by 1890, his defenders had "won the day." Meredith had a special appeal for a new generation which had outgrown Dickens and become tired of the praises lavished on George Eliot. His young defenders included Wilde, James Thomson, Barrie, and Stevenson. As one of them wrote concerning Oxford in the 1880's: "For us youngsters George Meredith was what Dickens had been to our seniors, and our joy in him was, I fear, just a little enhanced by his being—then, at least—caviare to the general." Although to an even later generation, the point may seem somewhat quaint, Meredith's value for the young was enhanced because he had daringly challenged Victorian prudery. "In 'Richard Feverel,' what a loosening of the bonds!" exclaimed Arnold Bennett. While Meredith's vogue lasted, Dickens seemed especially antiquated.

In his energetic effort to add seriousness to the novel not, like Henry James, by making it a serious art but by making it a device for testing serious ideas, Meredith paved the way

[10] *An Essay on Comedy* (New York, 1897), p. 99.

for such twentieth-century novels as *Howard's End* and *A Passage to India,* to say nothing of such extreme examples as *The Magic Mountain.* By making the readers of his novels accustomed to a fare of serious ideas, he even paved the way for writers as different from himself as Hardy and Dostovesky.

III

In the case of Hardy, Meredith's role was more obviously helpful. Of one of his own novels, Meredith once admitted: "This cursed desire I have haunting me to show the reason for things is a perpetual obstruction to movement. I *do* want the dash of Smollett and know it." [11] Perhaps with his own experience in mind, he advised Hardy to learn the art of narrative from Wilkie Collins. That Hardy profited from his advice is most evident in early novels such as *Desperate Remedies,* but there is a fondness for sensational narrative and melodramatic situation running through all his works, and he is much less concerned than Meredith or Eliot with a slow paced analysis of motives. Like Paul Dombey, Hardy had a somewhat old-fashioned air. George Eliot was to him one of the great "thinkers" of the century, superior to Newman and Carlyle, but "not a born storyteller." Throughout his scattered comments about the novel's having advanced to a thoughtful "analytic stage," Hardy still clung to a more primitive, Dickens-like belief in extraordinary incident. It is typical of his taste that he found realistic landscape-painting boring. "The much decried, mad, late-Turner rendering is now necessary to create my interest" he confessed in 1887.[12] For this reason the devoted reader of Hardy is much less apt to be allergic to Dickens' novels than is the devoted reader of Meredith.

In his admirable essay on "The Profitable Reading of Fiction" (1888), Hardy himself investigates the novel from the point of view of different levels of readers. He notes that the "perspicacious reader" may have insights into a novel's meaning of which the novelist himself is unaware. Unlike most artists, Hardy welcomed such insights and recommended that the perspicacious reader ought to look for a novelist's "special gift" which is "frequently not that feature in an author's work

[11] Quoted by Sassoon, *Meredith,* p. 33.
[12] Florence E. Hardy, *The Early Life of Thomas Hardy* (New York, 1928), pp. 129, 305; pp. 232, 268; cf. pp. 243, 189, 285.

which common repute has given him credit for." The "popular attribute" and "more obvious" talent may overshadow the author's true "specialty" which the critic ought to seek. "Behind the broad humour of one popular pen he discerns startling touches of weirdness." [13]

Hardy's comment seems almost a prophecy of the critical reinterpretations of Dickens in the 1940's and 1950's. It is also applicable to later evaluations of his own novels. In his provocative study of Hardy published in 1949, Albert Guerard argued that such readers as Lord David Cecil have been at fault in their dislike of Hardy's melodrama and in their attempt to circumvent it. Speaking for a later generation of readers, Guerard finds Hardy's "deliberate anti-realism" a virtue rather than a defect:

We have rediscovered, to our sorrow, the demonic in human nature as well as in political process; our everyday experience has been both intolerable and improbable, but even more improbable than intolerable. . . . Between the two wars the most vital literary movements . . . arrived at the same conclusions . . . that experience is more often macabre than not.

I cite this interesting passage partly because it effectively summarizes the direction being taken in recent interpretations of Dickens as well as of Hardy. Although Hardy, for the most part, worked independently of Dickens towards what Guerard calls the "grotesque, macabre and symbolic," he arrived at a similar juxtaposition of "the fantastic and everyday." [14]

Finally, according to this interpretation, Hardy was first of all a story-teller rather than a commentator upon Victorian problems. To thoughtful readers of an earlier period, as any list of books and articles about Hardy testifies, the contrary was true. Although he had arrived at different conclusions concerning the intentions of the President of the Immortals, Hardy was valued as George Eliot and Meredith were valued. He was a commentator upon the profound disturbance created by Darwin and his predecessors, a disturbance with which Dickens was apparently too ignorant to be concerned. Again the comparison was implicit. The philosophy of Dickens (what there was of it) was a philosophy for children. The philosophy of Hardy was a challenge to the adult.

[13] Hardy, *Life and Art* (New York, 1925), pp. 64, 58.
[14] *Thomas Hardy* (Cambridge, Mass., 1949), pp. 3-4, 39.

IV

When we turn to the reception of the Russian novelists in England, the word *adult* becomes even more prevalent. In an article published during the first World War entitled "Redemption and Dostoevsky," Rebecca West described *The Pilgrim's Progress* as an allegory for the world's childhood and *The Brothers Karamazov* as "an allegory for the world's maturity." [15] Much of the appeal of Russian fiction has been the sense it gives readers of a literature liberated not only from the butler's pantry but from the nursery. Two years after Dickens' death, Charles Yonge spoke of the novel as one of the "triumphs of British genius," and of British novelists as "certainly above all competition." Such insular confidence was to be sorely tried by successive invasions from abroad of French, Russian, and American novels. The effect of Russian novels in particular was to develop an inferiority complex among English readers which has had a marked effect on Dickens' status. In 1917, Somerset Maugham recorded in his notebook that his delight in Turgenev, Tolstoy, and Dostoevsky had made him unfair to such Victorian novelists as Dickens whose work seemed, by comparison, conventional and artificial. E. M. Forster's *Aspects of the Novel* (1927) opens with the airing of an "unpatriotic truth." "No English novelist is as great as Tolstoy— that is to say has given so complete a picture of man's life, both on its domestic and heroic side. No English novelist has explored man's soul as deeply as Dostoevsky." A similar point was made in 1947 by Clifford Bax who remarked, somewhat naively, that the Russian novelists who "mysteriously" admired Dickens have made it difficult for English readers to enjoy his novels any more.

---

[15] Quoted by Helen Muchnic, *Dostoevsky's English Reputation (1881-1936)*, *Smith College Studies in Modern Languages*, XX (1939), p. 86.

Perhaps the most remarkable of all the recent revaluations of anti-Victorian attitudes has been the brilliant revaluation of Dickens that started with Edmund Wilson's well-known essay, "Dickens: The Two Scrooges" in *The Wound and the Bow* (Boston, 1941). "The Bloomsbury that talked about Dostoevsky ignored Dostoevsky's master, Dickens," says Wilson; and he shows that Dickens was an even greater social realist than the Victorians understood, while at the same time he dramatized, through the symbolic structure of his novels, his own neuroses.

Victorian highbrows deserted Dickens because they were looking for the analysis of motives. But present-day critics, with their interest in the psychology of the unconscious, appreciate Dickens for the very qualities that caused the Victorian desertion—his apparent childishness, his extravagant plots, his apparent lack of concern for ideas and for moral and psychological complexity. Present-day critics appreciate what Dorothy Van Ghent here calls Dickens's "finely lucid atmosphere of fairy tale"; for they understand that the extravagant external events of fairy tale and romance symbolize the connection we make with the external world through our unconscious desires. In this chapter of 1953, Miss Van Ghent uses Marxist and Freudian concepts of alienation, neurosis and collective guilt to account for that which seems childish and improbable in Dickens's plotting and characterization—and to account especially for his celebrated humor.

DOROTHY VAN GHENT

On "Great Expectations"

"The distinguishing quality of Dickens's people," says V. S. Pritchett, 'is that they are solitaries. They are people caught living in a world of their own. They soliloquize in it. They do not talk to one another; they talk to themselves. The pressure of society has created fits of twitching in mind and speech, and fantasies in the soul . . . The solitariness of people is paralleled by the solitariness of things. Fog operates as a separate presence, houses quietly rot or boisterously prosper on their own . . . Cloisterham believes itself more important than the world at large, the Law sports like some stale and dilapidated circus across human lives. Philanthropy attacks people like a humor or an observable germ. The people and the things of Dickens are all out of touch and out of hearing of each other, each conducting its own inner monologue, grandiloquent or dismaying. By this dissociation Dickens brings to us something of the fright of childhood . . .[1]'

Some of the most wonderful scenes in *Great Expectations* are those in which people, presumably in the act of conversation, raptly soliloquize; and Dickens' technique, in these cases, is usually to give the soliloquizer a fantastic private language as unadapted to mutual understanding as a species of pig Latin. Witness Mr. Jaggers' interview with Joe Gargery, in which the dignified lawyer attempts to compensate Joe financially for his part in Pip's upbringing, and Joe swings on him with unintelligible pugilistic jargon.

"Which I meantersay . . . that if you come into my place bull-baiting and badgering me, come out! Which I meantersay as sech if you're a man, come on! Which I meantersay that what I say, I meantersay and stand or fall by!"

Or Miss Havisham's interview with Joe over the question of Pip's wages; for each question she asks him, Joe persists

[1] *The Living Novel* (New York, 1947), p. 88.

Dorothy Van Ghent, THE ENGLISH NOVEL: FORM AND FUNCTION (New York: Rinehart, 1953), pp. 125-38. Reprinted by permission of Holt, Rinehart and Winston, copyright 1953 by Dorothy Van Ghent. See also Steven Marcus, *Dickens: from Pickwick to Dombey* (New York, 1965); J. Hillis Miller, *Charles Dickens: The World of His Novels* (Cambridge, Mass., 1958).

in addressing his reply to Pip rather than herself, and his replies have not the remotest relation to the questions. Sometimes, by sheer repetition of a phrase, the words a character uses will assume the frenzied rotary unintelligibility of an idiot's obsession, as does Mrs. Joe's "Be grateful to them which brought you up by hand," or Pumblechook's mincing "May I?—May I?" The minimal uses of language as an instrument of communication and intellectual development are symbolized by Pip's progress in the school kept by Mr. Wopsle's great-aunt, where the summit of his education consists in his copying a large Old-English "D," which he assumes to be the design for a belt buckle; and by Joe's pleasure in the art of reading, which enables him to find three "J's" and three "O's" and three "J-O, Joes" in a piece of script.

"Give me [he says] a good book, or a good newspaper, and sit me down afore a good fire, and I ask no better. Lord! when you *do* come to a J and a O, and says you, 'Here, at last, is a J-O, Joe,' how interesting reading is!"

There is, perhaps, no purer expression of solipsism in literature. The cultivation of the peculiar Dickensian values of language reaches its apogee when the convict Magwitch, with a benefactor's proud delight, asks Pip to read to him from a book in a foreign language, of which he understands no syllable.

From *Don Quixote* on, the novels that we have read in this series of studies have frequently drawn our attention to the ambiguities of language and the varieties of its expressive relationship to life—from the incongruities between Quixote's and Sancho's understanding of the meaning of words, to the hopeless lapse of verbal understanding between Walter and Toby Shandy, and to the subtly threatening divergencies of meaning in the constricted language of Jane Austen's characters. Language as a means of communication is a provision for social and spiritual order. You cannot make "order" with an integer, one thing alone, for order is definitively a relationship among things. Absolute noncommunication is an unthinkable madness for it negates all relationship and therefore all order, and even an ordinary madman has to create a kind of order for himself by illusions of communication. Dickens' soliloquizing characters, for all their funniness (aloneness is inexorably funny, like the aloneness of the man who slips on a banana peel, seen from the point of view of togetherness), suggests a world of isolated integers, terrifyingly alone and unrelated.

The book opens with a child's first conscious experience of his aloneness. Immediately an abrupt encounter occurs —Magwitch suddenly comes from behind a gravestone, seizes Pip by the heels, and suspends him upside down.

"Hold your nose!" cried a terrible voice, as a man started up from among the graves at the side of the church porch. "Keep still, you little devil, or I'll cut your throat!"

Perhaps, if one could fix on two of the most personal aspects of Dickens' technique, one would speak of the strange languages he concocts for the solitariness of the soul, and the abruptness of his tempo. His human fragments suddenly shock against one another in collisions like those of Democritus' atoms or of the charged particles of modern physics. Soldiers, holding out handcuffs, burst into the blacksmith's house during Christmas dinner at the moment when Pip is clinging to a table leg in an agony of apprehension over his theft of the pork pie. A weird old woman clothed in decayed satin, jewels and spider webs, and with one shoe off, shoots out her finger at the bewildered child, with the command: "Play!" A pale young gentleman appears out of a wilderness of cucumber frames, and daintily kicking up his legs and slapping his hands together, dips his head and butts Pip in the stomach. These sudden confrontations between persons whose ways of life have no habitual or logical continuity with each other suggests the utmost incohesion in the stuff of experience.

Technique is vision. Dickens' technique is an index of a vision of life that sees human separatedness as the ordinary condition, where speech is speech *to* nobody and where human encounter is mere collision. But the vision goes much further. Our minds are so constituted that they insist on seeking in the use of language an exchange function, a delivery and a passing on of perceptions from soul to soul and generation to generation, binding them in some kind of order; and they insist on finding cause and effect, or *motivation,* in the displacements and encounters of persons or things. Without these primary patterns of perception we would not have what we call minds. And when these patterns are confused or abrogated by our experience, we are forced, in order to preserve some kind of psychic equilibrium, to

seek them in extraordinary explanations—explanations again
in terms of mutual exchange and cause and effect. Dickens
saw his world patently all in pieces, and as a child's vision
would offer some reasonable explanation of why such a world
was that way—and, by the act of explanation, would make
that world yield up a principle of order, however obscure or
fantastic—so, with a child's liberalism of imagination, he
discovered organization among his fragments.

Dickens lived in a time and an environment in which a
full-scale demolition of traditional values was going on,
correlatively with the uprooting and dehumanization of men,
women, and children by the millions—a process brought
about by industrialization, colonial imperialism, and the ex-
ploitation of the human being as a "thing" or an engine or
a part of an engine capable of being used for profit. This
was the "century of progress" which ornamented its steam
engines with iron arabesques of foliage as elaborate as the
antimacassars and aspidistras and crystal or cut-glass chan-
deliers and bead-and-feather portieres of its drawing rooms,
while the human engines of its welfare groveled and bred
in the foxholes described by Marx in his *Capital*. (Haunt-
ingly we see this discordance in the scene in *Great Expectations* where Miss Havisham, sitting in her satin and floral
decay in the house called Satis, points her finger at the child
and outrageously tells him to "play." For though the scene
is a potent symbol of childish experience of adult obtuseness and sadism, it has also another dimension as a social
symbol of those economically determined situations in which
the human soul is used as a means for satisfactions not its
own, under the gross and transparent lie that its activity is
its happiness, its welfare and fun and "play"—a publicity
instrument that is the favorite of manufacturers and insurance agencies, as well as of totalitarian strategists, with their
common formula, "We're just a happy family.") The heir
of the "century of progress" is the twentieth-century concentration camp, which makes no bones about people being
"things."

Dickens' intuition alarmingly saw this process in motion,
a process which abrogated the primary demands of human
feeling and rationality, and he sought an extraordinary explanation for it. People were becoming things, and things
(the things that money can buy or that are the means for
making money or for exalting prestige in the abstract) were

becoming more important than people. People were being de-animated, robbed of their souls, and things were usurping the prerogatives of animate creatures—governing the lives of their owners in the most literal sense. This picture, in which the qualities of things and people were reversed, was a picture of a daemonically motivated world, a world in which "dark" or occult forces or energies operate not only in people (as modern psychoanalytic psychology observes) but also in things: for if people turn themselves or are turned into things, metaphysical order can be established only if we think of things as turning themselves into people, acting under a "dark" drive similar to that which motivates the human aberration.

There is an old belief that it takes a demon to recognize a demon, and the saying illustrates the malicious sensibility with which things, in Dickens, have felt out and imitated, in their relationship with each other and with people, the secret of the human arrangement. A four-poster bed in an inn, where Pip goes to spend the night, is a despotic monster that straddles over the whole room,

> putting one of his arbitrary legs into the fireplace, and another into the doorway, and squeezing the wretched little washing-stand in quite a Divinely Righteous manner.

Houses, looking down through the skylight of Jaggers' office in London, twist themselves in order to spy on Pip-like police agents who presuppose guilt. Even a meek little muffin has to be "confined with the utmost precaution under a strong iron cover," and a hat, set on a mantelpiece, demands constant attention and the greatest quickness of eye and hand to catch it neatly as it tumbles off, but its ingenuity is such that it finally manages to fall into the slop basin. The animation of inanimate objects suggests both the quaint gaiety of a forbidden life and an aggressiveness that has got out of control—an aggressiveness that they have borrowed from the human economy and an irresponsibility native to but glossed and disguised by that economy.

Dickens' fairly constant use of the pathetic fallacy (the projection of human impulses and feelings upon the non-human, as upon beds and houses and muffins and hats) might be considered as incidental stylistic embellishment if his description of people did not show a reciprocal metaphor: people are described by nonhuman attributes, or by such an exaggeration of or emphasis on one part of their appearance that they seem to be reduced wholly to that part, with an effect of having become "thinged" into one of their own bodily members or into an article of their clothing or into some inanimate object of which they have made a fetish. Dickens' devices for producing this transposition of attributes are various. To his friend and biographer, Forster, he said that he was always losing sight of a man in his diversion by the mechanical play of some part of the man's face, which "would acquire a sudden ludicrous life of its own." Many of what we shall call the "signatures" of Dickens' people—that special exaggerated feature or gesture or mannerism which comes to stand for the whole person— are such dissociated parts of the body, like Jaggers' huge forefinger which he bites and then plunges menacingly at the accused, or Wemmick's post-office mouth, or the clockwork apparatus in Magwitch's throat that clicks as if it were going to strike. The device is not used arbitrarily or capriciously. In this book, whose subject is the etiology of guilt and of atonement, Jaggers is the representative not only of civil law but of universal Law, which is profoundly mysterious in a world of dissociated and apparently lawless fragments; and his huge forefinger, into which he is virtually transformed and which seems to act like an "it" in its own right rather than like a member of a man, is the Law's mystery in all its fearful impersonality. Wemmick's mouth is not a post-office when he is at home in his castle but only when he is at work in Jaggers' London office, where a mechanical appearance of smiling is required of him. And as Wemmick's job has mechanized him into a grinning slot, so oppression and fear have given the convict Magwitch a clockwork apparatus for vocal chords.

Or this general principle of reciprocal changes, by which things have become as it were daemonically animated and people have been reduced to thing-like characteristics—as if, by a law of conservation of energy, the humanity of which people have become incapable had leaked out into the external environment—may work symbolically in the association of some object with a person so that the object assumes his essence and his "meaning." Mrs. Joe wears a large apron, "having a square impregnable bib in front, that was stuck full of pins and needles"—she has no reason to wear it, and she never takes it off a day in her life. Jaggers flourishes a large white handkerchief—a napkin that is the mysterious complement of his blood-smeared engagements. Estella—who is the star and jewel of Pip's great expectations—wears jewels in her hair and on her breast; "I and the jewels," she says, as if they were interchangeable. The device of association is a familiar one in fiction; what distinguishes Dickens' use of it is that the associated object acts not merely to *illustrate* a person's qualities symbolically—as novelists usually use it— but that it has a necessary metaphysical function in Dickens' universe: in this universe objects actually usurp human essences; beginning as fetishes, they tend to—and sometimes quite literally do—devour and take over the powers of the fetish-worshiper.

The process of conversion of spirit into matter that operates in the Dickens world is shown working out with savage simplicity in the case of Miss Havisham. Miss Havisham has been guilty of aggression against life in using the two children, Pip and Estella, as inanimate instruments of revenge for her broken heart—using them, that is, as if they were not human but things—and she is being changed retributively into a fungus. The decayed cake on the banquet table acts, as it were, by homeopathic magic—like a burning effigy or a doll stuck with pins; its decay parallels the necrosis in the human agent. "When the ruin is complete," Miss Havisham says, pointing to the cake but referring to herself, she will be laid out on the same table and her relatives will be invited to "feast on" her corpse. But this is not the only conversion. The "little quickened hearts" of the mice behind the panels have been quickened by what was Miss Havisham, carried off crumb by crumb.

The principle of reciprocal changes, between the human and the nonhuman, bears on the characteristic lack of complex "inner life" on the part of Dickens' people—their lack of a personally complex psychology. It is inconceivable that the fungoid Miss Havisham should have a complex inner life, in the moral sense. But in the *art* of Dickens (distinguishing that moral dialectic that arises not solely from the "characters" in a novel but from all the elements in the aesthetic structure) there is a great deal of "inner life," transposed to other forms than that of human character: partially transposed in this scene, for instance, to the symbolic activity of the speckle-legged spiders with blotchy bodies and to the

gropings and pausings of the black beetles on Miss Havisham's hearth. Without benefit of Freud or Jung, Dickens
saw the human soul reduced literally to the images occupying
its "inner life."

Through the changes that have come about in the human,
as humanity has leaked out of it, the atoms of the physical
universe have become subtly impregnated with daemonic aptitude. Pip, standing waiting for Estella in the neighborhood
of Newgate, and beginning dimly to be aware of his implication in the guilt for which that establishment stands—
for his "great expectations" have already begun to make him
a collaborator in the generic crime of using people as means
to personal ends—has the sensation of a deadly dust clinging
to him, rubbed off on him from the environs, and he tries to
beat it out of his clothes. Smithfield, that "shameful place,"
"all asmear with filth and fat and blood and foam," seems to
"stick to him" when he enters it on his way to the prison.
The nettles and brambles of the graveyard where Magwitch
first appears "stretch up cautiously" out of the graves in an
effort to get a twist on the branded man's ankles and pull
him in. The river has a malignant potentiality that impreg-
nates everything upon it—discolored copper, rotten wood,
honey-combed stone, green dank deposit. The river is perhaps the most constant and effective symbol in Dickens,
because it establishes itself so readily to the imagination as
a daemonic element, drowning people as if by intent, dis-
gorging unforeseen evidence, chemically or physically changing all it touches, and because not only does it act as an
occult "force" in itself but it is the common passage and
actual flowing element that unites individuals and classes,
public persons and private persons, deeds and the results of
deeds, however fragmentized and separated. Upon the river,
one cannot escape its action; it may throw the murderer
and his victim in an embrace. At the end of *Great Expectations,* it swallows Compeyson, while, with its own obscure
daemonic motivation, though it fatally injures Magwitch, it
leaves him to fulfill the more subtle spiritual destiny upon
which he has begun to enter. The river scene in this section,
closely and apprehensively observed, is one of the most
memorable in Dickens.

It is necessary to view Dickens' "coincidences" under the
aspect of this wholesale change in the aptitudes of external
nature. Coincidence is the violent connection of the un-

connected. Life is full of violent connections of this sort, but one of the most rigorous conventions of fictional and dramatic art is that events should make a logically sequential pattern; for art is the discovery of order. Critics have frequently deplored Dickens' use of coincidences in his plots. But in a universe that is nervous throughout, a universe in which nervous ganglia stretch through both people and their external environment, so that a change in the human can infect the currents of the air and the sea, events and confrontations that seem to abrogate the laws of physical mechanics can logically be brought about. In this sense, the apparent coincidences in Dickens actually obey a causal order—not of physical mechanics but of moral dynamics.

What connection can there be [Dickens asks in another novel] between many people in the innumerable histories of this world, who, from opposite sides of great gulfs, have, nevertheless, been very curiously brought together!

What brings the convict Magwitch to the child Pip, in the graveyard, is more than the convict's hunger; Pip (or let us say simply "the child," for Pip is an Everyman) carries the convict inside him, as the negative potential of his "great expectations"—Magwitch is the concretion of his potential guilt. What brings Magwitch across the "great gulfs" of the Atlantic to Pip again, at the moment of revelation in the story, is their profoundly implicit compact of guilt, as binding as the convict's leg iron which is its recurrent symbol. The multiplying likenesses in the street as Magwitch draws nearer, coming over the sea, the mysterious warnings of his approach on the night of his reappearance, are moral projections as "real" as the storm outside the windows and as the crouched form of the vicious Orlick on the dark stairs. The conception of what brings people together "coincidentally" in their seemingly uncaused encounters and collisions—the total change in the texture of experience that follows upon any act, public or private, external or in thought, the concreteness of the effect of the act not only upon the conceiving heart but upon the atoms of physical matter, so that blind nature collaborates daemonically in the drama of reprisal—is deep and valid in this book.

In a finely lucid atmosphere of fairy tale, Dickens uses a kind of montage in *Great Expectations,* a superimposing of one image upon another with an immediate effect of hallucination, that is but one more way of representing his vision of a purely nervous and moral organization of reality. An instance is the scene in which Estella walks the casks in the old brewery. Estella's walking the casks is an enchanting ritual dance of childhood (like walking fence rails or railroad ties), but inexplicably present in the tableau is the suicidal figure of Miss Havisham hanging by her neck from a brewery beam. Accompanying each appearance of Estella—the star and the jewel of Pip's expectations—is a similarly disturbing ghost, an image of an unformed dread. When Pip thinks of her, though he is sitting in a warm room with a friend, he shudders as if in a wind from over the marshes. Her slender knitting fingers are suddenly horribly displaced by the marred wrists of a murderess. The technique of montage is that of dreams, which know with awful precision the affinities between the guilt of our desires and the commonplaces of our immediate perceptions.

This device, of doubling one image over another, is paralleled in the handling of character. In the sense that one implies the other, the glittering frosty girl Estella, and the decayed and false old woman, Miss Havisham, are not two characters but a single one, or a single essence with dual aspects, as if composed by montage—a spiritual continuum, so to speak. For inevitably wrought into the fascinating jewel-likeness of Pip's great expectations, as represented by Estella, is the falsehood and degeneracy represented by Miss Havisham, the soilure on the unpurchased good. The boy Pip and the criminal Magwitch form another such continuum. Magwitch, from a metaphysical point of view, is not outside Pip but inside him, and his apparition is that of Pip's own unwrought deeds: Pip, having adopted "great expectations," will live by making people into Magwitches, into means for his ends. The relationship between Joe Gargery, saintly simpleton of the folk, and Orlick, dark beast of the Teutonic marshes (who comes "from the ooze"), has a somewhat different dynamics, though they too form a spiritual continuum. Joe and Orlick are related not as two aspects of a single moral identity, but as the opposed extremes of spiritual possibility—the one unqualified love, the other unqualified hate—and they form a frame within which the actions of the others have their ultimate meaning. A commonplace of criticism is that, as Edmund Wilson puts it, Dickens was usually unable "to get the good and bad together in one character."[2] The criticism might be valid if Dickens' were a naturalistic world, but it is not very relevant to Dickens' daemonically organized world. In a naturalistic world, obeying mechanical laws, each character is organically discrete from every other, and presumably each contains a representative mixture of "the good and bad." But in Dickens' thoroughly nervous world, that does not know the laws of mechanics but knows only spiritual law, one simple or "flat" character can be superimposed upon another so that together they form the representative human complexity of good-in-evil and evil-in-good.

Two kinds of crime form Dickens' two chief themes, the crime of parent against child, and the calculated social crime. They are formally analogous, their form being the treatment of persons as things; but they are also inherent in each other, whether the private will of the parent is to be considered as depraved by the operation of a public institution, or the social institution is to be considered as a bold concert of the depravities of individual "fathers." In *Great Expectations* the private crime against the child is Mrs. Joe's and Pumblechook's and Wopsle's, all "foster parents" either by necessity or self-conceit; while the social crime is the public treatment of Magwitch. That the two kinds of crime are inherent in each other we are made aware of as we are led to identify Magwitch's childhood with Pip's; the brutality exercised toward both children was the same brutality, though the "parents" in the one case were private persons, and in the other, society itself. Complicating the meaning of "the crime" still further, Magwitch also has taken upon himself the role of foster parent to Pip, and whether, as parent, he acts in charity or impiousness, or both, is a major ambiguity which the drama sets out to resolve.

"The crime," in Dickens, is evidently a permutation of multiple motivations and acts, both public and private, but always with the same tendency to convert people into things, and always implying either symbolically or directly a child-parent situation. The child-parent situation has been disnatured, corrupted, with the rest of nature; or rather, since the child-parent situation is the dynamic core of the Dickens world, the radical disnaturing here is what has corrupted the

[2] *The Wound and the Bow* (Boston, 1941), p. 65.

rest. His plots seldom serve to canalize, with the resolution of
the particular set of plotted circumstances, the hysteria submerged in his vision of a nature gone thoroughly wrong; the
permutations of the crimes are too many, and their ultimate
cause or root is evasive, unless one would resort to some
dramatically unmanageable rationale such as original sin. The
Dickens world requires an act of redemption. A symbolic act
of this kind is again and again indicated in his novels, in the
charity of the uncherished and sinned-against child for the
inadequate or criminal father—which might be called the
theme of the prodigal father, Dickens' usual modification of
the prodigal son theme. But the redemptive act should be such
that it should redeem not only the individual "fathers," but
society at large. One might almost say—thinking of Dickens'
caricatures of the living dead, with their necrotic members
and organs, their identifications of themselves with inanimate
objects—that it should be such as to redeem the dead. *Great
Expectations* is an exception among his novels in that here
the redemptive act is adequate to and structural for both
bodies of thematic material—the sins of individuals and the
sins of society.

Pip first becomes aware of the "identity of things" as he is
held suspended heels over head by the convict; that is, in a
world literally turned upside down. Thenceforth Pip's interior
landscape is inverted by his guilty knowledge of this man
"who had been soaked in water, and smothered in mud, and
lamed by stones, and cut by flints, and stung by nettles, and
torn by briars." The apparition is that of all suffering that the
earth can inflict, and that the apparition presents itself to a
child is as much as to say that every child, whatever his innocence, inherits guilt (as the potential of his acts) for the condition of man. The inversion of natural order begins here with
first self-consciousness: the child is heir to the sins of the
"fathers." Thus the crime that is always pervasive in the
Dickens universe is identified in a new way—not primarily as
that of the "father," nor as that of some public institution, but
as that of the child—the original individual who must necessarily take upon himself responsibility for not only what is to
be done in the present and the future, but what has been done
in the past, inasmuch as the past is part and parcel of the
present and the future. The child is the criminal, and it is for
this reason that he is able to redeem his world; for the world's
guilt is his guilt, and he can expiate it in his own acts.

The guilt of the child is realized on several levels. Pip experiences the psychological *form* (or feeling) of guilt before he is capable of voluntary evil; he is treated by adults—Mrs. Joe and Pumblechook and Wopsle—as if he were a felon, a young George Barnwell (a character in the play which Wopsle reads on the night when Mrs. Joe is attacked) wanting only to murder his nearest relative, as George Barnwell murdered his uncle. This is the usual nightmare of the child in Dickens, a vision of imminent incarceration, fetters like sausages, lurid accusatory texts. He is treated, that is, as if he were a thing, manipulable by adults for the extraction of certain sensations: by making him feel guilty and diminished they are able to feel virtuous and great. But the psychological *form* of guilt acquires spiritual *content* when Pip himself conceives the tainted wish—the wish to be like the most powerful adult and to treat others as things. At the literal level, Pip's guilt is that of snobbery toward Joe Gargery, and snobbery is a denial of the human value of others. Symbolically, however, Pip's guilt is that of murder; for he steals the file with which the convict rids himself of his leg iron, and it is this leg iron, picked up on the marshes, with which Orlick attacks Mrs. Joe; so that the child does inevitably overtake his destiny, which was, like George Barnwell, to murder his nearest relative. But the "relative" whom Pip, adopting the venerable criminality of society, is, in the widest symbolic scope of intention, destined to murder is not Mrs. Joe but his "father," Magwitch—to murder in the socially chronic fashion of the Dickens world, which consists in the dehumanization of the weak, or in moral acquiescence to such murder. Pip is, after all, the ordinary mixed human being, one more Everyman in the long succession of them that literature has represented, but we see this Everyman as he develops from a child; and his destiny is directed by the ideals of his world—toward "great expectations" which involve the making of Magwitches—which involve, that is, murder. These are the possibilities that are projected in the opening scene of the book, when the young child, left with a burden on his soul, watches the convict limping off under an angry red sky, toward the black marshes, the gibbet, and the savage lair of the sea, in a still rotating landscape.

In Dickens' modification of the folk pattern of the fairy wishing, Magwitch is Pip's "fairy godfather" who changes the pumpkin into a coach. Like all the "fathers," he uses the child as a thing in order to obtain through him vicarious sensations of grandeur. In relation to society, however, Magwitch is the child, and society the prodigal father; from the time he was first taken for stealing turnips, the convict's career has duplicated brutally and in public the pathos of the ordinary child. Again, in relation to Pip, Magwitch is still the child; for, spiritually committed by his "great expectations" to that irresponsibility which has accounted for the Magwitches, Pip is projectively, at least, answerable for Magwitch's existence and for his brutalization. Pip carries his criminal father within him; he is, so to speak, the father of his father. The ambiguities of each term of the relationship are such that each is both child and father, making a fourfold relationship; and the act of love between them at the end is thus reinforced fourfold, and the redemption by love is a fourfold redemption: that is to say, it is symbolically infinite, for it serves for all the meanings Dickens finds it possible to attach to the central child-father situation, the most profound and embracing relationship that, in Dickens' work, obtains among men.

As the child's original alienation from "natural" order is essentially mysterious, a guilty inheritance from the fathers which invades first awareness, so the redemptive act is also a mysterious one. The mysterious nature of the act is first indicated, in the manner of a motif, when Mrs. Joe, in imbecile pantomime, tries to propitiate her attacker, the bestial Orlick. In Orlick is concretized all the undefined evil of the Dickens world, that has nourished itself underground and crept along walls, like the ancient stains on the house of Atreus. He is the lawlessness implied in the unnatural conversions of the human into the nonhuman, the retributive death that invades those who have grown lean in life and who have exercised the powers of death over others. He is the instinct of aggression and destruction, the daemonism of sheer external Matter as such; he is pure "thingness" emerging without warning from the ooze where he has been unconsciously cultivated. As Orlick is one form of spiritual excess—unmotivated hate—Joe Gargery is the opposed form—love without reservation. Given these terms of the spiritual framework, the redemptive act itself could scarcely be anything but grotesque —and it is by a grotesque gesture, one of the most profoundly intuitive symbols in Dickens, that Mrs. Joe is redeemed. What is implied by her humble propitiation of the beast Orlick is a recognition of personal guilt in the guilt of others, and of its dialectical relationship with love. The motif reappears in the moment of major illumination in the book. Pip "bows down," not to Joe Gargery, toward whom he has been privately and literally guilty, but to the wounded, hunted, shackled man, Magwitch, who has been guilty toward himself. It is in this way that the manifold organic relationships among men are revealed, and that the Dickens world—founded in fragmentariness and disintegration—is made whole.

Tennyson's *In Memoriam* (1850) has been called the Victorian *Essay on Man*, because like Pope Tennyson summarizes the scientific knowlege of his time and relates it to questions of religious and moral judgment. The difference is that for the Victorians scientific knowledge was antithetical to, rather than productive of, a religious and ethical position. In composing an elegy for his gifted young friend, Arthur Hallam, who died before he could fulfill his promise, Tennyson faced the question of all elegists. If this can happen, what is the value of life? Tennyson could not, like Milton in *Lycidas*, take over the orthodox Christian answer because the science of the time—Lyell's geology, for example, which showed how whole species had been destroyed—made it difficult to believe in a purposeful and moral universe. If man, too, Tennyson asks, were to leave as his only trace fossils in the rocks, what hope for the immortality of Hallam's soul or for the enduring value of one's love for him? One could no longer, like the Deists and Wordsworthians, find evidence in nature for the existence of God. But one could—these are Tennyson's answers—rely on the testimony of the heart and see, in the natural evolution of species, an analogue to social progress and man's spiritual evolution. Thus, Tennyson anticipated the discussion that was to follow the publication of Darwin's *Origin of Species* in 1859.

The mid-Victorians felt that *In Memoriam* provided answers to their religious doubts; but later generations came to feel that Tennyson's answers were entirely too facile. T. S. Eliot's essay of 1936 is part of the recent effort to salvage the enduring Tennyson from the late-Victorian and early twentieth-century image of him as the moralizing Laureate, the pronouncer of phony affirmations. Tennyson is a great poet, says Eliot, because of his technical mastery. *In Memoriam* is a religious poem not "because of the quality of its faith, but because of the quality of its doubt. Its faith is a poor thing, but its doubt is a very intense experience."

214

T. S. ELIOT

"In Memoriam"

Tennyson is a great poet, for reasons that are perfectly clear. He has three qualities which are seldom found together except in the greatest poets: abundance, variety, and complete competence. We therefore cannot appreciate his work unless we read a good deal of it. We may not admire his aims: but whatever he sets out to do, he succeeds in doing, with a mastery which gives us the sense of confidence that is one of the major pleasures of poetry. His variety of metrical accomplishment is astonishing. Without making the mistake of trying to write Latin verse in English, he knew everything about Latin versification that an English poet could use; and he said of himself that he thought he knew the quantity of the sounds of every English word except perhaps *scissors*. He had the finest ear of any English poet since Milton. He was the master of Swinburne; and the versification of Swinburne, himself a classical scholar, is often crude and sometimes cheap in comparison with Tennyson's. Tennyson extended very widely the range of active metrical forms in English: in *Maud* alone the variety is prodigious. But innovation in metric is not to be measured solely by the width of the deviation from accepted practice. It is a matter of the historical situation: at some moments a more violent change may be necessary than at others. The problem differs at every period. At some times, a violent revolution may be neither possible nor desirable; at such times, a change which may appear very slight is the change which the important poet will make. The innovation of Pope, after Dryden, may not seem very great; but it is the mark of the master to be able to make small changes which will be highly significant, as at another time to make radical changes, through which poetry will curve back again to its norm.

There is an early poem, only published in the official biog-

T. S. Eliot, SELECTED ESSAYS, New Edition (New York: Harcourt, Brace, 1950), pp. 286-95. Reprinted by permission of Harcourt, Brace and World. Copyright, 1932, 1936, 1950, by Harcourt, Brace and World; copyright, 1960, 1964, by T. S. Eliot. See also Jerome H. Buckley, *Tennyson: The Growth of a Poet* (Cambridge, Mass., 1961); Arthur J. Carr, "Tennyson as a Modern Poet," *University of Toronto Quarterly* XIX (1950), 361-82.

raphy, which already exhibits Tennyson as a master. According to a note, Tennyson later expressed regret that he had removed the poem from his Juvenilia; it is a fragmentary *Hesperides*, in which only the "Song of the Three Sisters" is complete. The poem illustrates Tennyson's classical learning and his mastery of metre. The first stanza of the "Song of the Three Sisters" is as follows:

> *The Golden Apple, the Golden Apple, the hallow'd fruit,*
> *Guard it well, guard it warily,*
> *Singing airily,*
> *Standing about the charmèd root.*
> *Round about all is mute,*
> *As the snowfield on the mountain peaks,*
> *As the sandfield at the mountain foot.*
> *Crocodiles in briny creeks*
> *Sleep and stir not; all is mute.*
> *If ye sing not, if ye make false measure,*
> *We shall lose eternal pleasure,*
> *Worth eternal want of rest.*
> *Laugh not loudly: watch the treasure*
> *Of the wisdom of the West.*
> *In a corner wisdom whispers. Five and three*
> *(Let it not be preach'd abroad) make an awful mystery:*
> *For the blossom unto threefold music bloweth;*
> *Evermore it is born anew,*
> *And the sap in threefold music floweth,*
> *From the root,*
> *Drawn in the dark,*
> *Up to the fruit,*
> *Creeping under the fragrant bark,*
> *Liquid gold, honeysweet through and through.*
> *Keen-eyed Sisters, singing airily,*
> *Looking warily*
> *Every way,*
> *Guard the apple night and day,*
> *Lest one from the East come and take it away.*

A young man who can write like that has not much to learn about metric; and the young man who wrote these lines somewhere between 1828 and 1830 was doing something new. There is something not derived from any of his predecessors. In some of Tennyson's early verse the influence of Keats is visible—in songs and in blank verse; and less successfully, there is the influence of Wordsworth, as in *Dora*. But in the lines I have just quoted, and in the two Mariana poems, *The Sea-Fairies, The Lotos-Eaters, The Lady of Shalott* and elsewhere, there is something wholly new.

> *All day within the dreamy house,*
> *The doors upon their hinges creak'd;*
> *The blue fly sung in the pane; the mouse*
> *Behind the mouldering wainscoat shriek'd,*
> *Or from the crevice peer'd about.*

The blue fly sung in the pane (the line would be ruined if you substituted *sang* for *sung*) is enough to tell us that something important has happened.

The reading of long poems is not nowadays much practised: in the age of Tennyson it appears to have been easier. For a good many long poems were not only written but widely circulated; and the level was high: even the second-rate long poems of that time, like *The Light of Asia,* are better worth reading than most long modern novels. But Tennyson's long poems are not long poems in quite the same sense as those of his contemporaries. They are very different in kind from *Sordello* or *The Ring and the Book,* to name the greatest by the greatest of his contemporary poets. *Maud* and *In Memoriam* are each a series of poems, given form by the greatest lyrical resourcefulness that a poet has ever shown. The *Idylls of the King* have merits and defects similar to those of *The Princess.* An idyll is a "short poem descriptive of some picturesque scene or incident"; in choosing the name Tennyson perhaps showed an appreciation of his limitations. For his poems are always descriptive, and always picturesque; they are never really narrative. The *Idylls of the King* are no different in kind from some of his early poems; the *Morte d'Arthur* is in fact an early poem. *The Princess* is still an idyll, but an idyll that is too long. Tennyson's versification in this poem is as masterly as elsewhere: it is a poem which we must read, but which we excuse ourselves from reading twice. And it is worth while recognizing the reason why we return again and again, and are always stirred by the lyrics which intersperse it, and which are among the greatest of all poetry of their kind, and yet avoid the poem itself. It is not, as we may think while reading, the outmoded attitude towards the relations of the sexes, the exasperating views on the subjects of matrimony, celibacy and female education, that make us recoil

from *The Princess*.[1] We can swallow the most antipathetic
doctrines if we are given an exciting narrative. But for narrative Tennyson had no gift at all. For a static poem, and a
moving poem, on the same subject, you have only to compare
his *Ulysses* with the condensed and intensely exciting narrative of that hero in the XXVIth Canto of Dante's *Inferno*.
Dante is telling a story. Tennyson is only stating an elegiac
mood. The very greatest poets set before you real men talking,
carry you on in real events moving. Tennyson could not tell
a story at all. It is not that in *The Princess* he tries to tell a
story and failed: it is rather that an idyll protracted to such
length becomes unreadable. So *The Princess* is a dull poem;
one of the poems of which we may say that they are beautiful
but dull.

But in *Maud* and in *In Memoriam,* Tennyson is doing what
every conscious artist does, turning his limitations to good
purpose. *Maud* consists of a few very beautiful lyrics, such as
*O let the solid ground, Birds in the high Hall-garden, and
Go not, happy day*, around which the semblance of a dramatic
situation has been constructed with the greatest metrical virtuosity. The whole situation is unreal; the ravings of the lover
on the edge of insanity sound false, and fail, as do the bellicose
bellowings, to make one's flesh creep with sincerity. It would
be foolish to suggest that Tennyson ought to have gone
through some experience similar to that described: for a poet
with dramatic gifts, a situation quite remote from his personal
experience may release the strongest emotion. And I do not
believe for a moment that Tennyson was a man of mild feelings or weak passions. There is no evidence in his poetry that
he knew the experience of violent passion for a woman; but
there is plenty of evidence of emotional intensity and violence
—but of emotion so deeply suppressed, even for himself, as to
tend rather towards the blackest melancholia than towards
dramatic action. And it is emotion which, so far as my reading of the poems can discover, attained no ultimate clear pur-
gation. I should reproach Tennyson not for mildness, or
tepidity, but rather for lack of serenity.

> *Of love that never found his earthly close,*
> *What sequel?*

[1] For a revelation of the Victorian mind on these matters, and of
opinions to which Tennyson would probably have subscribed, see the
Introduction by Sir Edward Strachey, Bt., to his emasculated edition
of the *Morte D'Arthur* of Malory, still current. Sir Edward admired
the *Idylls of the King*.

The fury of *Maud* is shrill rather than deep, though one feels in every passage what exquisite adaptation of metre to the mood Tennyson is attempting to express. I think that the effect of feeble violence, which the poem as a whole produces, is the result of a fundamental error of form. A poet can express his feelings as fully through a dramatic, as through a lyrical form; but *Maud* is neither one thing nor the other: just as *The Princess* is more than an idyll, and less than a narrative. In *Maud*, Tennyson neither identifies himself with the lover, nor identifies the lover with himself: consequently, the real feelings of Tennyson, profound and tumultuous as they are, never arrive at expression.

It is, in my opinion, in *In Memoriam*, that Tennyson finds full expression. Its technical merit alone is enough to ensure its perpetuity. While Tennyson's technical competence is everywhere masterly and satisfying, *In Memoriam* is the most unapproachable of all his poems. Here are one hundred and thirty-two passages, each of several quatrains in the same form, and never monotony or repetition. And the poem has to be comprehended as a whole. We may not memorize a few passages, we cannnot find a "fair sample"; we have to comprehend the whole of a poem which is essentially the length that it is. We may choose to remember:

> *Dark house, by which once more I stand*
> *Here in the long unlovely street,*
> *Doors, where my heart was used to beat*
> *So quickly, waiting for a hand,*
>
> *A hand that can be clasp'd no more—*
> *Behold me, for I cannot sleep,*
> *And like a guilty thing I creep*
> *At earliest morning to the door.*
>
> *He is not here; but far away*
> *The noise of life begins again,*
> *And ghastly thro' the drizzling rain*
> *On the bald street breaks the blank day.*

This is great poetry, economical of words, a universal emotion related to a particular place; and it gives me the shudder that I fail to get from anything in *Maud*. But such a passage, by itself, is not *In Memoriam: In Memoriam* is the whole poem. It is unique: it is a long poem made by putting together lyrics, which have only the unity and continuity of a diary, the concentrated diary of a man confessing himself. It is a diary of which we have to read every word.

Apparently Tennyson's contemporaries, once they had accepted *In Memoriam*, regarded it as a message of hope and reassurance to their rather fading Christian faith. It happens now and then that a poet by some strange accident expresses the mood of his generation, at the same time that he is expressing a mood of his own which is quite remote from that of his generation. This is not a question of insincerity: there is an amalgam of yielding and opposition below the level of consciousness. Tennyson himself, on the conscious level of the man who talks to reporters and poses for photographers, to judge from remarks made in conversation and recorded in his son's Memoir, consistently asserted a convinced, if somewhat sketchy, Christian belief. And he was a friend of Frederick Denison Maurice[2]—nothing seems odder about that age than the respect which its eminent people felt for each other. Nevertheless, I get a very different impression from *In Memoriam* from that which Tennyson's contemporaries seem to have got. It is of a very much more interesting and tragic Tennyson. His biographers have not failed to remark that he had a good deal of the temperament of the mystic—certainly not at all the mind of the theologian. He was desperately anxious to hold the faith of the believer, without being very clear about what he wanted to believe: he was capable of illumination which he was incapable of understanding. The "Strong Son of God, immortal Love," with an invocation of whom the poem opens, has only a hazy connexion with the Logos, or the Incarnate God. Tennyson is distressed by the idea of a mechanical universe; he is naturally, in lamenting his friend, teased by the hope of immortality and reunion beyond death. Yet the renewal craved for seems at best but a continuance, or a substitute for the joys of friendship upon earth. His desire for immortality never is quite the desire for Eternal Life; his concern is for the loss of man rather than for the gain of God.

> shall he,
> *Man, her last work, who seem'd so fair,*
> *Such splendid purpose in his eyes,*
> *Who roll'd the psalm to wintry skies,*
> *Who built him fanes of fruitless prayer,*

[2] [Christian Socialist, disciple of Coleridge.—Ed.]

> *Who trusted God was love indeed,*
> *And love Creation's final law—*
> *Tho' Nature, red in tooth and claw*
> *With ravine, shriek'd against his creed—*

> *Who loved, who suffer'd countless ills.*
> *Who battled for the True, the Just,*
> *Be blown about the desert dust,*
> *Or seal'd within the iron hills?*

That strange abstraction, "Nature," becomes a real god or goddess, perhaps more real, at moments, to Tennyson than God (*"Are God and Nature then at strife?"*). The hope of immortality is confused (typically of the period) with the hope of the gradual and steady improvement of this world. Much has been said of Tennyson's interest in contemporary science, and of the impression of Darwin. *In Memoriam*, in any case, antedates *The Origin of Species* by several years, and the belief in social progress by democracy antedates it by many more; and I suspect that the faith of Tennyson's age in human progress would have been quite as strong even had the discoveries of Darwin been postponed by fifty years. And after all, there is no logical connexion: the belief in progress being current already, the discoveries of Darwin were harnessed to it:

> *No longer half-akin to brute,*
> *For all we thought, and loved and did*
> *And hoped, and suffer'd, is but seed*
> *Of what in them is flower and fruit;*

> *Whereof the man, that with me trod*
> *This planet, was a noble type*
> *Appearing ere the times were ripe,*
> *That friend of mine who lives in God,*

> *That God, which ever lives and loves,*
> *One God, one law, one element,*
> *And one far-off divine event,*
> *To which the whole creation moves.*

These lines show an interesting compromise between the religious attitude and, what is quite a different thing, the belief in human perfectibility; but the contrast was not so apparent to Tennyson's contemporaries. They may have been taken in by it, but I don't think that Tennyson himself was, quite: his feelings were more honest than his mind. There is evidence elsewhere—even in an early poem, *Locksley Hall*, for example—that Tennyson by no means regarded with complacency all the changes that were going on about him in the progress of industrialism and the rise of the mercantile and manufacturing and banking classes; and he may have contemplated the future of England, as his years drew out, with increasing gloom. Temperamentally, he was opposed to the doctrine that he was moved to accept and to praise.

Tennyson's feelings, I have said, were honest; but they were usually a good way below the surface. *In Memoriam* can, I think, justly be called a religious poem, but for another reason than that which made it seem religious to his contemporaries. It is not religious because of the quality of its faith, but because of the quality of its doubt. Its faith is a poor thing, but its doubt is a very intense experience. *In Memoriam* is a poem of despair, but of despair of a religious kind. And to qualify its despair with the adjective "religious" is to elevate it above most of its derivatives. For *The City of Dreadful Night,* and *A Shropshire Lad,* and the poems of Thomas Hardy, are small work in comparison with *In Memoriam:* It is greater than they and comprehends them.[3]

In ending we must go back to the beginning and remember that *In Memoriam* would not be a great poem, or Tennyson a great poet, without the technical accomplishment. Tennyson is the great master of metric as well as of melancholia; I do not think any poet in English has ever had a finer ear for vowel sound, as well as a subtler feeling for some moods of anguish:

> *Dear as remember'd kisses after death,*
> *And sweet as those by hopeless fancy feign'd*
> *On lips that are for others; deep as love,*
> *Deep as first love, and wild with all regret.*

And this technical gift of Tennyson's is no slight thing. Tennyson lived in a time which was already acutely time-

---

[3] There are other kinds of despair. Davidson's great poem, *Thirty Bob a Week,* is not derivative from Tennyson. On the other hand, there are other things derivative from Tennyson besides *Atalanta in Calydon.* Compare the poems of William Morris with *The Voyage of Maeldune,* and *Barrack Room Ballads* with several of Tennyson's later poems.

conscious: a great many things seemed to be happening, railways were being built, discoveries were being made, the face of the world was changing. That was a time busy in keeping up to date. It had, for the most part, no hold on permanent things, on permanent truths about man and God and life and death. The surface of Tennyson stirred about with his time; and he had nothing to which to hold fast except his unique and unerring feeling for the sounds of words. But in this he had something that no one else had. Tennyson's surface, his technical accomplishment, is intimate with his depths: what we most quickly see about Tennyson is that which moves between the surface and the depths, that which is of slight importance. By looking innocently at the surface we are most likely to come to the depths, to the abyss of sorrow. Tennyson is not only a minor Virgil, he is also with Virgil as Dante saw him, a Virgil among the Shades, the saddest of all English poets, among the Great in Limbo, the most instinctive rebel against the society in which he was the most perfect conformist.

Tennyson seems to have reached the end of his spiritual development with *In Memoriam;* there followed no reconciliation, no resolution.

> *And now no sacred staff shall break in blossom,*
> *No choral salutation lure to light*
> *A spirit sick with perfume and sweet night,*

or rather with twilight, for Tennyson faced neither the darkness nor the light in his later years. The genius, the technical power, persisted to the end, but the spirit had surrendered. A gloomier end than that of Baudelaire: Tennyson had no *singulier avertissement*. And having turned aside from the journey through the dark night, to become the surface flatterer of his own time, he has been rewarded with the despite of an age that succeeds his own in shallowness.

The dramatic monologue, which was brought to perfection by Browning and Tennyson, is the only new poetic form of the Victorian age. It is the appropriate form of an age in which all dogmatic values had been called into question; so that it became more important to understand points of view than to judge. Since everything we know in a dramatic monologue comes through the speaker who looms disproportionately large, the dramatic monologue derives its special effect from the disequilibrium and sometimes even the conflict between our sympathetic engagement with the speaker and our judgment of him. This dual effect is achieved through mixing drama and lyric; so that Eliot, in objecting to the mixture in Tennyson's *Maud* (p. 219), shows that he does not understand the *structure* of dramatic monologues, though he himself wrote them.

In his magnum opus, *The Ring and the Book* (1868-69), Browning tells us the same story over through ten dramatic monologues projecting ten different points of view. Although the poem takes place in Italy in 1698 and does not, like *In Memoriam*, deal overtly with the issues of Victorian England, it is, according to this chapter, a characteristically Victorian poem in its attempt to establish truth as *relative* to psychological and historical conditions, and in its attempt to salvage essential Christian truth from historically obsolete formulations and institutionalizations of that truth. In his stridently realistic purpose, his attempt to pull out of a forgotten and sordid old Roman murder case the Christian scheme of sin and redemption, Browning was trying to write a long poem that would meet the conditions the realistic novelists were meeting. If Browning is in *The Ring and the Book* working toward the novel, he is working toward George Eliot's kind of novel rather than Dickens's.

Robert Langbaum

"The Ring and the Book": A Relativist Poem

In the same sense that Dante's great poem can be said to derive its meaning from a Catholic, and Milton's from a Protestant, ethos—so Browning's *The Ring and the Book* derives its meaning from the relativist ethos predominant in Western culture since the Enlightenment. The first sign of the poem's relativism is in Browning's use of dramatic monologues to tell his story. For though he does not entirely succeed, his aim at least, in telling the same story eleven times over through ten dramatic monologues and his own account in Book I, was to replace the objective view of events of traditional drama and narrative with points of view. Such a method can be justified only on the relativist assumption that truth cannot be apprehended in itself but must be "induced" from particular points of view, and that there can be sufficient difference among the points of view to make each repetition interesting and important as a psychological fact.

Another sign of relativism is that Browning counted it such a virtue for his poem to be based on "pure crude fact." Facts figure as pure gold in the analogy of the ring, which Browning uses to justify stamping an interpretation upon the facts. The poet's imagination, the "something of mine," is likened to the alloy which the goldsmith uses to shape the gold into a ring. But the ring once made, the goldsmith bathes it in acid to free the gold from the alloy; so that in the end, we are assured, "the shape remains,"

> Gold as it was, is, shall be evermore:
> Prime nature with an added artistry.   (I, 28-29)

It is significant that Browning should have felt it necessary to justify a liberty of interpretation which has always been granted poets.

Robert Langbaum, THE POETRY OF EXPERIENCE: THE DRAMATIC MONOLOGUE IN MODERN LITERARY TRADITION (New York: Random House, 1957), pp. 109-36. Reprinted, with author's revisions, by permission of the publisher and the Modern Language Association. The chapter first appeared in PMLA LXXI (March 1956), 131-54. All rights reserved. See also W. C. DeVane, *A Browning Handbook*, Second Edition (New York, 1955); Philip Drew, ed., *Robert Browning: A Collection of Critical Essays* (London, 1966).

But it was just the imputation of poetic licence, relegating his work to the realm of fancy, entertaining but unimportant, that he did not want. His truth had to be taken seriously, which meant in a positivist age that it had to have the facts behind it, had to emerge from the facts. In answer to the difficult question, "Why take the artistic way to prove so much?"—Browning, speaking again in his own voice in the concluding passage of the poem, says the artistic way is best for criticizing a whole false view of things. Since falsehood is formulation that has got too far from the facts, to attack it with another formulation is to awaken resistance and have your true formulation judged false by the logical criteria that established the false formulation. "But Art," he says.

> may tell a truth
> Obliquely, do the thing shall breed the thought,
> Nor wrong the thought, missing the mediate word.
> So may you paint your picture, twice show truth,
> Beyond mere imagery on the wall,—
> So, note by note, bring music from your mind,
> Deeper than ever e'en Beethoven dived,—
> So write a book shall mean beyond the facts,
> Suffice the eye and save the soul beside.   (XII, 859-67)

Art, then, is truer than philosophical discourse because it is closer to the facts, taking into account more complexities, breeding the thought precisely. It shows the truth twice in that it shows the physical facts and the metaphysical meaning behind them—opening out an extra dimension "beyond . . . the wall" because it brings to the business of understanding the mind's deepest resource, imagination, what Wordsworth called "Reason in her most exalted mood." Above all, art is more convincing than philosophical discourse because, confronting false formulations with facts, it causes us to start again with the facts and construct the truth for ourselves.

Yet the judgments of *The Ring and the Book* are by no means "relative"—if we mean by the word that no one is either good or bad but a bit of both. Pompilia, Count Guido's young wife whom he murders, is presented in the final judgment as nothing short of a saint; while Guido is an incarnation of evil. His being evil remains as the real motive and the only one that can explain all the facts of his behaviour—when, after two monologues totalling more than 4500 lines, the complex layers of rationalized motivations have been finally stripped away. What he comes to understand, and we along with him, is that he has hated Pompilia for no other reason than that she is good. Let no one, he says,

> think to bear that look
> Of steady wrong, endured as steadily
> —Through what sustainment of deluding hope? ...
> This self-possession to the uttermost,
> How does it differ in aught, save degree,
> From the terrible patience of God?   (XI, 1373-80)

And he cries out in an unguarded moment:

> Again, how she is at me with those eyes!
> Away with the empty stare! Be holy still,
> And stupid ever!   (XI, 2076-78)

He hates her, he reveals, because she did not hate him in return, did not wish him harm. But not until the end, when the blackhooded Brotherhood of Death has come to take him to execution, when the railing and the spite are no longer of use, nor the steadily shifting arguments ever retreating toward confession of his wolf nature—not until the extreme moment does he strip himself bare in a desperate call for help. He calls, in psychologically ascending order, upon the Abate and Cardinal who have attended him in the death cell, upon Christ, Maria, God, and in the final line:

> Pompilia, will you let them murder me?   (XI, 2427)

That cry is his salvation, acknowledging for the first time, without qualification or self-defence, Pompilia's goodness and his own evil. The implication is that he dies repentant.

Between the moral poles of Pompilia and Guido, the other characters are assigned no less definite places. Caponsacchi, the young priest who helps Pompilia escape from Guido, possesses the heroic as distinguished from the saintly virtues; he possesses, too, the weaknesses of the heroic character when its potentiality is unemployed—dandyism and gallantry with women. But being good in the purely human way, Caponsacchi has a capacity for development not required by Pompilia's unchanging perfection. She is for him the *donna angelicata,* providing him with the crucial opportunity of his life—the chance for heroic exploit and the chance to recognize in her, embodied goodness, and to be thus recalled to his priestly vows and the true meaning of Christianity.

Corresponding in moral position to Caponsacchi is the
Pope, who represents the highest moral attainment of human
wisdom as Caponsacchi represents the highest in manliness
and courage. Although not vessels of Divine Grace, like
Pompilia, it is their distinction to be the only ones (except
for Guido in his final line) who recognize her pre-eminence
and learn from her. It is the Pope in his capacity of final
court of appeal for Guido, who pronounces all the authoritative judgments of the poem—"the ultimate/Judgment save
yours" (I, 1220-21) Browning calls it, addressing the reader.
But if the reader has read correctly, his judgments should
coincide with the Pope's; and to allow no mistake Browning
tells the main events of the story in his own voice in Book I,
in such a way as to shape our judgments of the speakers
before we have met them. The judgments of the poem are
obviously not intended to be "relative"—if we mean by the
word *indefinite* or a *matter of opinion*.

To be sure, there are the characters of indefinite moral
position. They people the world in which the significant
action of the poem takes place; they are the poem's common
clay, its chorus. Browning dubs in the "world" by means of
the three speakers who represent the three lines of Roman
opinion, the pro-Guido, the pro-Pompilia, and the impartial;
by means of the two lawyers, prosecution and defence; and
although they never speak, by means of Pompilia's parents,
the Comparini who, through their mixture of motives and
consistent pettiness, make the mistakes that involve their
daughter in tragedy. But if these characters are in themselves
indefinite, the judgment of them is quite definite. The Pope
condemns the Comparini in terms general enough to apply
to all the small-souled, morally indefinite inhabitants of the
"world." "Sadly mixed natures," he calls the Comparini, who
troop

> somewhere 'twixt the best and worst,
> Where crowd the indifferent product, all too poor
> Makeshift, starved samples of humanity! (X, 1213-15)

Nor are they less culpable because indefinite:

> White shall not neutralize the black, nor good
> Compensate bad in man, absolve him so:
> Life's business being just the terrible choice. (X, 1236-38)

What the Pope understands about the whole tragic Pompilia story, and what Guido also acknowledges in his final moments, is that it is sheer miracle that just this once the good has been vindicated and Pompilia's true worth recognized. All the established institutions for distinguishing right from wrong—the law, the Church, the authority of parents and husband—all have been either entirely wrong, or if partly right have still missed the main point, Pompilia's absolute goodness and Guido's badness. The courts, the lawyers, the representative of the impartial line of Roman opinion, all have committed the "relativist" fallacy of supposing that there must be both right and wrong on each side. Caponsacchi complains to the court of their "relativist" obtuseness. If I insist, he says, that my motives in helping Pompilia to escape were entirely pure and Christian, you cry "absurd!" But if I

> own flaws i' the flesh, agree
> To go with the herd, be hog no more nor less,
> Why, hogs in common herd have common rights:
> (VI, 1722-24)

why then you are indulgent of what you consider my peccadillo with a pretty woman. For the Pope it is precisely the moral of the story that the good was vindicated by just the dandy priest doing what his vows and the laws of Church and State expressly forbid, running away with a married woman. "Be glad," says the Pope apostrophizing Caponsacchi,

> thou hast let light into the world
> Through that irregular breach o' the boundary.
> (X, 1205-06)

And this brings us to the proper sense in which *The Ring and the Book* can be called a relativist poem. It is relativist in that the social and religious absolutes are not the means for understanding the right and wrong of the poem; they are for the most part barriers to understanding. Pompilia is misled by all the constituted authorities, by "foolish parents" and "bad husband" as the Pope puts it, as well as by Church and State in the persons of the Archbishop and the Governor of Arezzo who send her back to Guido when she appeals to them for help. She even turns out to have been the offspring of vice, since Violante Comparini alleges in the course of the poem that she bought Pompilia from her real mother, a Roman prostitute. Nevertheless, in spite of all the wrong external influences, Pompilia finds the right way because her instinct is right. The Pope marvels at the flowering, just where the odds against it were greatest, of this one shining example of goodness vouchsafed his reign, while the plants so carefully nurtured by Church and respectability came to nought:

> While—see how this mere chance-sown cleft-nursed seed
> That sprang up by the wayside 'neath the foot
> Of the enemy, this breaks all into blaze,
> Spreads itself, one wide glory of desire
> To incorporate the whole great sun it loves
> From the inch-height whence it looks and longs!
> (X, 1041-46)

In the same way, the Pope sees that Caponsacchi was in the position for "catching quick the sense of the real cry" just because he had strayed, had his "sword-hand" on the "lute" and his "sentry-station" at some "wanton's gate"; he had therefore a fresh ear for the contrasting moral cry, while pious Christians had grown "too obtuse/Of ear, through iteration of command" (X, 1198-99). Caponsacchi did right not to reason on the merits of Pompilia's case but to follow with passionate spontaneity his immediate perception of the good. "Blind?" asks the Pope,

> Ay, as a man would be inside the sun,
> Delirious with the plenitude of light
> Should interfuse him to the finger-ends—
> Let him rush straight, and how shall he go wrong?
> (X, 1562-65)

Caponsacchi himself tells the court how in deciding to rescue Pompilia he came to see that what official morality called sin was in this case virtue, that death was in this case life, salvation:

> Death was the heart of life, and all the harm
> My folly had crouched to avoid, now proved a veil
> Hiding all gain my wisdom strove to grasp.   (VI, 954-56)

Not only are the judgments of *The Ring and the Book* independent of official morality, they are for the most part in conflict with it and in this sense *relative* to the particular conditions of the poem and to the motives and quality of the characters. Browning is not saying that all discontented wives are to be rescued from their husbands, but just this particular wife from her particular husband. Why? Because of what we understand Pompilia and Guido to *be*. Hence the use of repetition and the dramatic monologue—not because the judgments are a matter of opinion but because we must judge what is being said by who is saying it. The point is that all the speakers are eloquent to a fault and make the best possible case consistent with their own prepossessions and the facts accessible to them. Our judgments depend, therefore, on what we understand of them as people—of their motives, sincerity and innate moral quality. Judgment goes on, in other words, below the level of the argument and hence the dramatic monologue, which makes it possible for us to apprehend the speaker totally, to subordinate what he says to what we know of him through sympathy.

Browning makes it clear, speaking in his own voice in Book I, that the judgments of the "world" are inadequate because of the personal inadequacies of the "worldly" speakers. The speaker who represents the Half-Rome that favours Guido is honest enough in his "feel after the vanished truth," but harbours all the same in that feel "A hidden germ of failure," "Some prepossession" that causes

> The instinctive theorizing whence a fact
> Looks to the eye as the eye likes the look.   (I, 863-64)

In recognizing the inevitability of personal distortion, Browning does not mean, as I understand it, that there is no truth, but that truth depends upon the nature of the theorizing and ultimately upon the nature of the soul of which the theorizing is a projection. After all, Browning justifies by the analogy of the ring his own instinctive theorizing of the facts of the Roman murder case, and there is disparity between the accounts of even such admirable characters as Pompilia and Caponsacchi. But the pro-Guido speaker of the monologue called *Half-Rome* reveals a prepossession hardly adequate to understanding Pompilia's story. He reveals toward the end that he is a married man worried about his wife's fidelity, and that his whole account, with its emphasis on Guido's just revenge, is by way of a warning that he wants delivered to his rival.

The pro-Pompilia speaker of the monologue called *The Other Half-Rome* is, instead, a sentimental bachelor, yet no more adequate as a judge. He represents

> the opposite feel
> For truth with a like swerve, like unsuccess,—
> Or if success, by no skill but more luck
> This time, through siding rather with the wife,
> Because a fancy-fit inclined that way,
> Than with the husband.   (I, 883-88)

Critics have objected to this unfavourable introduction of a speaker who in his monologue strikes us as intelligent, sensitive and sincere; and it must be admitted that we would probably not discern the limitations of the pro-Pompilia speaker were we not specifically alerted to look for them. But it is to alert us that Browning speaks in his own voice in Book I; he wants us to see that the speaker's interest in Pompilia is sentimental and literary rather than moral, and hence a "fancy-fit." The speaker conceives Pompilia as the beautiful wronged heroine of what he himself calls the "romance-books." He characterizes her as

> the helpless, simple-sweet
> Or silly-sooth, unskilled to break one blow
> At her good fame, by putting finger forth.   (III, 805-07)

This is to miss the hard moral core of the saint, diluting her into mere negative and vapid weakness; the conception, in fact, matches Guido's when he pictures an Ovidian metamorphosis in which Pompilia will turn into water after her death (XI, 2050-55).

The speaker is preoccupied with Pompilia's beauty and the theatrical effect of her death-bed scene. He is as inadequate as the rest of the "world" in judging her relation with Caponsacchi:

> Men are men: why then need I say one word
> More than that our mere man the Canon here
> Saw, pitied, loved Pompilia?   (III, 880-82)

though he is too well-versed in the conventions of the romance-books to suppose, like the others, that their love has not been technically innocent:

> oh, called innocent love, I know!
> Only, such scarlet fiery innocence
> As most folk would try to muffle up in shade.
> (III, 894-96)

Just as he casts Pompilia and Caponsacchi in the roles of romance hero and heroine, so he casts Guido as a romance villain at some points, and at others as comic cuckold—in both roles Guido is to be hated by literary convention. Guido is himself aware of literature's antipathy to the betrayed husband, and complains that literary and stage precedents have turned opinion against him. The speaker of *The Other Half-Rome* is so much concerned with the melodramatic surface of the story, and so little with its moral meaning, that he makes no moral distinction between Pompilia and the Comparini, characterizing the parents along with the daughter as innocent lambs ravaged by the Franceschini wolves, Guido and his family.

Whether or not we grant that Browning has successfully dramatized the limitations of the pro-Pompilia speaker, we must agree that in its intention at least *The Other Half-Rome* is perhaps the poem's boldest stroke. For at the risk of confusing us utterly, the poet forestalls just the facile judgment the casual reader is likely to make; he takes a stand not only against wrong judgments but against the right judgment on the wrong grounds. "So listen," he says in concluding his introduction of the pro-Pompilia speaker,

> how, to the other half of Rome,
> Pompilia seemed a saint and martyr both!   (I, 908-09)

and there is, in the context of what has preceded, a note of sarcasm in the last line. Yet the last line does not differ from the Pope's "ultimate judgment" of Pompilia. The point for us, the point that explains the use of the dramatic monologue in this poem, is that the judgments are different because the men who pronounce them are different.

If the first two Roman speakers go wrong through their prepossessions, Tertium Quid, the representative of cultivated Roman opinion, goes wrong through his attempt to evade moral judgment altogether. Browning introduces him with evident sarcasm:

> Here, after ignorance, instruction speaks;
> Here, clarity of candour, history's soul,
> The critical mind in short.   (I, 924-26)

The speaker's assumption that there is neither right nor wrong in the case, but self-interested motives on both sides, is itself a prepossession that leaves him in the end as "wide o' the mark" as the other two. Besides, he reveals an aristocratic bias that covertly favors Guido.[1]

As the institutional mechanism by which the "world" passes judgment, law and the lawyers cannot be ignored, though they are included only to be satirized. "Ignore law," asks Browning with mock surprise,

> the recognized machine,
> Elaborate display of pipe and wheel
> Framed to unchoke, pump up and pour apace
> Truth till a flowery foam shall wash the world?
> The patent truth-extracting process,—ha?   (I, 1110-14)

Law is too mechanical to deal adequately with moral issues, while the lawyers are immediately disqualified as judges of the moral issue by the professional nature of their motives. They speak for hire and subordinate the truth-extracting process to winning the case and advancing their careers. Arcangeli, the Procurator of the Poor who defends Guido, has not only to win the case but also

> All kind of interests to keep intact,
> More than one efficacious personage
> To tranquillize, conciliate and secure,
> And above all, public anxiety
> To quiet,   (I, 1138-42)

and to render absurd his mixture of motives, he has in addition domestic burdens, a birthday-banquet to prepare for his only son, "Paternity at smiling strife with law" (I, 1146).

His opponent, Bottini, the Fisc, because he is prosecuting Guido finds himself

> Pompilia's patron by the chance of the hour
> To-morrow her persecutor,   (I, 1173-74)

her persecutor, we learn in a postscript to the poem in the last Book, when after Pompilia's death he prosecutes a suit for her property, which requires that he prove her to have been a fallen woman. In prosecuting Guido, however, his job is to vindicate Pompilia's fame; but even in doing this, he grants so much against her that his "best defence"—as is pointed out by the Augustinian monk who heard Pompilia's last confession—is itself a calumny. A bachelor, he has not

---

[1] James F. Loucks demonstrates this bias in Chapter II of *Browning's Roman Murder Story: A Reading of "The Ring and the Book,"* written with Richard D. Altick (Chicago, 1968).

the domestic preoccupations of Arcangeli, but is preoccupied instead with his own eloquence and ingenuity and with the frustrating awareness that his masterly argument is only to be read by the court and will never enjoy the advantage of his oral delivery. Bottini's extra preoccupations, like Arcangeli's, obscure the moral issue:

> ah, the gift of eloquence!
> Language that goes, goes, easy as a glove,
> O'er good and evil, smoothens both to one. (I, 1179-81)

Arcangeli and Bottini disqualify not only as lawyers but as men, and it was probably to reveal their personal inadequacies that Browning gave their pleas private and dramatic settings. (Arcangeli is doing a first draft of his plea at home; Bottini is rehearsing his aloud at home.) Arcangeli is much too normal, fat, domestic and contented to appreciate the emotional and moral intensities of the case; while Bottini is the young-old man, disproportioned between emotional and intellectual development, a child with an old and corrupt mind:

> Just so compounded is the outside man,
> Blue juvenile pure eye and pippin cheek,
> And brow all prematurely soiled and seamed
> With sudden age, bright devastated hair. (I, 1196-99)

With his intellectual virtuosity, he manipulates passions and moral meanings he cannot begin to understand.

No less than the lawyers, the representatives of Roman opinion speak to show off their virtuosity. They all reveal at the end of their monologues self-interested motives which disqualify them as judges of the moral issue. The pro-Guido speaker has a vested interest in the authority of the marriage bond; the pro-Pompilia speaker is a bachelor with a sentimental, if not an active, interest in melodramatic violations of the marriage bond; and Tertium Quid reveals in his last two lines that he has been the whole time speaking to impress certain Princes and Cardinals:

> (You'll see, I have not so advanced myself,
> After my teaching the two idiots here!) (IV, 1639-40)

he mutters after an Excellency and a Highness have departed.

By their motives shall ye know them! This is Browning's injunction throughout. In contrast to the inadequate motives of the "world," we have the Pope's high seriousness as he sits out

<blockquote>
the dim
Droop of a sombre February day   (I, 1235-36)
</blockquote>

With winter in my soul beyond the world's.   (X, 213)

The Pope is aware of his responsibility as Christ's Vicar in making the ultimate judgment, and knows also that his judgment is fallible. He is confident, however, for even if it should turn out that he has made a mistake in judging Guido, he knows he has judged according to the light given him, that his motives have been pure:

<blockquote>
For I am ware it is the seed of act,
God holds appraising in His hollow palm,
Not act grown great thence on the world below,
Leafage and branchage, vulgar eyes admire.
Therefore I stand on my integrity,
Nor fear at all.   (X, 272-77)
</blockquote>

To add to the solemnity of the Pope's motives, he is eighty-six and aware that Guido's death may just precede his own, that his judgment of Guido may be his last official act, closely bound up with his own salvation.

The Pope's confidence in his judgment does not rest on the supposition that the truth is directly or easily apprehensible; but neither does he suppose that the truth cannot be found in the "pleadings and counter-pleadings" he has before him:

<blockquote>
Truth, nowhere, lies yet everywhere in these—
Not absolutely in a portion, yet
Evolvible from the whole: evolved at last
Painfully, held tenaciously by me.   (X, 229-32)
</blockquote>

Truth is not in any one argument but can be "induced" from the particular points of view, the way Browning expects us to "induce" it from the ten dramatic monologues. And the judgments the Pope pronounces as evolved truth are the kind the dramatic monologue offers—judgments of character. The Pope does not weigh argument against argument, fact against fact, but cuts right through the facts to a sympathetic apprehension of the motives and essential moral qualities behind the deeds. He relies not upon logic to make his judgments but upon talent, intuition, insight, the advantages of his own character gained through long experience of life and people:

> dark, difficult enough
> The human sphere, yet eyes grow sharp by use,
> I find the truth, dispart the shine from shade,
> As a mere man may,

with "well-nigh decayed intelligence," if what the populace says of his senility is true, but "What of that?"

> Through hard labour and good will,
> And habitude that gives a blind man sight
> At the practised finger-ends of him, I do
> Discern, and dare decree in consequence,
> Whatever prove the peril of mistake. (X, 1241-52)

Thus he decrees:

> First of the first,
> Such I pronounce Pompilia, then as now
> Perfect in whiteness: (X, 1004-06)

Caponsacchi sprang forth "the hero," and in spite of the compromising look of the facts,

> In thought, word and deed,
> How throughout all thy warfare thou wast pure,
> I find it easy to believe: (X, 1169-71)

while in spite of all the arguments and legal rights that Guido can adduce, "Not one permissible impulse moves the man" (X, 537).

All the morally significant characters of the poem cut through facts in the same way. As soon as Pompilia and Caponsacchi lay eyes on each other, each recognizes the other's distinction. And their subsequent relation is carried on by means of such intuitive perceptions. Guido forges letters of crude solicitation which he has carried between them in order to compromise Pompilia. But each knows the other incapable of such letters. "As I," says Caponsacchi,

> Recognized her, at potency of truth,
> So she, by the crystalline soul, knew me,
> Never mistook the signs. (VI, 931-34)

Their relation develops by means of the letters in a direction contrary to the purport of the letters. In the course of receiving them and sending back refusals, Pompilia comes to realize that Caponsacchi is the honourable man she can trust to rescue her, while he comes to realize that she is the virtuous woman whom it would not be a sin to rescue. Guido himself cuts through his own false defences to see in the end the moral truth. He stands for this reason a better chance of salvation than the inhabitants of the "world" who, by flattening out the moral issue, miss the final truth.

Thus, truth is psychologized in the sense that the facts do not reveal it, nor is it arrived at by any external yardstick, whether legal, Christian, or conventional. The moral judgments are definite and extreme, but they depend upon our total apprehension of the characters themselves. What we arrive at in the end is not *the* truth, but truth as the worthiest characters of the poem see it.

Truth is historicized as well, the historical meaning running parallel to the psychological. Just as the facts and arguments do not adequately reveal the moral issue between Pompilia and Guido, so the legal and ecclesiastical machinery of the time proves inadequate to reveal and judge the moral issue. The Pope is distressed by the failure of the instituted machinery because he sees its significance in terms of historical dialectics. "We have got too familiar with the light" (X, 1794), he says comparing his own time, when Christianity is respectable and necessary for getting on in the world, with apostolic times, when as a minority sect it could attract no one not sincerely committed to its essential meaning.

The time is 1698, almost the end of the seventeenth century and of the pontificate of Innocent XII (died 1700); almost the end, as the Pope points out, of Christianity's period of triumph, of the age when for all the heresies and theological disputes the authority of Christianity itself remained uncontested. The Pope foresees a new age to be ushered into life by his death, and asks whether it will be the mission of that age "to shake"

This torpor of assurance from our creed,
Re-introduce the doubt discarded, bring
That formidable danger back, we drove
Long ago to the distance and the dark? (X, 1853-57)

He draws from Pompilia's case both despair and hope. On the one hand, her case presented a challenge which the instituted machinery showed itself unable to meet. The machinery of Christianity showed itself to be by now almost completely at odds with the meaning of Christianity. For was it not by daring to break the Christian rules ;hat Caponsacchi came to virtue's aid, while where, asks the Pope, were "the Christians in their panoply?" "Slunk into corners!" (X, 1566-71).

On the other hand, there is hope in the fact that Pompilia and Caponsacchi did find the right way in spite of all the wrong external guidance. Even in the anarchic age ahead when men shall reject dogma and declare themselves a law unto themselves, some one Pompilia will keep essential Christianity alive through sheer right instinct:

> At least some one Pompilia left the world
> Will say "I know the right place by foot's feel,
> "I took it and tread firm there; wherefore change?"
> (X, 1885-87)

just as in the past Euripides anticipated Christian morality without benefit of Christian revelation. Thus, the Pope comes to see that the truth is something other than the machinery by which men try to understand it. He sees what is pointed out by St John in Browning's *A Death in the Desert*—that "the proofs shift," that myth, dogma, the machinery changes, but truth remains, never in equilibrium with the machinery and sometimes in direct conflict with it. He draws dialectical comfort from the necessary disequilibrium, for injustice shows up the old machinery as inadequate and helps

> to evolve,
> By new machinery in counterpart,
> The moral qualities of man.   (X, 1378-80)

In trying, in other words, to adapt the machinery of understanding to the truth, which remains always in advance of the machinery, man advances his moral understanding.

Just as, psychologically, the truth about a man is larger and always in advance of our formulated understanding of him; so, historically, truth is larger and in advance of the formulations and institutions of any age. Fra Celestino, the Augustinian monk who was Pompilia's last confessor, carries this idea beyond the possibility of dialectical comfort in a sermon, some paragraphs of which are quoted as execrable in a letter of Bottini in Book XII. Let no one suppose, says the Augustinian in his sermon, that Pompilia's vindication proves man capable of discerning truth or his judgments trustworthy. Let us rather draw from the case the contrary lesson that "God is true and every man a liar." For the fact that such a case has come to our attention should warn us of all the Pompilias who have died wronged and unknown. Nor is her vindication to the credit of human institutions, public opinion or

> The inadequacy and inaptitude
> Of that self-same machine, that very law
> Man vaunts,   (XII, 576-78)

but the work of the Pope's miraculous insight, as much a gift of God as Pompilia's goodness itself:

> What I call God's hand,—you, perhaps,—mere chance
> Of the true instinct of an old good man
> Who happens to hate darkness and love light,—
> In whom too was the eye that saw, not dim,
> The natural force to do the thing he saw,
> Nowise abated,—both by miracle.   (XII, 592-97)

The conclusion to be drawn both from the Pope's dialectical perception of the developing disequilibrium between truth and machinery, and Fra Celestino's somewhat Antinomian perception of their eternal opposition, is that fixed principles and the institutions which embody them can never be adequate to judge the truth. Judgment must remain what it is in the Pope—a matter of talent, insight and the essential moral quality of the judge. It must remain what it is in the dramatic monologue—a matter of total apprehension to which formulation is secondary and in some degree of disequilibrium. Truth in other words is relative—psychologically, to the nature of the judge and person being judged; historically, to the amount of disequilibrium in any given age between truth and the institutions by which truth is understood.

Not only does Browning show the inadequacy of most people to judge Pompilia, but he sets the action against a detailed historical background the purpose of which is to show how far the disequilibrium between truth and machinery has gone by 1698. From every side it is made clear that the Church has become a centre of wealth and power, attracting to its service men whose motives are anything but religious. Guido's two younger brothers are priests as the only means of livelihood for younger sons of an impoverished noble family, and it is only the need to produce an heir for the family that has kept Guido himself from turning priest. He has, however, taken minor orders and served for thirty years as toady to a Cardinal in the hope of making his fortune. It is when the hope fails that he marries Pompilia for her money. The Pope finds it indicative of the condition of the Church that Guido has the effrontery to claim clerical privilege in appealing to the Pope the decision of the secular court of Rome. The Pope sees that the clerical privilege is now being used to protect crime.

Guido also expected the nobleman's privilege: "Who, using the old licence, dreamed of harm" (XI, 780), he complains; and he cites as the kind of precedent he has in mind the brutal story of a stableman, Felice, who in the reign of the last Pope was beheaded for daring to strike a Duke who had abducted his sister. "Ah, but times change," Guido complains.

> there's quite another Pope,
> I do the Duke's deed, take Felice's place. (XI, 276-77)

Both Guido and the Pope are aware that the general corruption of the time ought to have guaranteed Guido protection, and that justice in this case is unaccountable miracle, "luck" as Guido calls it:

> What was there wanting to a masterpiece
> Except the luck that lies beyond a man? (XI, 1566-67)

The Pope knows that a routine bribe would unquestionably have obtained for Guido the scrap of paper necessary to leave Rome with horses and so escape to his native Tuscany, where the Grand Duke's court had already declared in his favour and the Papal court could not touch him. That Guido, a thirty-years' resident of Rome and wise to its inside track, should have neglected to provide for such an obvious contingency, the Pope can only attribute to an act of God. And Guido completes the story by telling how, in his frantic efforts to use bribery for obtaining horses without the necessary scrap of paper, it was his bad luck to have encountered just "the one scrupulous fellow in all Rome" (XI, 1639).

It is a nice stroke, however, that the same general corruption which ought to have protected Guido would in any case have undone him in the end. For it is revealed in the Pope's monologue and again in Guido's second monologue that the four peasants from Guido's estate, who helped in the murder, were planning to murder him on the road from Rome to Arezzo, because he had not paid them the money promised. Although in his first monologue Guido speaks of their feudal loyalty and keen sense of their lord's honour, which caused them to volunteer vengeance for his wife's infidelity, the Pope reveals that they cared no more for feudal loyalty and honour than did their lord. "All is done purely for the pay," says the Pope,

> which, earned,
> And not forthcoming at the instant, makes
> Religion heresy, and the lord o' the land
> Fit subject for a murder in his turn.   (X, 952-55)

And Guido, complaining in his second monologue of his bad luck, says that even if all else had gone well, there were still these "rustic four o' the family, soft swains," planning to cut his throat.

In this second monologue Guido again goes over the story of the murder, this time to show that he committed not a "crime" but a "blunder"; for the practice, as distinguished from the professed ideals, of his time gave him every reason to pursue the course he did. He complains of his trial in terms that make clear his disrespect for the legal machinery of the time. Were not his lawyers sufficiently "fools" to satisfy the "foolishness set to decide the case?" Did the lawyers lack skill in law, Latin, logic? Did they neglect to feign and flatter, and were not the judges clearly moved by the flattery? How then did the decision go against him? And in appealing finally to the Pope, had he not reason to expect indulgence from an old man about to die, who professed to be "pity's source and seat"? What is more to the point, he had every reason to expect

> A little indulgence to rank, privilege,
> From one who is the thing personified,
> Rank, privilege, indulgence, grown beyond
> Earth's bearing, even, ask Jansenius else!   (XI, 1778-81)

Actually, Guido and the Pope make the same historical observations, though for opposite reasons and with opposite judgments. Both see the age, to the Pope's distress and Guido's encouragement, as corrupt from top to bottom, and the murder case as symptomatic of the corruption. But they also see in the murder case, to the Pope's comfort and Guido's chagrin, signs that the corruption of the old order is giving birth to a regenerated new order. The ultimate origin of the crime in the poverty and vice out of which Pompilia was born, and in the property system which caused the Comparini to acquire Pompilia in order to preserve their claim to an inheritance; the cynical marriage barter of Pompilia's money for Guido's title; the precedents of injustice and abuse of privilege that Guido relied on and that were amply fulfilled by the decision of the Tuscan court in his favour; the failure of Church and State authorities to help Pompilia, forcing her to turn to Caponsacchi; the shameful conduct of the Roman convent that sheltered Pompilia, then sought after her death to defame her in order to inherit her property; the presence in the Church of men like Guido and his brothers; the brutality of Guido's peasants, which Guido first used to his advantage then found turned against him—these are signs that the ecclesiastical and feudal sanctions have ceased to apply, that the old order has died from within though the dead machinery still grinds. On the other hand, the unexpected accidents of which Guido complains, the approximately right judgment of the Roman court and the precisely right judgments of Fra Celestino and the Pope, even the exceptional scruples of the official who refused Guido the horses—these are signs that within the old institutions themselves lie the seeds of regeneration.

Psychologically, the right instinct of Pompilia and Caponsacchi is a guarantee that truth maintains itself in the human heart *in spite of* history, of external change. But historically, the murder case shows that truth maintains itself *by means of* history. The general corruption that made Guido's crime possible would also have destroyed him in the end, as it is destroying the old order he relied on. In addition, his crime aroused the almost forgotten conscience of the age to condemn him and the old order. That Pompilia and Caponsacchi found the right way in spite of the age, as Euripides found it in a pre-Christian era and some other Pompilia will find it in the coming post-Christian era, means that truth is different from and anterior to any cultural expression of it, and that the cultural expression must be renewed by testing against truth's source in the human heart. But the dying order makes its own contribution to truth, by dying, and by summoning up its own conscience to condemn itself to death. By isolating the truth within itself against itself, the old order hands on essential truth to find embodiment in a new order.

The Pope is aware of the social and revolutionary impli-

cations of the murder case. He is aware that the privileged
class expects him to uphold authority by declaring Guido to
have acted within his rights as lord and husband. That is
why the Pope has Guido executed not in the usual place
but in the Square frequented by the nobility: "So shall the
quality see, fear and learn" (X, 2114)—learn that the age
of special privilege is over. The Pope sacrifices the social
order, and even the Christian era, to Christian truth. The
act by which he condemns Guido and vindicates Pompilia
is the great final act of his life, his gift as dying leader of the
old order to the new order.

The historical meaning of the poem is symbolized by the
references to Molinism, which recur like a leitmotif throughout.[2] Molinism was a fashionable sect in Italy during the
1670's and 1680's; "the sect for a quarter of an hour,"
Browning calls it. Since it was declared heretical and its
leader, Molinos, condemned and imprisoned in 1687, it was
undoubtedly by the time of the murder case in 1698 a lost
cause from which everyone would be naturally eager to dissociate himself, if indeed people still spoke of it as ubiqui-
tously as Browning makes out. But the very question of
Browning's historical accuracy in giving so much emphasis
in 1698 to Molinism is a sign that the short-lived heresy had
advantages for his historical meaning. First, the restricted
life of the heresy and its obscurity in the modern recollec-
tion help localize the poem historically, supplying the detail
appropriate to no other time and place, and the authentic
detail, since there it was though now almost forgotten. Second, the nature of the heresy suggests the stirrings within
the Church that foreshadow the new order. Since Molinos
was a Quietist who taught direct apprehension of God apart
from ritual, Church, and even in certain instances the inter-
mediary contemplation of the humanity of Christ, the heresy
has affinities not only with Evangelical Protestantism but
more to the point with the kind of essential Christianity that
the Pope finds in Pompilia, Euripides and the future Pompilia of the post-Christian era.

Actually, the poem tells us nothing directly about Molinos'
doctrine; we gather its purport indirectly from the characters
who condemn as Molinism actions which strike us as ad-
hering to the spirit, in opposition to the dogma and ma-

[2] See A. K. Cook, "Molinos and the Molinists," *A Commentary
Upon Browning's "The Ring and the Book"* (London, 1920), Ap-
pendix VIII.

chinery, of Christianity. It is this pejorative use of Molinism as a recognition that the times are evil, and as a scapegoat on which to hang the evils of the time, that is its third and most important advantage in the poem. Molinism and the murder case are linked together as signs that "Antichrist surely comes and domesday's near," Guido's crime cropping forth

> I' the course of nature when Molinos' tares
> Are sown for wheat.   (II, 175-76)

We can almost rank the characters morally by the degree of their preoccupation with Molinism and the extent to which they use it as a scapegoat. On the one hand, Guido, the lawyers, and the pro-Guido speaker of *Half-Rome* find Molinists in every bush. Guido links the case against him with Molinism; Arcangeli, in defending Guido, calls it Molinist doctrine that would "bar revenge," the "natural privilege of man"; the Fisc, Bottini, calls Fra Celestino's sermon, "Molinism simple and pure!" Caponsacchi's cynical old bishop, aware of the use to which charges of Molinism are put, half-jestingly accuses him of turning Molinist because he plays "truant in church all day long" from the more worldly duties laid upon him by the Church—duties of society priest and apostle to rich ladies. (To which Caponsacchi replies, "Sir, what if I turned Christian?") Pompilia, too, is jestingly accused of dipping into Molinist books, because she is reluctant to give herself up to Guido's loveless embraces.

On the other hand, Pompilia, Caponsacchi, Fra Celestino and the pro-Pompilia speaker of *The Other Half-Rome* talk little about Molinism and say nothing against it; and the Pope even defends it:

> Leave them alone . . . those Molinists!
> Who may have other light than we perceive.   (I, 315-16)

The Pope sees the Molinists as heralds of the new era, who break up "faith in the report" to return to "faith in the thing." Remembering how Christianity broke up the "old faith of the world," the Pope wonders if it will be necessary in the new era for everyone to deny "recognized truths," as the Molinists do now, in favour of

> some truth
> Unrecognized yet, but perceptible?—
> Correct the portrait by the living face,
> Man's God, by God's God in the mind of man?
> (X, 1871-74)

Just as Guido and the Pope display the same historical understanding of the age, so both the characters who condemn and those who do not condemn Molinism understand it in the same way—as an attempt to purify religion and as a herald of revolutionary changes to come. Whatever Molinos' actual doctrine, Molinism in Browning stands for an anti-dogmatic, an empirical and relativist, a psychological and historical approach to religion. Faith in the report must be replaced by faith in the thing; and the thing, the unformulated but perceptible truth, "God's God in the mind of man," is a step ahead of formulated truth, "man's God." Truth's ultimate source is in the individual mind; so that judgment of truth rests on judgment of character. Thus, the Pope is impressed by Molinism because its adherents make their denials "at peril of their body and soul," while the motives of orthodox Christians are questionable since orthodoxy is prudent for body and soul.

Nor is Browning's Molinism an anti-historical heresy that condemns the past as a mistake. It makes its protest within the limited historical context of 1698, a time when the disequilibrium between the thing and the report had grown too great. The Pope sees Molinism and the post-Christian era it foreshadows as history's way of producing again

> the Christian act so possible
> When in the way stood Nero's cross and stake,—
> So hard now when the world smiles "Right and wise!"
>   (X, 1832-34)

The Church's heresy-hunting impedes the historical process by obscuring the truth, but it also advances history by advancing the decay of the old order. For the Pope sees that while the Church concentrates its attention on the frontier between orthodoxy and heresy, the Christian mainland inside, "quite undisputed-for," decays (X, 1605-13). The historical point is that heresy was not required in Nero's time when no one was likely to profess Christian dogma who had not the faith, and will not be required in the new era when there will again be no disparity between dogma and faith. We hear of no new Molinist dogma to replace the old Church dogma. Browning's Molinism would seem to leave truth at its source in the individual mind, to develop where and as the man of right instinct finds it.

Thus, by precept and example, by its ideas and structure,

The Ring and the Book achieves its meaning through meeting the conditions of modern psychological and historical relativism. If Browning's poem does not offer the same order of satisfaction as Dante's or Milton's, or for that matter Homer's or Virgil's, it must be remembered that he starts with an almost opposite set of conditions, conditions unprecedented in major poetry before *Faust*.

First of all, Browning starts with Goethe's condition that the poem is not to derive meaning from any external standard of judgment, but is to be the empiric ground giving rise to its own standard of judgment. (Faust spends the whole poem evolving the law by which his actions are to be judged, so that we have really to suspend judgment until the end.) Then Browning imposes upon Goethe's condition another still harder one, in that he does not take off from traditional categories, does not like Goethe give new meaning to an old myth, but draws his meaning out of "pure crude fact." He starts with history, and not even official history with its incrustation of myth, but with just the unmoralized and unhistoricized remains of the life that goes on below the level of history, with an old and forgotten scandal.

It is impossible to overemphasize the importance Browning attached to the crudely and even sordidly realistic quality of his story, since he himself recurs to its rock-bottom factuality over and over again in Book I as though he could not exult enough about it. In his exultation he tosses the Old Yellow Book into the air, catches it again and twists it about by the crumpled vellum covers, all because it is "pure crude fact," likened to the "pure gold" of a ring. It has the shape of a book, he says returning to the subject, but is

> really, pure crude fact
> Secreted from man's life when hearts beat hard,
> And brains, high-blooded, ticked two centuries since.
> Give it me back! The thing's restorative
> I' the touch and sight.   (I, 86-90)

And again, with naive wonder, as though he could hardly believe in his good fortune:

> So, in this book lay absolutely truth,
> Fanciless fact, the documents indeed,
> Primary lawyer-pleadings . . .
> > real summed-up circumstance.   (I, 143-46)

The book is an index to a much larger life situation, and Browning exults because he has found for his magnum opus a subject out of life not literature.

In an experience of illumination, Browning saw through the jumbled facts to the truth of the real life situation. To do this he used the alloy of imagination, not as an interpretive but as a projective function: "I fused my live soul and that inert stuff."

> The life in me abolished the death of things,
> Deep calling unto deep: as then and there
> Acted itself over again once more
> The tragic piece.   (I, 520-23)

But for the repristination, the separation of the alloy from the gold once the ring has been shaped, Browning says he retained the sense and manner of the documentation:

> I disappeared; the book grew all in all;
> The lawyers' pleadings swelled back to their size—
> Doubled in two, the crease upon them yet.   (I, 687-89)

For Browning's purpose was to make us repeat his experience of seeing through the facts by projection into the life situation. He had, therefore, to restore the surface jumble; at the same time that he had, in order to convey his understanding, to make certain changes from the account in The Old Yellow Book and to give the facts what they notably did not have, literary form.

He had, in other words, to dramatize the story, not to impose truth upon it but to make the truth accessible, as the smith makes the gold accessible by shaping it into a ring. For though the truth is all set down in the bookful of facts, what has hitherto come of it? Who remembers Guido and Pompilia?

> Was this truth of force?
> Able to take its own part as truth should,
> Sufficient, self-sustaining? Why, if so—
> Yonder's a fire, into it goes my book,
> As who shall say me nay, and what the loss?   (I, 372-76)

No loss because the poet adds nothing to the truth. In imitating in due proportion God's creativeness, man "Creates, no, but resuscitates, perhaps."

Man, bounded, yearning to be free,
May so project his surplusage of soul
In search of body, so add self to self
By owning what lay ownerless before,—
So find, so fill full, so appropriate forms—
That, although nothing which had never life
Shall get life from him, be, not having been,
Yet, something dead may get to live again,
Something with too much life or not enough,
Which, either way imperfect, ended once:
An end whereat man's impulse intervenes,
Makes new beginnings, starts the dead alive,
Completes the incomplete and saves the thing. (I, 718-34)

Here is the new nineteenth-century theory of the nature and function of poetry. The poet is neither the "creator" of one traditional poetic theory, nor yet the "mirror" or "imitator" of another. For while he works only with extant facts, his meaning is not quite there for imitation; he must find his meaning by restoring to the facts a concreteness they have lost in the process of becoming facts, of being abstracted from their original human and historical situations. Thus the poet as "resuscitator" is the superlatively effective psychologist and historian, the arch-empiricist who works toward greater concreteness and not, as in traditional poetic theory, toward general truths. His talent lies in the "surplusage of soul" which enables him to project himself into the facts, apprehend them sympathetically in other words, and thus apprehend their life. His poem establishes a pole for sympathy, so that the reader, too, can project himself into the facts and apprehend their life. For both poet and reader, to "see into the life of things" is to see their meaning. Meaning comes not from theoretical interpretation but from the intensest concreteness.

Thus, meaning is not separable from the facts, and is in that sense psychological and historical, co-extensive with the facts of character and setting. Any formulation of the meaning in terms applicable beyond the conditions of the poem remains partial and problematical as an account of the poem. Even the Pope's interpretation of the events is presumably partial and problematical, though we favour it above other interpretations because of what we apprehend about him as a person. Hence Browning's use of dramatic monologues, to make clear that no point of view is identifiable with the truth. "The same transaction," Browning said of the poem, "seen from a number of differing points of view, or glimpses in a mirror."[3] Just as we perceive the third dimension because each eye gives a different report, so the disparity in points of view gives the lifelike effect. Our apprehension of the total three-dimensional picture is the meaning. But when we try to rationalize our apprehension, break it up into moral or legal judgments or even judgments of fact, we are reduced to partial views, the variegated refractions of truth in the mirror.

These then are the unprecedented conditions of *The Ring and the Book*—not only that the poem was to be no mere illustration of an external principle from which the facts would derive meaning, but that the facts themselves, all of them, unselected and as they came to hand (their sordidness was all the better as a guarantee that they were unselected), were to seem to yield the meaning. It can be argued that Browning does not entirely let the facts speak for themselves; for he not only speaks in his own voice in Books I and XII, but he makes the Pope too authoritative.[4] It is certainly a valid criticism of *The Ring and the Book* that good and evil are not sufficiently interfused. Our judgment is forced from the beginning, whereas it would seem to be peculiarly the genius of a poem treating different points of view toward the same story to treat each point of view impartially, allowing judgment to arise out of the utmost ambiguity.

But such a criticism raises the question whether facts really can speak for themselves; whether a poet can, with the mere accumulation of prosaic details and a workable middle style seldom rising to passages which can in themselves be called poetry, achieve the high transcendental meaning Browning wanted. For he wanted nothing less than to portray in Pompilia the most exalted saintliness (Dante's Beatrice was not, I should imagine, beyond his mark), revealing itself amid and by means of the ordinarily vicious human motives and judgments. The poetry, the total illumination, lies in the dynamism of the whole scheme, really in the backward glance, the reader's sense of having come a long way.

[3] Quoted in Betty Miller, *Robert Browning: A Portrait* (London, 1952), p. 231.

[4] Henry James, who saw a point-of-view novel in *The Ring and the Book*, considers dropping the Pope from his hypothetical novelized version—"as too high above the whole connection functionally and historically for us to place him within it dramatically." ("The Novel in 'The Ring and the Book'," *Notes on Novelists*, London, 1914, p. 316.)

However we measure Browning's achievement, his aim—to make poetry rise out of prose and spirituality out of the world's common clay, to meet in other words the conditions for modern intellectual and moral conviction as Tennyson in the *Idylls,* Arnold in *Sohrab* and Morris in *Sigurd* do not—would have to be the aim, I should think, of any genuinely modern literature. If his method seems to pertain more closely to the novel than to poetry, so much the better for my point. For to judge Browning's poem adequately, we would want to know whether other poets have managed to pitch their meaning higher, given the same weight of clay; or whether the long poem is, for that matter, the vehicle for sublimating a weight of clay.

The relativist conditions for modern conviction might explain, for example, the decline of the long poem and the rise of the novel in the nineteenth century, as well as the almost universal retreat by twentieth-century poets into short poetry —the poetry of momentary illumination in which the illumination is made possible through a personal and temporary rejection of the facts, or rather of the prevailing system of ideas through which we perceive the facts. Certainly, the relativist conditions make the virtues of classical narrative and dramatic poetry difficult to achieve. The weight of clay makes difficult what Arnold, protesting against the effect on poetry of modern culture, called the "grand style"; while the differing points of view, the variegated refractions in the mirror are, according to the new *ars poetica,* a virtue— though a virtue quite opposite from that singleness of view Arnold admired and envied so much in Sophocles, "who saw life steadily and saw it whole."

If we think of the novel as anti-epic and anti-romance, then George Eliot is the most novelistic of Victorian novelists. For she excludes heroes and villains and all violent, colorful contrasts; she tries to do without sensational events and big scenes in which crucial moral choices are made. Her serious characters divide, says John Holloway, "into the good and the weak"; and her weak characters succumb to small temptations that through a process of slow and imperceptible change carry them into wrong positions they never meant to take. Her view comes as close as any novelist's can to that of the social historian; for she sees character as determined by slow, imperceptible natural and social changes —as, in her words, the "sum of conditions."

Like the other Victorian sages with whom Holloway connects her—Carlyle, Disraeli, Newman, Arnold and Hardy—George Eliot compounds out of the science and thought of her time a world-view which seems to make inevitable the morality she preaches. She preaches resignation and renunciation as a duty— because nature is the way it is, because our life is largely determined for us.

JOHN HOLLOWAY

George Eliot

(i) *Preliminary: "Silas Marner"*

George Eliot is quite plainly a novelist who is also a sage. She speaks in her letters of "The high responsibilities of literature that undertakes to represent life"; she writes "it is my way . . . to urge the human sanctities . . . through pity and terror, as well as admiration and delight," or "My books have for their main bearing a conclusion . . . without which I could not have dared to write any representation of human life—namely, that . . . fellowship between man and man . . . is not dependent on conceptions of what is not man: and that the idea of God, so far as it has been a highly spiritual influence, is the ideal of a goodness entirely human." [1] But there is really no need to turn to the letters. The didactic intention is perfectly clear from the novels alone.

In *Adam Bede*, for example—and it is George Eliot's first full-length work—she says that so far from inventing ideal characters, her "strongest effort is . . . to give a faithful account of men and things as they have mirrored themselves in my mind." Realistic pictures of obscure mediocrity serve a didactic purpose: "these fellow-mortals, every one, must be accepted as they are . . . these people . . . it is needful you should tolerate, pity and love: it is these more or less ugly, stupid, inconsistent people whose movements of goodness you should be able to admire." Finally, she gives the lesson an autobiographical import: "The way in which I have come to the conclusion that human nature is lovable—. . . its deep pathos, its sublime mysteries—has been by living a great deal among people more or less commonplace and vulgar."

But George Eliot is not interested only in people and in their good and bad qualities; she wishes, beyond this, to

[1] Quoted in J. W. Cross, *George Eliot's Life*, ii, 293, 442; iii, 245.

John Holloway, THE VICTORIAN SAGE: STUDIES IN ARGUMENT (New York: Macmillan, 1953), pp. 111-28. Reprinted by permission of The Shoe String Press (Hamden, Conn.), which republished the book in 1962. See also F. R. Leavis, *The Great Tradition: George Eliot, Henry James, Joseph Conrad* (London, 1950); Barbara Hardy, *The Novels of George Eliot* (London, 1959).

impart a vision of the world that reveals its whole design and value. Her teaching may be partly ethical, but it is ethics presented as a system and grounded on a wider metaphysical doctrine. Her early novels emphasize how an integrated scheme of values is a help to man—"No man can begin to mould himself on a faith or an idea without rising to a higher order of experience"—and she vividly indicates the forces in her own time that impelled men to seek such a scheme. For one class to be cultured and sophisticated another must be "in unfragrant deafening factories, cramping itself in mines, sweating at furnaces . . . or else, spread over sheep-walks, and scattered in lonely houses and huts . . . where the rainy days look dreary. This wide national life is based entirely on . . . the emphasis of want. . . . Under such circumstances there are many . . . *who have absolutely needed an emphatic belief*: life in this unpleasurable shape demanding some *solution* even to unspeculative minds . . . something that good society calls "enthusiasm," something that will present motives in an entire absence of high prizes . . . that includes resignation for ourselves and active love for what is not ourselves." This is an interesting passage for the social historian, and for the critic of nineteenth-century capitalism too; but its present importance lies in showing what was of concern to George Eliot as she wrote, and how we are justified in searching her novels for philosophy as well as ethics.

Moreover, she clearly saw that these principles did not lend themselves to abstract presentation; to be convincing they needed the methods of the imaginative writer. A striking passage in *Janet's Repentance* asserts that the influence which really promotes us to a higher order of experience is "not calculable by algebra, not deducible by logic, but mysterious . . . ideas are often poor ghosts . . . they pass athwart us in thin vapour, and cannot make themselves felt. But sometimes they are made flesh; they . . . speak to us in appealing tones; they are *clothed in a living human soul, with all its conflicts, its faith. . . .* Then their presence is a power . . . and we are drawn after them with gentle compulsion." [2] We cannot but recognize, even in passing, how Dinah Morris, Maggie, Dorothea and others of George Eliot's characters are just such incarnations. And when, in *The Mill on The Floss,* she writes of the influence of Thomas à Kempis, this appeal of a nonlogical kind is related directly to how books

---

[2] *Scenes of Clerical Life* (1858), my italics.

are written. The *Imitation* still "works miracles" because "written down by a hand that waited for the heart's prompting"; expensive sermons and treatises that lack this essential carry no "message," no "key" to "happiness" in the form of a key to understanding; their abstractions consequently cannot persuade.

Thus it is clear that George Eliot wished to convey the kind of message, and knew that she must use the distinctive methods, with which this enquiry is concerned. But in examining how her novels are moulded to conform to these requirements, there is something which is here of first importance as it was not with Disraeli. For George Eliot was a profoundly, perhaps excessively serious writer, and her novels are coloured through and through by her view of the world, and devoted in their whole dimensions to giving it a sustained expression, whereas most of Disraeli's novels are of lighter weight, and give expression to his more serious views more or less fitfully. It would, with George Eliot, be therefore a mistake to begin by noticing incidents, metaphors, snatches of conversation, or similar details. What must be given primary stress is the broad outline, the whole movement of her novels as examples of life that claim to be typical. "How unspeakably superior," wrote Matthew Arnold, "is the effect of the one moral impression left by a great action treated as a whole, to the effect produced by the most striking single thought or by the happiest image." [3] This is as true of the work of the sage-novelist as it is of classical drama or the epic poem. To ignore it is to miss the wood for the trees.

Silas Marner, perhaps because it is simple and short, shows this most plainly. It is worth examining in some detail. Silas the weaver, expelled from his little nonconformist community through a trick of blind chance, settles as a lonely bachelor in the obscure Midland village of Raveloe; one son of the local landlord steals his savings but is unsuspected, and Eppie, the daughter of another by a secret marriage, appears as a foundling at his cottage and he adopts her. Many years after, when she is a young woman about to marry, and her father Godfrey is middle-aged and has married again, the truth about her birth and about the robbery comes at last to light. Various things lend the tale its distinctive quality. First, the characters and their doings seem to belong to the same order of things as the non-human

[3] Preface to the 1853 Edition of the poems.

world that surrounds them. The little village, off the beaten track in its wooded hollow, is half submerged in the world of nature. The villagers are "pressed close by primitive wants." The passage of time and the rotation of the seasons affect humans and animals and plants all alike. Individuals are dominated by their environment. "Marner's face and figure shrank and bent themselves into a constant mechanical relation to the objects of his life, so that he produced the same sort of impression as a handle or a crooked tube, which has no meaning standing apart." It follows from this that all the people in the book are humble and obscure; they may be attractive or virtuous, but they are all nobodies. Silas is a poor weaver who finds hard words in the prayerbook, Godfrey Cass is a squireen's son and a barmaid's husband, Eppie marries a gardener—even Nancy Lammeter, Godfrey's second wife, is only a trim farmer's daughter who does the baking and says " 'oss." Such, the tale implies, is the staple of men and women.

The pattern of events in which these people are involved is one of "poetic justice": vice suffers, virtue is rewarded. Silas, though unfortunate at first, is a good man, and at last is made happy. Godfrey Cass, who refused to acknowledge his daughter, has no children by his second marriage. Dunstan Cass the rake, stealing Silas's money at night, falls into the pond and is drowned. But this justice is rough and partial. It is not vindictively stern, so much as impersonal and aloof and half-known; it takes a slow chance course, and meets human imperfections not with definite vengeance but with a drab pervasive sense of partial failure or limited success. For the peasantry of such places as Raveloe "pain and mishap present a far wider range of possibilities than gladness and enjoyment." For Silas in his time of misfortune the world is a strange and hopeless riddle. His money is taken, Eppie arrives, through the operation of forces that he venerates without comprehending. Done injustice by a sudden twist of fate, he comes to trust in the world again over a long period of years, as the imperceptible influence of Eppie gradually revives long-dead memories and emotions; over the same period his estrangement from the other villagers is slowly replaced by intimacy. His life is governed by habit, and so is theirs. We never learn whether his innocence ever became clear to the congregation that expelled him as a thief.

Though the book is so short, its unit of measurement is the generation: Silas young and old, Eppie the child and the bride, Godfrey the gay youth and the saddened, childless husband. The affairs of one generation are not finally settled except in the next, when Silas's happiness is completed by Eppie's marriage, and Godfrey's early transgressions punished by her refusal to become Miss Cass. Dunstan Cass's misdeeds are not even discovered until, twenty years after the robbery, his skeleton is found clutching the money-bags when the pond is drained; and this is brought to light through, of all things, Godfrey's activities as a virtuous, improving landlord. Well may the parish-clerk say "there's windings i' things as they may carry you to the fur end o' the prayer-book afore you get back to 'em." All in all, the world of the novel is one which, in its author's own words, "never *can* be thoroughly joyous." The unhappiness in it comes when natural generous feelings are atrophied by selfishness: Dunstan steals, Godfrey denies his daughter. And the consequences of sin are never quite obliterated; Godfrey must resign himself to childlessness, though resignation is itself a kind of content. Real happiness comes when numb unfeeling hardness, the state of mind for example of the grief-stricken and disillusioned Silas, slowly thaws to warmer emotions of kindliness and love.

This novel contains, therefore, though in little, a comprehensive vision of human life and the human situation. It does so through its deep and sustained sense of the influence of environment and of continuity between man and the rest of nature, through its selection as characters of ordinary people living drab and unremarkable lives, and through the whole course of its action, working out by imperceptible shifts or unpredictable swings of chance to a solution where virtue is tardily and modestly rewarded, and vice obscurely punished by some dull privation. The details of George Eliot's treatment operate within this broader framework.

(ii) *General Features of the Novels*

Most of George Eliot's other books express the same vision of life, some of them amplifying it through their greater length or complexity. All except *Romola* and *Daniel Deronda* are set in the same historical period—that of the immediate past. This choice is significant. It is a time sufficiently near the present for manners to be familiar, dull and unremarkable, and for nothing to have the excitement or glamour of the remoter past; and yet sufficiently remote for the rhythm of life to be slower, and for man to be more fully subservient to nature. *Felix Holt* (1866) has the 1830's for its period. "The glory had not yet departed from the old coach-roads." But besides their glories, the coaches evoke other memories; they take us back to the shepherd "with a slow and slouching walk, timed by the walk of grazing beasts . . . his glance accustomed to rest on things very near the earth . . . his solar system . . . the parish," back to the great straggling hedgerows that hid the cottages, to the hamlet that "turned its back on the road, and seemed to lie away from everything but its own patch of earth and sky," and the villagers, free alike from popish superstition, and from "handlooms and mines to be the pioneers of Dissent." The third chapter of this book is devoted entirely to a survey of historical trends at the time of the story, with the comment, "These social changes in Treby parish are comparatively public matters . . . but there is no private life which has not been determined by a wider public life . . . that mutual influence of dissimilar destinies which we shall see gradually unfolding itself." *Adam Bede* (1859) opens in the year 1799, when the village carpenter sings hymns as he works in his shop, and travellers go a-horseback, and "there was yet a lingering after-glow" from the time of Wesley. The actions of *Middlemarch* (1871-72) and *The Mill on the Floss* (1860) seem to be set in the 1830's; while *Silas Marner* (1861) is a story of the early nineteenth century "when the spinning wheels hummed busily in the farmhouses" and pallid weavers, "like the remnants of a disinherited race," were to be seen "far away among the lanes, or deep in the bosom of the hills" and "to the peasants of old times, the world outside their own direct experience was a region of vagueness and mystery."

The total impact of the novels also owes much to the sense they create of historical change; and of how, slowly, indirectly, in unexpected ways, it touches the lives of the characters. Inconspicuous as it is, this does much to suggest an integrated social continuity, of which personal relations between characters are only one part. *Janet's Repentance* portrays the gradual permeation of rural life by Evangelicalism; it records one instance of a general social change. The background of *The Mill on the Floss* is the expanding prosperity and material progress of the whole nation; and when the fortunes of the Tulliver family are at their lowest, Tom is carried up again by the rising prosperity of the firm he works for, with its many interrelated and developing commercial activities. At one point the story hangs upon whether or not to install steam plant in the Tulliver's old watermill. When Silas Marner goes back at last to the chapel in Lantern Yard where he worshipped as a young man, he finds everything swept away to make room for a modern factory with its crowds of workpeople. In *Felix Holt,* personal experience is determined by the Reform Bill's gradually taking effect, and still more by the slow shift of population from agriculture to industry.

But in this respect there is a more massive contribution. Real historical change is quite important in these novels, but it is less important than the complex interaction of town and countryside, of the pleasures or amusements of life with its work and business, of various classes of society, and of social institutions like the church, the village inn, the bank, the chapel, the manor, the schools and the workshop. It is an interesting contrast with Dickens. Varied though his social panorama may be, he is really interested in the occupations of only one social class—his business men are rarely seen in their offices, and if they are, it is usually not to work—and an occupation interests him not for its distinctive niche in the scheme of things, but for what it has of odd or picturesque or *macabre.* His characters sell curiosities or optical instruments or skeletons; they drive coaches or keep inns; they are ham actors, dancing-masters, fishermen; or if simply clerks or schoolmasters, they tend to be oddities or rogues in themselves. But for George Eliot every character has his distinctive occupational niche, and it is this which determines his nature and gives him what leverage he has upon the course of the action. Lawyer Dempster in *Janet's Repentance,* Mr. Tulliver in *The Mill on the Floss,* Lawyer Jermyn in *Felix Holt,* Bulstrode and Mr. Vincy and Caleb Garth and Lydgate in *Middlemarch,* Tito in *Romola* even—all of them have their livelihoods to earn, and their actions are largely governed by the need to do so in a world that is complex and slow to change.

Often these complexities are not treated fully in the novel, but they lend it a depth and variety of social colour. Adam Bede's getting a wife and following a career are not two processes, but one; and as the story proceeds, the relation between him and Arthur Donnithorne is a product of how they stand as rival lovers, and how they stand as landlord and bailiff. In *Middlemarch,* the love-affair of Lydgate and Rosamond is largely a projection of their social and economic standing. Similarly in a minor work like *Brother Jacob*: [4] the story centres upon how a new shopping habit gradually spreads through a country town. "In short," writes George Eliot, "the business of manufacturing the more fanciful viands was fast passing out of the hands of maids and matrons in private families, and was becoming the work of a special commercial organ." Mr. Freely, who is responsible for this "corruption of Grimworth manners," "made his way gradually into Grimworth homes, as his commodities did." His engagement to a prosperous farmer's pretty daughter is an aspect of economic success.

Seeing the characters thus enmeshed in a wider context develops in George Eliot's readers the sense of a tortuous, half-unpredictable, slowly changing world of a thousand humdrum matters. "Anyone watching keenly the stealthy convergence of human lots, sees a slow preparation of effects from one life on another . . . old provincial society had its share of this subtle movement; had not only its striking downfalls . . . but also those less marked vicissitudes which are constantly shifting the boundaries of social intercourse, and begetting new consciousness of interdependence . . . municipal town and rural parish gradually made fresh threads of connection—gradually, as the old stocking gave way to the savings-bank, and the worship of the solar guinea became extinct . . . settlers, too, came from distant counties, some with an alarming novelty of skill, others with an offensive advantage in cunning." Lydgate exemplifies the first of these types, Bulstrode the second. The author, illustrating the general order of life by particular cases, is at pains to ensure that we see the wider drift.

George Eliot also uses the temporal scale of her novels for didactic ends. The slow movement of the natural world is stressed by the great span of time with which every novel deals—a span not packed with events in their variety, but necessary if we are to watch the full working out of even one event. *Silas Marner, The Mill on the Floss* and *Amos Barton* (if we take count of its epilogue) actually narrate events over a full generation. All of the other novels or *Scenes,* except *Adam Bede,* plunge back a full generation to depict the circumstances that originally created the situa-

⁴ Printed in *Silas Marner.*

tion of the novel. In *Felix Holt,* for example, the fortunes of all the chief characters except Felix are settled by the liaison, thirty-five years ago, between the local landowner's wife and her lawyer, and by the elderly minister's marriage as a young man to a Frenchwoman whose infant daughter is now a grown woman. *Daniel Deronda* tells how Daniel recovered the Judaic heritage of which he was deprived at birth. It is the same with the others.

The sense of a deterministic world where everything happens of necessity is increased in these novels by their stress on kinship. George Eliot is never tired of emphasizing how the nature of the parents fixes that of their children. *Felix Holt* depends for its climax on a visible resemblance between father and son. The earlier pages of *The Mill on the Floss* are full of the power of family tradition, the manner in which children reproduce and yet modify their parents' characters, and above all, the sense that kinship by blood is the basis of just such a slowly operating, half-inarticulate interdependence between things as George Eliot desires us to recognize everywhere. The reader who responds to this will see an added point when Maggie rescues Tom from the flood. The details of the narrative may leave much to be desired. But Maggie's action shows how a deep sentiment of kinship may overcome years of hostility; and in essence, it is apt in the same way as Aunt Glegg's sudden change to helpfulness when her niece is in trouble. It is not pure melodrama or pure sentimentalism at all. Again, in *Adam Bede,* the author is careful to bring out the partial resemblance and partial contrast between Adam and his mother, or Mr. Irwine and old Mrs. Irwine, or Mrs. Poyser and her niece Dinah the Puritan. There is a sustained sense of continuity by blood decisive in its influence but almost too obscure and subtle for observation. If there were any doubt that this contributes to a general impression of nature, the point is made explicitly in *Daniel Deronda.* When Daniel tells Mordecai, his Jewish future brother-in-law, that he too is a Jew, Mordecai's first words indicate how this kinship adumbrates a wider system: "we know not all the pathways . . . all things are bound together in that Omnipresence which is the plan and habitation of the world, and events are as a glass wherethrough our eyes see some of the pathways." Kinship is an aspect of the system of Nature.

(iii) *The Basic Selection*

The chief general feature which gives expression to George Eliot's view of things has yet to be mentioned. It is the very strict selection she makes of what characters or events she is prepared to tell of at all.[5] This preliminary selection, necessarily made by almost any artist, is easily overlooked; but of crucial importance. We may perhaps allow the amplitude and solidity of George Eliot's best work to blind us to all that is rigidly excluded from it; yet a large part of human nature she never touches. In all her work, no one is coolly, calmly, deliberately selfish, like Becky Sharp;[6] the least lovable characters are merely half-aware of the pain they cause others. No one except Mr. Tulliver and Baldassare are even alleged to know real hatred, and their feelings are constantly thwarted and attenuated by the course of events. Apart from them, no one feels the sudden, violent passions of anger, or jealousy, or revenge, or spitefulness, or infatuation. (Stephen Guest perhaps feels this for Maggie at one instant, when he kisses her arm, but in the main the situation between them is different.) No one consciously finds pleasure in doing wrong, or in inflicting pain on themselves or others. No one is savage, no one is depraved. The world of serious characters divides into the good and the weak; being weak is essentially being stupid, being blinded to all the consequences.

Necessarily, the incidents are as distinctive as the characters. There are no adventures, almost no scenes of violence, no picaresque episodes or isolated romances. The staple of the books lies in slowly ripening, intermittent, half-unconscious things like disillusion, the quest for insight, growing affection, reformation, or, above all, temptation. Dorothea slowly learns that Casaubon is a false god; Maggie, and Gwendolen Harleth in *Daniel Deronda,* learn that happiness lies in renunciation; Silas's starved affections unfold again in the presence of Eppie; Fred Vincy reforms. To the

[5] *The Lifted Veil,* in many respects quite exceptional, is not taken into account here.

[6] "Rosamond . . . think no unfair evil of her, pray: she had no wicked plots, nothing sordid or mercenary . . . she never thought of money except as something necessary which other people would always provide"; "there may be coarse hypocrites, who consciously affect beliefs and emotions for the sake of gulling the world, but Bulstrode was not one of them. He was simply a man whose desires had been stronger than his theoretic beliefs" (*Middlemarch*). (Compare the account of real heroes in *Janet's Repentance, Scenes of Clerical Life.*)

slow mounting of temptation George Eliot returns again and again. It is a temptation like this which makes Arthur Donnithorne seduce Hetty and Hetty abandon her child; Maggie and Stephen Guest yield to a similar erosive process; so too with Bulstrode, at both the beginning of his life when he makes his fortune at the expense of others, and later when he occasions the death of his former confederate. It is through this kind of slow weakening, even, that Gwendolyn Harleth fails to throw the rope to her drowning husband. So it is with Dunstan Cass stealing Silas's money. *Romola*, of course, is more than anything else an account of how Tito sins more and more deeply without ever really intending evil at all. No one, in the moment of yielding, fully sees the significance of his act; insight is dulled by the pressure of circumstance.

When George Eliot is thinking of how her characters relate to each other, though, two processes interest her chiefly, and they are of this same gradual and half-unseen kind. They are, estrangement, and—in its widest sense—endearment. *The Mill on the Floss* depicts the growth of affection between Maggie and Phillip Wakem, and then Maggie and Stephen Guest; and the waning of affection, except at the end, between Maggie and her brother. *Romola* records how Tito's position is slowly consolidated in his marriage with Romola, and then how she gradually becomes estranged from him. The relations between Adam and Dinah, or Arthur and Hetty in *Adam Bede*, between Felix Holt and Esther, between Gwendolen Harleth and her husband in *Daniel Deronda*, or between Dorothea and Casaubon and Ladislaw and Rosamond and Lydgate in *Middlemarch*, are of a similar kind. They are not phases or episodes, their resolution makes the substance of these novels from beginning to end. George Eliot cares for those aspects of human nature which come nearest to the *geological*. Such relationships may be crucial, but they are certainly distinctive. That by virtually confining herself to them she suggests that they are typical, is what contributes so much to her view of the human situation.

To sum up, then, George Eliot gives expression to her "philosophy of life" by such broad and general features of her work as its characteristic setting in the recent past; its habit of linking a particular story to known historical conditions; its meticulous charting of social and economic patterns; its interest in slow changes and events that have remote consequences; its pervasive sense of the tie of kinship;

and its being rigorously confined to characters and happen-
ings of a quite distinctive kind. If we now turn from these
features to the details of presentation, we find that they too
play an important part; but as might be expected, they in-
doctrinate us less with the speculative than with the moral
aspect of the author's teaching. In doing so they reveal
that, as is natural but important, this moral teaching is at
all points a consequence and inference from her metaphysics.

The general reason why this is so could not be clearer.
For George Eliot, Man is a part of Nature, and Nature is a
vast and complex system of which the parts are subordinate
to impersonal forces governing the whole. The individuals
that belong to such a system cannot be heroes; they have
to be obscure and petty, and their characters cannot but
mingle good and bad. George Eliot never tires of saying
so. In *Mr. Gilfil's Love-Story,* describing Tina at the height
of her grief, she interrupts the story with "Nature was holding on her calm inexorable way"; and in this "mighty torrent"
Tina is no more important than an amoeba or a sparrow.
And in *The Mill on the Floss* she writes, "It is a sordid life
. . . this of the Tullivers and Dodsons—irradiated by no
sublime principles, no romantic visions . . . emmet-like
. . . oppressive narrowness." But if we have a full understanding, we see fine human qualities, though they are inevitably moulded and adjusted by the system. "In natural
science . . . there is nothing petty to the mind that has a
large vision of relations, and to which every single object
suggests a vast sum of conditions. It is surely the same with
the observation of human life." In *Middlemarch* ordinari-
ness actually creates the remarkable: "That element of
tragedy which lies in the very fact of frequency, has not yet
wrought itself into the coarse emotion of mankind." But in
Amos Barton another point is made: people of this "insignificant stamp," even so "bear a conscience, and have felt the
sublime prompting to do the painful right." What is crucial
is that George Eliot's preoccupation with those whose life
is obscure or frustrated determines her portrait of human
duty.

(iv) *The Ethics*

First of all, in this complex world, duty is not always easy
to recognize.[7] We might expect not. But sometimes it *is* easy.

[7] "A thick mist seemed to have fallen where Mr. Lyon was looking
for the track of duty" (*Felix Holt*).

As Mrs. Farebrother is made to say, "Keep hold of a few plain truths, and make everything square with them. When I was young, Mr. Lydgate, there never was any question about right and wrong." This proud, kindly, distinguished old lady is a reliable authority. George Eliot is fairly clear about what leads in moral questions to definite answers. Objectively, duty is settled by fixed and unalterable circumstances—by the constants in the system of Nature. We require "that knowledge of the irreversible laws within and without . . . which, governing the habits, becomes morality." Sometimes the relevant circumstance is an established human tie or bond. "She had rent the ties that had given meaning to duty"; "It was as if he had found an added soul in finding his ancestry."[8] But duty is determined, in the sense of *recognized,* less by ingenuity or logical acumen than by deep true feeling. "That signifies nothing—what other men would think," says honest Caleb Garth in *Middlemarch,* "I've got a clear feeling inside me, and that I shall follow." In *Theophrastus Such* comes the formal—and as it is called, "persuasive"—definition: *"Let our habitual talk give morals their full meaning* as that conduct which . . . would follow from the fullest knowledge and the fullest sympathy."[9] Knowledge itself, if we may judge from an observation in *Middlemarch,* is in these matters a kind of feeling; and the passage quoted from *Theophrastus Such* goes on immediately to relate duty to the natural system, for it says that this "meaning" is "perpetually corrected and enriched by a more thorough appreciation of dependence in things, and a finer sensibility to both physical and spiritual fact." The word "sensibility" is significant. According to George Eliot, we cannot fully unravel the system of "dependence"; we must know it by the partly non-logical comprehension appropriate to it.

So much for what factors determine duty and what processes of thought discover it. In both, George Eliot's view follows from her whole metaphysics. This is true also of what she says about the behaviour that constitutes duty. To her, dutiful behaviour is renouncing pleasures in excess of our

[8] *Daniel Deronda;* see George Eliot's Notes to *The Spanish Gypsy:* "Meanwhile the subject had become more and more pregnant to me. I saw *it might be taken as a symbol* of the part which is played in the general human lot by hereditary conditions in the largest sense, and of the fact that what we call duty is entirely made up of such conditions." (Cross, *Life,* iii, 43; my italics.)
[9] My italics.

obscurity and unimportance, and resigning ourselves to the privations of a system of nature where personal happiness is subordinate and accidental. Resignation is a duty because Nature is as it is. "Our life is determined for us," says Maggie, "and it makes the mind very free when we give up wishing and only think of bearing what is laid upon us"; "She was experiencing some of that peaceful melancholy which comes from the renunciation of demands for self, and from taking the ordinary good of existence . . . as a gift above expectation." Renunciation, for George Eliot, is the essential part of virtue; and it is the chief moral reality implied by her whole outlook.

Vice and virtue contrast with each other point by point. Wrong actions, like right ones, are determined by all the slow complexity of events: this determines them, however, not in the sense of making them wrong, but in the plainer sense of bringing them about. Lydgate sees himself "sliding into that pleasureless yielding to the small solicitations of circumstance, which is a commoner history of perdition than any single momentous bargain." This too is how the thought of a sinful course of action grows in the mind. There is no need to reflect; sin proffers itself freely as what is most attractive. But according to George Eliot, what makes it possible for the sinful thought to dawn and to influence is the converse of what enables us to see the path of righteousness. It is not deep feeling but a lack of feeling, it is an insensibility blinding us to feelings and sufferings in others, and causing us to face life with excessive demands. "He was . . . back in those distant years when he and another . . . had seen no reason why they should not indulge their passion and their vanity, and determine for themselves how their life should be made delightful in spite of unalterable external conditions." Bulstrode, in *Middlemarch,* could combine wrong-doing with evangelicalism because "he had argued himself into not feeling it incompatible . . . the years had been perpetually spinning . . . intricate thickness, like masses of spider's web, padding the moral sensibility." And it is emphasized that his aptitude for wrong followed from a combination of excessive demand and defective emotion: ". . . age made egoism more eager but less enjoying." Every word of that phrase directs us to something in the outlook of the author.

The consequences of virtue and of vice are the one point in George Eliot's view that remains to be stated. Here the case of vice is clearer. Righteousness may be rewarded, or may have to be its own reward, but the ultimate consequences of wickedness are never in doubt. No one in George Eliot's novels ever sins and escapes; even though punishment may be long delayed and its local source quite unexpected. Tito Melema, Mrs. Transome, Bulstrode, in a sense Lydgate, Grancourt—however tardily or unpredictably, Fate ultimately chastises them all. The fate of other sinners is of course less circuitous. And clearly enough, the general action of her stories is largely modified to bring this about. At the close of *Brother Jacob* she says plainly that this is something to make a story worth telling: "Here ends the story of Mr. David Faux . . . and we see in it, I think, an admirable instance of the unexpected forms in which the great Nemesis hides itself."

Thus George Eliot has a detailed theory of human morality, and a detailed account of how it follows from what the world is like. It may seem as though in summarizing this outlook we have first surreptitiously wandered quite away from the methods of presenting it, and then, in the final quotation from *Brother Jacob,* wandered surreptitiously back. But a fuller survey of the confirmatory passages quoted throughout the discussion disproves this: for the great majority of those passages were not isolated reflections, but embedded in the texture of the novels. They commented upon a concrete situation, were uttered by a distinctive character, or appeared in a fictitious argument with a definite pattern of its own. Their significance was always controlled by methods of suggestion that are George Eliot's because she is a novelist.

Hardy's good fortune was that he grew up in a rural backwater, Dorset of the 1840's. He thus "experienced as a powerful reality," says Irving Howe in his book on Hardy, the "organic culture" that elsewhere in England was a nostalgic memory, almost by now a myth. Exposed to the most advanced post-Darwinian thought, the mature Hardy used his experience of Dorset (the Wessex of his novels) as "something equivalent to a moral absolute," or still point, from which to define a changing world.

But by the time of his last novel, *Jude the Obscure* (1895), Hardy, says Howe in this selection, "could no longer find in the world of Wessex a sufficient moral and emotional support." Because Wessex had receded too far into the past to matter, society in *Jude* lacks sufficient definition for the hero and heroine even to rebel against it. Utterly isolated, "Jude and Sue are lost souls . . . their goals are hardly to be comprehended in worldly terms at all"; and this leads to a new kind of characterization and to the diminished importance of plot or external action. For this reason, and because the problem of Jude and Sue is mainly sexual, Howe sees *Jude* as pointing toward the twentieth-century novel. Certainly, the objections to the sexual explicitness of Hardy's previous novel, *Tess of the D'Urbervilles* (1891), and the uproar over *Jude* (unequaled since the attacks on Swinburne's 1866 *Poems and Ballads*) show the accumulating interest of writers, as we approach the twentieth century, in sexual problems and their need to fight for the freedom to treat sex frankly.

IRVING HOWE

THOMAS HARDY

["Jude the Obscure"]

In Hardy's diary for 1888 there appears a note for "a short story of a young man who could not afford to go to Oxford." It would deal with "his struggles and ultimate failure. Suicide. There is something this world ought to be shown, and I am the one to show it . . ." Six years later the projected story had grown into a novel, Hardy's last and most bitter, *Jude the Obscure*. By 1895, the year *Jude* came out, Hardy was in his mid-fifties, an established writer who had composed two great novels [1] and several of distinction. But he was more than a famous or honored writer. For the English-speaking world he had become a moral presence genuinely affecting the lives of those who read him.

When Hardy first printed *Jude the Obscure* as a monthly serial in *Harper's Magazine* between December 1894 and November 1895, he agreed to cut some of its most vital parts: those which showed Jude to be harried by sexual desire, others reporting that Jude and Sue Bridehead did finally go to bed together, and still others displaying Hardy's gift for a muted but humorous earthiness. In the serial Jude and Sue did not have a child; more demurely, they adopted one. Arabella, when she got Jude back and flooded him with liquor, ended the evening by tucking him into bed in a spare room. Today such mutilations by a serious writer would provoke an uproar of judgment; but Hardy, not being the kind of man who cared to languish in a garret, did what he had to do in order to sell the serial rights. In any case, he knew that his true novel, the one later generations would read and judge him by, was soon to appear in hard covers.

[1] [*The Mayor of Casterbridge* (1886) and *Tess of the D'Urbervilles* (1891).—Ed.]

Irving Howe, THOMAS HARDY (New York: Macmillan; London: Collier-Macmillan, 1967), pp. 132-46. Reprinted by permission of the publisher. Copyright © 1967 by The Macmillan Co.; © 1966 by Irving Howe. See also "Study of Thomas Hardy" in *D. H. Lawrence: Selected Literary Criticism*, ed. Anthony Beal (New York, 1956), pp. 116-228; Albert J. Guérard, *Thomas Hardy* (New York, 1964).

Some months later, when the book came out, it stirred up a storm of righteousness. Many of the reviewers adopted a high moral tone, denouncing Hardy's apparent hostility to the institution of marriage while choosing to neglect the sympathy he showed toward people caught up in troublesome relationships, whether in or out of marriage. One true-blooded Englishman, the Bishop of Wakefield, publicly announced that he "was so disgusted with [the book's] insolence and indecency that I threw it into the fire." To which Hardy added that probably the bishop had chosen to burn the book because he could not burn the author.

Later, writing to his friend Edmund Gosse, Hardy denied that the novel was "a manifesto on the marriage question, although, of course, it involves it." This is precisely the kind of distinction that most of the contemporary reviewers neither could nor wished to understand: they were, like most reviewers of any age, blunt-minded journalists who demanded from a work of art that it confirm the settled opinions they already had. What Hardy was getting at in his letter to Gosse is an idea now commonly accepted by serious writers: that while a work of fiction may frequently raise social and moral problems, the artist's main intention is to explore them freely rather than take hard-and-fast public positions. In his 1895 preface to *Jude the Obscure* Hardy made quite clear his larger purpose in composing the book:

. . . to deal unaffectedly with the fret and fever, derision and disaster, that may press in the wake of the strongest passion known to humanity; to tell, without a mincing of words, of a deadly war waged between flesh and spirit; and to point the tragedy of unfulfilled aims.

Nor were these new concerns for Hardy. In his earlier novels he had already shown what a torment an ill-suited marriage can be; he had known himself, through much of his first marriage, the dumb misery that follows upon decayed affections. By the 1890's, when England was beginning to shake loose from the grip of Victorian moralism, the cultivated minority public was ready for his gaunt honesty, even if the bulk of novel readers was not. That marriage had become a *problem,* that somehow it was in crisis and need of reform, was an idea very much in the air. During the 1890's the notorious Parnell case, involving an adultery suit against the leader of Irish nationalism, split the English-

speaking world into hostile camps but also forced a relatively candid discussion of the realities of conjugal life. The
plays of Ibsen were being performed in English translation
during the years *Jude* was written, and their caustic inquiry
into the evasions and repressions of middle-class marriage
may have found an echo in Hardy's book. And through the
late 1880's Hardy had been reading the work of Schopenhauer and von Hartmann, pessimistic German philosophers
who had recently been translated into English; he did not
need their help, or anyone else's, in order to reach his "twilight view" of man's diminished place in the universe, but
he did find in their philosophic speculations a support—he
might have said a confirmation—for his own temperamental
bias.

Hardy's last novel was not quite the outcry of a lonely
and embittered iconoclast that it has sometimes been said
to be. *Jude* displeased official opinion, both literary and
moral; it outraged the pieties of middle-class England to an
extent few of Hardy's contemporaries were inclined to risk;
but it also reflected the sentiments of advanced intellectual
circles in the 1890's. Thus while it is true that *Jude* was not
meant to be "a manifesto on the marriage question," the
book could hardly have been written fifteen or twenty years
earlier. Coming at the moment it did, *Jude* played a part
in the modern transformation of marriage from a sacred
rite to a secular and thereby problematic relationship—just
as those nineteenth century writers who tried to salvage
Christianity by scraping it of dogma and superstition un-
wittingly helped to undermine the whole structure of theism.

Jude the Obscure is Hardy's most distinctly "modern"
work, for it rests upon a cluster of assumptions central to
modernist literature: that in our time men wishing to be
more than dumb clods must live in permanent doubt and
intellectual crisis; that for such men, to whom traditional
beliefs are no longer available, life has become inherently
problematic; that in the course of their years they must face
even more than the usual allotment of loneliness and anguish;
that in their cerebral overdevelopment they run the danger
of losing those primary appetites for life which keep the
human race going; and that courage, if it is to be found at
all, consists in a readiness to accept pain while refusing the
comforts of certainty. If Hardy, excessively thin-skinned as
he was, suffered from the attacks *Jude* brought down upon
his head, he should have realized—as in his moments of

shrewdness he did—that attack was precisely what he had
to expect. For he had threatened his readers not merely in
their opinions but in their deepest unspoken values: the first
was forgivable, the second not.

In its deepest impress *Jude the Obscure* is not the kind of
novel that compels one to reflect upon the idea of history,
certainly not in the ways that Tolstoy's *War and Peace* or
Stendhal's *The Red and the Black* do. Nor is it the kind of
novel that draws our strongest attention to the causes, patterns and turnings of large historical trends as these condition the lives of a few centered characters. The sense *Jude*
leaves one with, the quality of the pain it inflicts, has mostly
to do with the sheer difficulty of human beings living elbow
to elbow and heart to heart; the difficulty of being unable
to bear prolonged isolation or prolonged closeness; the difficulty, at least for reflective men, of getting through the
unspoken miseries of daily life. Yet to grasp the full strin-
gencies of Jude's private ordeal, one must possess a strong
historical awareness.

The English working class, coming to birth through the
trauma of the Industrial Revolution, suffered not merely
from brutality, hunger and deprivation, but from an oppressive snobbism, at times merely patronizing and at other
times proudly violent, on the part of the "superior" social
classes. By the middle of the nineteenth century a minority
of intellectuals and reformers had begun to display an active
sympathy for the workers: they could not live in peace while
millions of countrymen lived in degradation. But meanwhile,
and going as far back as the late eighteenth century, something far more important had begun to happen among the
English workers themselves—the first stirrings of intellectual
consciousness, the first signs of social and moral solidarity.
Workingmen began to appear who sought to train their
minds, to satisfy their parched imaginations, to grasp for
themselves a fragment of that traditional culture from which
Western society had coldly locked them out.

The rise of the self-educated proletarian is one of the most
remarkable facts in nineteenth century English history. Frequently this new man discovered himself through the trade
union and socialist movements, which brought to him a
sense of historical mission, an assignment of destiny and role;
but he could also be found elsewhere. Struggling after long
hours of labor to master the rudiments of learning, he

flourished in the dissident chapels which had shot up in England beyond the privileged ground of the Anglican Church; in the lecture courses and night schools that were started by intellectual missionaries; [2] in little reading "circles" that were formed amidst the degradation of the slums. For some of these men education meant primarily a promise of escape from their cramped social position; for others, no doubt a minority, it could approximate what it meant to Jude Fawley—a joy, pure and disinterested, in the life of the mind. [3]

English fiction was slow to absorb this remarkable new figure, just as it was slow to deal with the life of the working class as a whole. There are glimpses of the self-educated worker in the novels of George Gissing; he appears a bit more fully in the "Five Towns" fiction of Arnold Bennett, and still more impressively in D. H. Lawrence's early novels; and in recent years, as he begins to fade from the social scene, he is looked back upon with nostalgia in novels about the early English Labor movement written by Raymond Williams and Walter Allen.

Now Jude Fawley is not himself a character within this tradition. But he is close to it, a sort of rural cousin of the self-educated worker; and I think it can be said that unless the latter had begun to seem a significant type in late nineteenth century England, Hardy could not have imagined as strongly as he did the intellectual yearnings of Jude. That in his last novel Hardy should have turned to a figure like Jude is itself evidence of a major shift in outlook. The fixity of Hardy's rural attachments was, in the previous Wessex novels, so deep as to provide him with something equivalent to a moral absolute, a constant of moral security through which to set off—yet keep at a manageable distance—those of his characters troubled by unrest. But Hardy, by the point he had reached in *Jude the Obscure,* could no longer find in the world of Wessex a sufficient moral and emotional support. His feelings had come to a pained recognition that Wessex and all it stood for was slipping out of his fingers, changing shape beyond what he remembered from his youth,

[2] [Most notably, the Workingmen's College, London, started in 1854 by F. D. Maurice, Charles Kingsley and other Christian Socialists. Ruskin and D. G. Rossetti taught art there.—Ed.]

[3] In 1912 Hardy remarked, with forgivable pride, that "some readers thought . . . that when Ruskin College was . . . founded it should have been called the College of Jude the Obscure." Ruskin College at Oxford was the first English college designed to enable needy but gifted working-class boys to attend a university.

receding into history. And as for Jude, though he comes from the country, he spends most of his life in the towns. The matter upon which Jude's heart and mind must feed, the matter which rouses him to excitement and then leaves him broken, is the intellectual disturbance of modern life—and that, for good or bad, can be found only in the towns. Not born a worker, and without the political interests which usually spurred the self-educated proletarian to read and study, Jude nevertheless shares in the latter's passion for self-improvement, as well as in the pathos of knowing that never can he really know enough. Jude is Hardy's equivalent of the self-educated worker: the self-educated worker transplanted into the Wessex world. So that when Hardy first conceived of Jude in that notable clause, "a young man who could not go to Oxford," he was foreshadowing not merely one man's deprivation but the turmoil of an entire social group.

Socially, Jude hovers somewhere between an old-fashioned artisan and a modern worker. The kind of work he does, restoring old churches, pertains to the traditional English past, but the way he does it, hiring himself out for wages, points to the future. His desire for learning, both as a boy trying to come by a Greek grammar and then as a man walking awestruck through the chill streets of Christminster (Oxford), is portrayed by Hardy with enormous sympathy. But to stress this sympathy is not at all to share the view of some critics that Hardy is so deeply involved with Jude's yearnings, he cannot bring to bear upon them any critical irony. What but somberly ironic is the incident in which Jude receives a crushing reply from the Christminster master to whom he has applied for advice, and what but devastatingly ironic is the scene in which Jude drunkenly flaunts his Latin before the good-natured uncomprehending artisans at the Christminster tavern? Jude is a thoroughly individualized figure, an achievement made possible by Hardy's balance of sympathy and distance; but Jude's personal drama is woven from the materials of historical change, the transformation and uprooting of traditional English life.

The same holds true for Sue Bridehead. She is a triumph of psychological portraiture—and to that we shall return. But the contours of her psychology are themselves shaped by a new historical situation. She could not possibly appear in a novel by Jane Austen or Dickens or Thackeray; her style of thought, her winsome charms and maddening indecisions, are all conditioned by the growth of intellectual skepticism and modernist sensibility. She is the first major anticipation in the English novel of that profoundly affecting and troublesome creature: the modern girl. If she could not appear in an earlier nineteenth century novel, she certainly could in a twentieth century one—the only difference would probably be that now, living in her neat brownstone apartment in Manhattan or stylish flat in London and working for a publishing house or television company, she would have learned to accept a "healthier" attitude toward sex. Or at the least, she would have learned to pretend it.

In the' last third of the nineteenth century, the situation of women changed radically: from subordinate domesticity and Victorian repression to the first signs of emancipation, leading often enough to the poignant bewilderments of a Sue Bridehead. So that while Sue, like Jude, is an intensely individualized figure, she is also characteristic of a moment in recent history; indeed, the force with which Hardy has made her so uniquely alive depends a great deal on the accuracy with which he has placed her historically.

Between Jude and Sue there is a special closeness, and this too has been historically conditioned. It is the closeness of lovers, but more than that. It is the closeness of intellectual companions, but more again. In Jane Austen's *Pride and Prejudice* Elizabeth Bennet and Mr. Darcy make their way past comic misunderstandings to a happy marriage, for they share a sense of superior cultivation and, with the additional advantage of status, can expect to keep themselves in a semi-protected circle, a little apart from the dull but worthy people surrounding them. At home in their society, they can yet maintain a comfortable distance from it. In Emily Brontë's *Wuthering Heights* Heathcliff and Cathy, in their moments of ecstasy, cut themselves off from common life, neither accepting nor rebelling against society, but refusing the very idea of it. In George Eliot's *Middlemarch* Dorothea Brooke and Lydgate, the two figures who should come together but through force of circumstances and vanity do not, envision a union in which they would struggle in behalf of those serious values their society disdains. They know the struggle would be difficult, but do not regard it as impossible. But by *Jude the Obscure* there is neither enclave nor retreat, evasion nor grasped opportunity for resistance. Jude and Sue are lost souls; they have no place in the world they can cherish or to which they can retreat;

their goals are hardly to be comprehended in worldly terms at all. Lonely, distraught, rootless, they cling to one another like children in the night. Exposed to the racking sensations of homelessness, they become prey to a kind of panic whenever they are long separated from each other. The closeness of the lost—clutching, solacing and destroying one another— is a closeness of a special kind, which makes not for heroism or tragedy or even an exalted suffering, but for that somewhat passive "modern" sadness which suffuses *Jude the Obscure*.

Now it would be foolish to suppose that the social history of nineteenth century England can be neatly registered in this sketch of changing assumptions from Jane Austen to Thomas Hardy—though by 1900 there was, I think, good reason for cultivated persons to feel more estranged from their society than their great-grandparents might have felt in 1800. What can plausibly be assumed is that there were serious historical pressures behind the increasingly critical attitudes that nineteenth century English novelists took toward their society. Hardy comes at the end of one tradition, that of the solid extroverted English novel originating mostly with Henry Fielding; but he also comes at the beginning of another tradition, that of the literary "modernism" which would dominate the twentieth century. In personal background, novelistic technique, choice of locale and characters, Hardy remains mostly of the past; but in his distinctive sensibility, he is partly of the future. He moves somewhat beyond, though he does not quite abandon, the realistic social novel such as George Eliot and Thackeray wrote, and by *Jude the Obscure* he is composing the kind of fiction about which one is tempted to employ such terms as expressionist, stylized, grotesque, symbolic distortion and a portrait of extreme situations. None of these is wholly to the point, yet all suggest that this last of Hardy's novels cannot be fully apprehended if read as a conventional realistic work. Not by its fullness or probability as a rendering of common life, but by its power and coherence as a vision of modern deracination—so must the book be judged. It is not a balanced or temperate work; it will not satisfy well-adjusted minds content with the blessings of the wholesome; it does not pretend to show the human situation in its many-sidedness. Committed to an extreme darkness of view, a promethean resistance to fatality, *Jude the Obscure* shares in the spirit of the Book of Job, whose author seems also to have been a pessimist. In the history of Hardy criticism *Jude the Obscure* provides a touchstone of taste: the older and more traditional critics, loving Hardy for the charm and comeliness of his Wessex portraiture, have usually disparaged the book as morbid, while the more recent and modern critics are inclined to regard its very starkness as a sign of truth.

To present *Jude the Obscure* as a distinctively modern novel is surely an exaggeration; but it is an exaggeration I think valuable to propose, since it helps to isolate those elements which make the book seem so close to us in spirit. There is, in regard to *Jude the Obscure,* an experience shared by many of its readers: we soon notice its fragility of structure, we are likely to be troubled by its persistent depressiveness and its tendency to prompt a fate already more than cruel, yet at the end we are forced to acknowledge that the book has moved and shaken us. This seeming paradox is almost impossible to explain if *Jude* is regarded as a conventional realistic novel; it becomes easier to account for if the book is read as a dramatic fable in which the traditional esthetic criteria of unity and verisimilitude are subordinated to those of a distended expressiveness.

In Hardy's earlier novels, as in most of nineteenth century English fiction, characters tend to be presented as fixed and synthesized entities, as knowable public events. They function in a social medium; they form the sum or resultant of a set of distinguishable traits; they act out, in their depicted conduct, the consequences and implications of these traits; and their very "meaning" as characters in a novel derives from the action to which they are entirely bound. In a book like *The Mayor of Casterbridge* the central figure, Michael Henchard, becomes known to us through his action: what he does is what he is. It would be impudent to suppose that in writing *The Mayor* Hardy did not realize that human beings have a complex inner life, or that there are discrepancies between one's inner and outer, private and public, experience. Of course he knew this, and so did such novelists as Fielding, Jane Austen and Thackeray. But in their work, as a rule, the inner life of the characters is to be inferred from their public behavior, or from the author's analytic synopses.

By *Jude the Obscure* Hardy is beginning to move away from this mode of characterization. He is still quite far from that intense hovering scrutiny to which James subjects

his figures, nor does he venture upon that dissolution of
public character into a stream of psychic notation and event
which can be found in Virginia Woolf and James Joyce.
Yet we are made aware, while reading *Jude the Obscure,*
that human character is being regarded as severely problematic, open to far-reaching speculative inquiry, and perhaps beyond certain knowledge; that the character of some-
one like Sue Bridehead must be seen not as a coherent
force realizing itself in self-consistent public action, but as
an amorphous and ill-charted arena in which irrational impulses conflict with one another; and that behind the interplay of events occupying the foreground of the novel there
is a series of distorted psychic shadows which, with some
wrenching, can be taken to provide the true "action" of
the book.

Thinking, for example, of Jude Fawley, we are inclined
to see him as a man whose very being constitutes a kind of
battlefield and who matters, consequently, more for what
happens within him than for what happens to him. He is
racked by drives he cannot control, drives he barely understands. Powerfully sexed, drawn immediately to Arabella's
hearty if somewhat soiled physical life, Jude is in constant
revolt against his own nature. (That revolt comprises a
major portion of the novel's inner action "behind" its visible
action.) Jude responds far more spontaneously to Arabella
than to Sue, for Arabella is unmistakably female and every
now and then he needs a bit of wallowing in sex and drink
to relieve him from the strain of his ambition and spirituality.
At the same time Jude is forever caught up with Sue, who
represents an equivalent or extension of his unsettled consciousness, quick and brittle as he is slow and cluttered,
and therefore all the more attractive to him, as a vivid bird
might be to a bear. The two of them are linked in seriousness, in desolation, in tormenting kindness, but above all,
in an overbred nervousness. Theirs is a companionship of
the nerves.

At least in part, Jude seems an anticipation of modern
rationality struggling to become proudly self-sufficient and
thereby cutting itself off from its sources in physical life.
Though he is born in the country and lives mostly in towns,
Jude could soon enough adapt himself to the twentieth
century city: his mental life, in its creasing divisions and
dissociations, is that of the modern metropolis. Destined
to the role of stranger, he stops here and rests there, but

without community, place or home. His frustration derives not so much from a denial of his desires as from their crossing and confusion; and as he struggles to keep in harmony his rumbling sensuality, his diffused ambition and his high ethical intent, one is reminded a little of St. Augustine's plaint to God: "Thou has counselled a better course than thou hast permitted."

Even more than Jude, Sue Bridehead invites psychological scrutiny; indeed, she is one of the great triumphs of psychological portraiture in the English novel. Sue is that terrifying specter of our age, before whom men and cultures tremble: she is an *interesting* girl. She is promethean in mind but masochist in character; and the division destroys her, making a shambles of her mind and a mere sterile discipline of her character. She is all intellectual seriousness, but without that security of will which enables one to live out the consequences of an idea to their limit. She is all feminine charm, but without body, without flesh or smell, without femaleness. Lacking focused sexuality, she casts a vaguely sexual aura over everything she touches. Her sensibility is kindled but her senses are mute. Quite without pride in status or self, she is consumed by vanity, the vanity of the sufferer who takes his suffering as a mark of distinction and bears a cross heavier than even fate might demand. Sue cannot leave anything alone, neither her men nor herself: she needs always to be tampering and testing, communicating and quivering. D. H. Lawrence, quick to see in Sue Bridehead the antithesis of his idea of the woman, writes of her with a fascinated loathing:

She is the production of the long selection by man of the woman in whom the female is subordinate to the male principle. . . .
Her female spirit did not wed with the male spirit . . . Her spirit submitted to the male spirit, owned the priority of the male spirit, wished to become the male spirit. . . .
One of the supremest products of our civilization is Sue, and a product that well frightens us. . . .
She must, by the constitution of her nature, remain quite physically intact, for the female was atrophied in her, to the enlargement of the male activity. Yet she wanted some quickening for this atrophied female. She wanted even kisses. That the new rousing might give her a sense of life. But she could only *live* in the mind . . .
Here, then, was her difficulty: to find a man whose vitality could infuse her and make her live, and who would not, at

the same time, demand of her a return of the female impulse into him. What man could receive this drainage, receiving nothing back again? He must either die or revolt.

Yet one thing more, surely the most important, must be said about Sue Bridehead. As she appears in the novel itself, rather than in the grinder of analysis, she is an utterly charming and vibrant creature. We grasp directly, and not merely because we are told, why Jude finds himself unable to resist Sue. Hardy draws her with a marvelous plasticity, an affectionate yet critical attentiveness. She is happily charming when she first encounters Jude at the martyr's cross: "I am not going to meet you just there, for the first time in my life! Come farther on." She is pathetically charming when she escapes the training school and, dripping wet, comes to Jude's chambers. And there is even charm of a morbid kind when she rehearses in church with Jude the wedding she is soon to seal with Phillotson. "I like to do things like this," she tells him, " in the delicate voice of an epicure in emotions"—and in that remark lives a universe of unrest and perversity.

What has been said here about the distinctively "modern" element in *Jude the Obscure* holds not merely for its characterization but also for its narrative structure. The novel does not depend primarily on a traditional plot, by means of which there is revealed and acted out a major destiny, such as Henchard's in *The Mayor of Casterbridge*. A plot consists of an action purposefully carved out of time, that is, provided with a beginning, sequence of development and climax, so that it will create the impression of completeness. Often this impression comes from the sense that the action of a novel, as given shape by the plot, has exhausted its possibilities of significant extension; the problems and premises with which it began have reached an appropriate terminus. Thus we can say that in the traditional kind of novel it is usually the plot which carries or releases a body of meanings: these can be profound or trivial, comic or tragic. *The Mayor of Caster-bridge* contains a plot which fulfills the potential for self-destruction in the character of Henchard—but it is important to notice that in *this* kind of novel we would have no knowledge of that potential except insofar as we can observe its effects through an action. Plot here comes to seem inseparable from meaning, and meaning to inhere in plot.

When a writer works out a plot, he tacitly assumes that

there is a rational structure in human conduct, that this structure can be ascertained, and that doing so he is enabled to provide his work with a sequence of order. But in "modernist" literature these assumptions come into question. In a work written on the premise that there is no secure meaning in the portrayed action, or that while the action can hold our attention and rouse our feelings, we cannot be certain, indeed must remain uncertain, as to the possibilities of meaning—in such a characteristically modern work what matters is not so much the plot but a series of *situations,* some of which can be portrayed statically, through tableaux, set-pieces, depth psychology, and others dynamically, through linked episodes, stream of consciousness, etc. Kafka's fiction, Joyce's novels, some of Faulkner's, like *The Sound and the Fury*—these all contain situations rather than plots. *Jude the Obscure* does not go nearly so far along the path of modernism as these works, but it goes as far as Hardy could. It is consistently a novel in which plot does not signify nearly so much as in his more traditional novels.

With a little trouble one could block out the main lines of a plot in *Jude the Obscure*: the protagonist, spurred by the dominant needs of his character, becomes involved in a series of complications, and these, in turn, lead to a climax of defeat and death. Yet the curve of action thus described would not, I think, bring one to what is most valuable and affecting in the novel—as a similar kind of description would in regard to *The Mayor of Casterbridge*. What is essential in *Jude,* surviving and deepening in memory, is a series of moments rather than a sequence of actions. These moments—one might also call them panels of representation—tend to resemble snapshots rather than moving pictures, concentrated vignettes rather than worked-up dramatic scenes. They center upon Jude and Sue at critical points in their experience, at the times they are together, precious and intolerable as these are, and the times they are apart, necessary and hateful as these are. Together, Jude and Sue anticipate that claustrophobic and self-destructive concentration on "personal relationships" which is to be so pervasive a theme in the twentieth century novel. They suffer, as well, from another "modern" difficulty: that of thoughtful and self-reflective persons who have become so absorbed with knowing their experience, they become unable to live it. Their predicament is "tragic" in that deeply serious and modern sense of the word which teaches us that human waste, the waste of spirit and potential, is a terrible thing. Yet a tragedy in any classical sense *Jude* is not, for it directs our attention not to the fateful action of a looming protagonist but to the inner torments of familiar contemporaries. In classical tragedy, the hero realizes himself through an action. In the modern novel, the central action occurs within the psyche of the hero. And *Jude*, in the last analysis, is a novel dominated by psychology.

It is not the kind of book that can offer the lure of catharsis or the relief of conciliation. It does not pretend to satisfy the classical standard of a composure won through or after suffering: for the quality it communicates most strongly is that of naked pain. Awkward, subjective, over-wrought and embittered, *Jude the Obscure* contains moments of intense revelation, at almost any point where the two central figures come together, and moments of glaring falsity, as in the botched incident of Father Time's death. (Botched not in conception but in execution: it was a genuine insight to present the little boy as one of those who were losing the will to live, but a failure in tact to burden him with so much philosophical weight.) Such mixtures of psychological veracity and crude melodrama are characteristic of Hardy, a novelist almost always better in parts than the whole. Yet the final impact of the book is shattering. Here, in its first stirrings, is the gray poetry of modern loneliness, which Jude brings to apotheosis in the terrible words, *"Let the day perish wherein I was born, and the night in which it was said, There is a man child conceived."*

The mid-Victorian passion for realistic detail went with a militant disregard for artistic conventions. The result was the notorious bad taste of the period, which showed up particularly in ornament—where literalism created a world in which a critic could ask, of a table supported by swans, "why swans should make their nests under a table at the risk of having their necks broken by everyone seated at it." In this witty and wide-ranging chapter, Jerome Buckley relates the industrial designers who "sought to conceal the function of their machines with the intricacies of machine-made ornament" to certain bad mid-century poets, the so-called Spasmodics, who wanted, on the one hand, to be realistic and, on the other, to spiritualize with irrelevant ornament their prosaic subject matter.

But even the best writers of the time prided themselves on factual accuracy. So did the Pre-Raphaelite painters. Yet the long-range effect of Pre-Raphaelite art, if we trace the effect from Rossetti through Morris and Burne-Jones to Beardsley, was surely to increase the respect for design or pattern; just as the long-range effect of Ruskin and Morris was, in spite of their misguided hatred of machine production, to increase the respect for functionalism in architecture and interior decoration. It is against the background of mid-Victorian literalism that we should understand late-Victorian aestheticism—Pater's pronouncement in the 1877 "School of Giorgione" (*The Renaissance*) that art tries to obliterate the distinction between content and form, that *"All art constantly aspires toward the condition of music"*; or Oscar Wilde's brilliantly paradoxical attack, in "The Decay of Lying" (1889), on writers who have lost the art of lying, and on readers who think art is to be valued for its ability to tell the literal truth about things.

JEROME HAMILTON BUCKLEY

Victorian Taste

Then came that great event, the Exhibition,
When England dared the world to competition. . . .
But still, I hold, we were triumphant seen
In iron, coal, and many a huge machine. . . .
Peace-men had then their beatific vision;
And Art-schools were to render earth Elysian.
            —PHILIP JAMES BAILEY

Though hardly a Christian Socialist, Prince Albert was almost as eager as Kingsley himself to quicken the moral conscience of an industrial England. While he could have no recourse to direct attack upon the abuses of capital, he could at least rebuke the insularity of British manufacturers who remained suspicious of his alien tastes. Accordingly, guided by the vision of a universal brotherhood to be grounded upon civilized technology and peaceful commerce, he informed all plans for the Great Exhibition of 1851 with his own "religious" impulse; and ultimately on the memorable opening day he presided over this first world's fair with true Christian humility amid all the pageantry of pomp and circumstance. If few of the exhibitors he attracted to London shared the purity of his motives, none entirely escaped the sense of interdependence which Albert sought earnestly to engender. Even the official catalogue bore some impress of his moral purpose; its very title page announced—in Latin and in English—a divine sanction for the miracles of the nineteenth century's inventive genius:

Say not the discoveries we make are our own—
The germs of every art are implanted within us,
And God our instructor, out of that which is concealed,
Develops the faculties of invention.

Not all, to be sure, among the thousands who converged on Hyde Park were moved to religious awe by the visible triumph of the machine; for the actual "works of industry

Jerome Hamilton Buckley, THE VICTORIAN TEMPER: A STUDY IN LITERARY CULTURE (Cambridge, Mass.: Harvard University Press, 1951), pp. 124-42. Reprinted by permission of the publisher, copyright 1951 by the President and Fellows of Harvard College. See also Kenneth Clark, *The Gothic Revival: An Essay in the History of Taste* (New York, 1929).

of all nations," for which the Crystal Palace had been designed, were in truth largely void of spiritual intent. But many felt dwarfed by the huge glass house and at the same time strangely exalted by the vague awareness that a destiny too large for their comprehension was shrinking the limits of the world community. On Sundays countless pilgrims to the shrine of industry crowded the metropolitan churches to offer thanks to the favoring Providence that had vouchsafed the incredible progress of man; and even St. Paul's and Westminster, closed to worshipers for many generations, were temporarily opened for public services. William Whewell, D.D., the Master of Trinity College, Cambridge, was quite overpowered by the spectacle of "millions upon millions, streaming to [the fair], gazing their fill, day after day, at this wonderful vision, . . . comparing, judging, scrutinizing the treasures produced by the all-bounteous earth, and the indomitable efforts of man, from pole to pole." And as he himself measured the science of the West against all the products of the gorgeous East, the Reverend Dr. Whewell felt that "surely that mighty thought of a PROGRESS in the life of nations is not an empty dream; and surely our progress has carried us beyond them"; for "there," he said, "Art labours for the rich alone; here she works for the poor no less; . . . here the man who is powerful in the weapons of peace, capital and machinery, uses them to give comfort and enjoyment to the public whose servant he is, and thus becomes rich while he enriches others with his goods."[1] In the presence of such reassuring optimism, the congregation assembled in St. Margaret's four days after the grand opening of the Exhibition was naturally rather puzzled to make sense of Kingsley's bitter warning that no scientific advance could long conceal the fundamental atheism of modern culture.[2]

As newly appointed Laureate, Tennyson felt it only proper to commend Victoria's share in having

> *brought a vast design to pass,*
> *When Europe and the scattered ends*
> *Of our fierce world were mixt as friends*
> *And brethren, in her halls of glass.*[3]

[1] William Whewell, "The General Bearing of the Great Exhibition on the Progress of Art and Science," in *Lectures on the Results of the Great Exhibition of 1851* (London, 1852), pp. 12, 18-19.

[2] See Mrs. Kingsley, ed., *Charles Kingsley, His Letters and Memories of His Life* (New York, 1877), p. 140.

[3] Stanza added to "To the Queen," dedication to *In Memoriam*, 1851; the lines were later dropped. See also Hallam Tennyson, *Memoir*, I, 340.

But for his own part, he thought the halls themselves more remarkable than all the ingenious exhibits they sheltered. And however frequent his lapses as a judge of things aesthetic, his enthusiasm for the Crystal Palace was not misplaced. Long after Ruskin had dismissed the great greenhouse as "neither a palace nor of crystal," as merely a glass envelope built "to exhibit the paltry arts of our fashionable luxury,"[4] Joseph Paxton's original plans were to find a vital place in the story of a new architecture.[5] For the Crystal Palace was on many counts the most revolutionary building of the Victorian era, the one most daring in its use of "functional" materials. The masters of an older style had thought that the outer wall must serve always as a weighty and weight-bearing mass designed with due proportion to enclose finite space. But the Crystal Palace, breaking all orthodox precedent, raised its airy shell, supported by a vertebrate structure of light blue iron girders, as a thin transparent cover assembled from light but strong portable units and shaped not to shut off an interior volume but rather to suggest all the unlimited outer world by the space within. Had the space within been filled with objects fashioned as organically as the great frame, the Exhibition might have effected a reformation of public taste which artisans far more pretentious than Paxton could not achieve with all their laborious contrivance. Unfortunately, however, the quality of its contents —at least viewed from a vantage point in time—merely helped explain Ruskin's disgust with the building itself.

But, despite the misgivings of the critical few, most visitors to the Crystal Palace stood long enraptured before the marvels of mechanical craftsmanship. Everywhere in the exhibits, said the sanguine Dr. Whewell, lay incontestable evidence that the inventive machinist might prove himself again and again the true Poet or Maker, since "man's power of making," he insisted, "may show itself not only in the beautiful *texture* of language, the grand *machinery* of the epic, the sublime display of poetical *imagery;* but in these material works."[6] Many of the "makers" themselves must have felt the praise well merited; for their wares alone were ample proof that they deemed their talents in the highest sense "creative." Not content with illustrating the range of applied

[4] See Ruskin, *Works*, X, 114; XII, 419-20.
[5] See Walter Curt Behrendt. *Modern Building* (New York, 1937), pp. 42-43; and Christopher Hobhouse, *1851 and the Crystal Palace* (New York, 1937).
[6] Whewell in *Lectures on the Great Exhibition*, p. 5.

science, they strove to make of their looms and reapers, their grates and boilers, obvious works of art. Impatient with the simpler devices of clean line and natural curve, they repeatedly sought to conceal the function of their machines with the intricacies of machine-made ornaments. Like the exhibitors at every world's fair, they sacrificed the beautiful to the ingenious; and their search for the novel led inevitably to fantastic creation. One manufacturer, for instance, proudly displayed a walnut-wood couch, serviceable as a bed but stuffed with his own patent cork fiber to make it buoyant when placed in water—for the couch, "in case of danger at sea," was instantly convertible into a life raft with a floating surface of fifty square feet; and to this versatile piece were attached two cabinets of fine walnut, one hiding "a self-acting washing stand" and the other "as a Davenport, forming a patent portable water-closet."[7]

Less ambitious craftsmen, who had perhaps not learned the merits of cork fiber, devoted themselves to painful experiment with *papier-mâché*, the malleable pulp glued and shellacked, out of which they could shape vases and footstools and even pianofortes, all lacquered, tinted, and grained, bespangled with gilt or inlaid with mother-of-pearl.[8] Eventually the multiple-purpose furniture like the couch-bed-lifepreserver-watercloset would suggest the more immediately practical appointments of the Pullman car,[9] just as the manufacture of *papier-mâché* might foreshadow the elaborate processes by which a less synthetic plywood could be molded. But the artisans of 1851 felt little of the pioneer's humility; far from tentative, their works were designed as end products and so accorded final embellishment.

Whether working with strange or familiar materials, nearly all the exhibitors who brought their produce to the Crystal Palace struggled to achieve something of "the sublime display of poetical imagery" that betokened the "maker." With the intensity of the Spasmodic poets, whose impulses were indeed rather similar, they strained after fanciful "conceits" in plastic form, ornaments wrought in lush detail, existing for their own sake, often quite unrelated to the "prose meaning" of the chair or table or chimney piece they adorned. To beds

[7] See *Official Descriptive and Illustrated Catalogue*, 3 vols. (London, 1852), II, 730.
[8] See Rita Wellman, *Victoria Royal* (New York, 1939), pp. 55-58. Miss Wellman's general account of the Exhibition is both amusing and informative.
[9] See Sigfried Giedion, "Railroad Comfort and Patent Furniture," *Technology Review*, XLVII (1944-45), 97-98, 137-38.

and bookcases, to whatnots and newel posts, to twenty-foot mirrors and many-drawered chests, they applied their "metaphors" of wood and iron and plaster, Gothic peaks and finials, arches, arcatures, and arabesques, symbolic griffins and naturalistic camels, acorns and fish and twisted vines, ruddy cherubim and reclining elephants. Inevitably, the desire for copious "illustration" fought down all respect for unified design, until the various motifs that bedecked a single article of furniture might be not only irrelevant to the piece as a whole but also ill-proportioned to each other. Since the new machines of Birmingham could turn forth the florid as inexpensively as the simple, the manufacturer yielded readily to the demand of an uncritical public for size and quantity of ornament rather than balance and harmony.

Though many of the official judges were happy to think that the factory had thus brought culture to the multitude by cheaply reproducing "the noblest works of art," several charged the British industrialist with some lack of restraint in his enthusiasm for the ornate. It might be, they mused, that English taste, generally, was inferior to French. For certainly no native artisan had created an original work so noble as "the grand buffet of M. Fourdinois," which was awarded the Council Medal as a piece "of rare excellence and merit in design, and of skilful and artistic execution as to carving."[10] But if the sideboard seemed a most effective antidote to excessive *décor,* it was nonetheless itself sufficiently complex to require descriptive commentary and interpretation. At its base, six dogs, "emblematical of the chace," rested on a parquet floor, supporting a slab fronted by a finely carved molding and inlaid "in geometric forms." Above the slab, standing on four pedestals were "female figures, gracefully designed as emblems of the four quarters of the world each bearing the most useful production of their climate as contributions to the feast"—European wine, Asiatic tea, African coffee, and American sugar cane. And in the center the products of the chase were "poured out on the very board," above which the space was "filled with a framed picture of rare fruits, giving an opportunity to enliven the work by the addition of colour, without militating against good taste." The figure of Plenty crowned the piece, and the bracketed cornice beside her carried boys "with the implements of the vineyard and of agriculture," while the ends bore figures with "the implements of fishing on the one side and of the chace on the other." All in all, the buffet—at least in the opinion of Richard Redgrave, R.A., the eminent authority on design—was "consistent and free from puerilities," and though "thoroughly fitted for its purpose as a sideboard, . . . at the same time of a highly ornamental character, without any of its decoration being overdone or thrown away."

By limiting his *décor* to motifs more or less closely associated with the festal rites, M. Fourdinois attained the coherence of "intellectual" pattern that had eluded most British craftsmen. But it hardly occurred to the judges that his motifs might be intrinsically ludicrous in their naturalism or that the over-all effect of his neo-baroque style might not represent the highest achievement in pure design. For his "simplicity" stuck fiery off indeed beside far more ornate examples of "spasmodic" artistry. In evaluating the exhibits, even Redgrave became at times "tired altogether of ornament" and eager for an absolute utility "where use is so paramount that ornament is repudiated."[11] His fellow critic, Owen Jones, saw the source of a confusion worse confounded in the failure of the artisans to agree on an aesthetic standard. "We have," Jones wrote, "no principles, no unity; the architect, the upholsterer, the paper-stainer, the weaver, the calico-printer, and the potter run each their independent course; each struggles fruitlessly, each produces in art novelty without beauty, or beauty without intelligence."[12] Though more inclined to applaud British invention, the *Spectator* admitted that the displays at the Crystal Palace betrayed "the chaotic condition of the civilized mind in respect to canons of taste."[13] And Bailey, whose *Festus* had not been distinguished for economy of selection, lamented a common deficiency of his countrymen:

> *What England as a nation wants, is taste;*
> *The judgment that's in due proportion placed;*
> *We overdo, we underdo, we waste.*[14]

Years later, on looking back from a new era, Frederic Harrison pointed to his revulsion, as a youth of nineteen, from the "appalling vulgarity" of the Exhibition, as proof that he had never been in spirit an "Early Victorian."[15] He felt it

[11] See *Exhibition of Works of Industry*, p. 708.
[12] Jones, "Colour in the Decorative Arts," in *Lectures on the Great Exhibition*, 2d ser. (London, 1853), p. 256.
[13] *Spectator*, XXIV (1851), 663.
[14] Bailey, *The Age*, p. 28.
[15] Harrison, *Autobiographic Memoirs*, I, 88-89.

clearly necessary to acquit himself of that label; for the attack of the Edwardians on all the values of their grand-fathers, and even on the standards of Harrison's generation, was stimulated in large part by the legacy of tangible un-loveliness which the middle decades of the nineteenth century had left behind. Yet many of the Victorians themselves could recognize in their own time a complete failure of the plastic arts; and many could accept Kingsley's charge that the "mass of the British people . . . sits contented under the imputation of 'bad taste.' "[16] It was not for lack of criticism that the "bad taste" so long persisted. It was merely that the sanctions of the ornate and the ugly were too widely diffused and defended to be easily destroyed.

"If people only knew as much about painting as I do," said Edwin Landseer, "they would never buy my pictures."[17] But few among the middle-class public that most cherished his work could be expected to bring to any canvas any more than a sharp eye for lifelike detail. The same "puritan" disci-plines that had abetted their rise in a mercantile world had from the first inculcated in them a distrust of all that was purely "aesthetic." Not before they had won financial security and political independence could they afford even to consider the claim of art as a means of a more abundant living. And then, unfamiliar with the proven standards that had long guided the judgment of the aristocrat, they were driven to their own trial-and-error attempts at culture. In control of industrial empires vaster than all the estates of the landed gentry, the upper middle classes sought to establish their own tradition of opulent elegance, an outward sign of their eco-nomic triumph. And the aspiring many below them, the smaller tradesmen and foremen, the shopkeepers and clerks, for the most part quite innocent of any trained tastes, set out to garner unto themselves such objects of intricate design and impressive bulk as it was within their means to procure—inexpensive replicas of the "finer things," produced in quan-tity to demonstrate that their purchasers were not exclusively devoted to the gross and the useful.

All levels of bourgeois society exercised their acquisitive powers at leisure moments in amassing great stores of bric-a-brac, wax flowers, ormolu candelabra, porcelain vases, plas-ter busts of literary idols, and iron or lead statuettes of pagan

[16] Kingsley, *Plays and Puritans* (London, 1873), p. 4.
[17] Quoted by W. P. Frith, *My Autobiography and Reminiscences*, 2 vols. (New York, 1888), I, 223.

deities. For the sheer joy of possession, they accumulated innumerable oddments, especially novelties in glass—glass ducks and dogs and roosters, glass hats and slippers and sea shells, glass bowls in the "daisy-and-button" pattern, glass cups large and small, warted and welted with the "thousand-eye" design or branched and veined like the "tree of life."[18] They lined their shelves and spread their walls with tiny miniatures and huge prints in heavy frames as numerous as the characters in their three-volume novels. If they knew little of painting, they were nonetheless enthusiastic collectors of cheap engravings which preserved a wealth of gesture and sentiment for their constant perusal. And on occasion they could measure their own graphic treasures against enormous originals; when W. P. Frith first exhibited his "Derby Day" (1858), they came in such droves to the Royal Academy that the canvas had to be railed off to keep the picture-readers from "smelling" out its detail "like bloodhounds."[19] Ill-informed yet eager, many argued about styles in furniture and building with the determined assurance which a culti-vated few brought to the elucidation of Browning's verse. Though the machine age was robbing their labors of diver-sity, their tastes in art and ornament reflected no willingness to accept the monotones of order.

Despite his sensitive responses to literature, Newman com-plained, in prefacing his own poems, of his ignorance of any fixed aesthetic values. Unable to find a standard "by which to discriminate aright between one poetical attempt and another,"[20] he feared that all criticism of verse must remain personal and so more or less arbitrary and unscientific. In religion he could invoke the authority of dogma to confute the anarchy of dissent; but in art he felt forced to accept the canon of a nonconformist individualism. Much of the con-fusion that attended judgments of taste throughout the Vic-torian era arose from the failure of the artisan and his public to discover a common body of principles or to question the validity of their personal reactions. In the building trades, *laissez-faire* economics encouraged *laissez-faire* aesthetics; as long as the state refused to place controls on private construc-tion or to assume responsibility for town planning, the jerry-builder was left as free as the conscientious architect to follow his own "designs." If individual enterprise determined the

---

[18] See Ruth Webb Lee, *Victorian Glass: Specialties of the Nineteenth Century* (Northborough, Mass., 1944).

[19] See Frith, *Autobiography*, I, 202-03.

[20] Newman, 1867 dedication, *Verses on Various Occasions*, pp. vi-vii.

progress of industry, individual performance seemed largely
to guide the course of music and the drama. From the forties
on, the average concert audience was much less interested in
abstract harmonies of sound than in the particular charms of
the artiste occupying the center of the stage. The wide popularity of the Italian opera stemmed mainly from the occasions for emotional display which it afforded highly paid and
highly eccentric prima donnas. And a native composer could
enjoy great acclaim only if his work, like *The Bohemian
Girl* (1843) of Michael William Balfe, showed sufficient
technical virtuosity to strain the operatic talents of its principal singers. The theater, likewise, from Macready to Irving,
was completely dominated by the star system; the play as a
rule was written for the leading actor, adapted to his peculiar
mannerisms, and directed to his best advantage. Since pro-
ducer and spectator were alike more concerned with the
versatile protagonist than with coherent theme or firm structure, most significant attempts at dramatic art were doomed
from the first to failure. Tennyson, who could secure tragic
effect in isolated scenes, knew no practicing playwright able
to teach him the first essentials of serious stagecraft. And
George Meredith, who might, in the opinion of Harley
Granville-Barker,[21] have proven himself the great comic
dramatist of the period, was quite unable to find the public
that the comic muse demanded.

Unfamiliar with the formal conventions that governed the
various aesthetic media, the middle-class critic would frequently resort to the sanction of verisimilitude. In judging
ornament he would attach less value to the pleasing line than
to a "truth to nature" quite literally conceived. He could,
therefore, approve of such preposterous objects as the center-
piece designed by Prince Albert,[22] which arrayed upon ornate
pedestals the Queen's favorite dogs, modeled from life, together with a dead hare, a caged rat, and the remains of a
dead one, the actual tokens of happy hunting. Prince Albert
had clearly "gone to nature"; yet he had made no attempt to
deceive: the dogs on the pedestals were obviously not real
dogs, since the metal of which they were molded could not
be "mistaken for that which it professe[d] to imitate." In any
other material, too direct an imitation of nature might have

---

[21] See his "Tennyson, Swinburne, Meredith—and the Theatre,"
Eighteen Seventies, pp. 161-91.
[22] See *Art Journal,* I (1849), 159; the art critic called the piece "in
all respects so worthy a specimen of his Royal Highness's taste and
skill in designing."

been misleading,[23] for, as a popular aesthetician explained, "the perfect reproduction of the form would lead to demands for reality"—and the dogs themselves had no place on the tablecloth.

All successful ornament was thus expected not only to attain the appearance of actuality, but also to suggest that the illusion was merely illusion. Even the picture most admirable for its realistic detail was to remain a picture; heavily matted, it was to be hung in an embellished frame "to keep it totally distinct from its surroundings," lest it be mistaken for a window opening unto an illusory world.[24] For the Victorian of taste was loath to be betrayed by a wayward fancy; and he allowed the "lamp of literalism" to guide his judgment in queer directions. Redgrave at the Crystal Palace, for instance, objected to a table supported by swans, not so much because the piece was graceless and cumbersome, as because he himself was perplexed to know "why swans should make their nests under a table at the risk of having their necks broken by everyone seated at it."[25] Actuated by a like regard for truth, a later consultant on decoration saw fit to praise a bowl enlivened by cherubs clustering about its stem; for the bowl was supported by the stem *"resting upon a solid basis"* and not by the frail infants who could scarcely have sustained such weight.[26] Craftsmanship so faithful to the realities of experience, he thought, deserved special commendation at a time when most designers seemed content to violate all laws of "Common Sense" in their search for lifelike detail. "It might be too much to say," he wrote, "that one may knock for admittance with the head of a goat, wipe one's 'feet' upon a Newfoundland dog, approach the hostess over a carpet strewn with bouquets, converse with one foot upon a Bengal tiger, and contemplate birds of paradise upon the walls; that one may be called upon to interpose the Bay of Naples between an elderly lady and the fireplace, to slice a pine-apple upon a humming-bird, and place one's finger-glass upon the countenance of a Tyrolese peasant. Yet this as fairly describes the popular taste as when we say that the English people have a decided predilection for the imbibition of beer." What disturbed the critic, however, was not that

[23] On imitation and the use of metal, see M. Digby Wyatt, "An Attempt to define the Principles which should determine Form in the Decorative Arts," *Lectures on the Great Exhibition*, 2d ser., pp. 233-40.
[24] See *The Science of Taste* "by G.-L." (London, 1879), p. 105.
[25] See *Exhibition of Works of Industry*, p. 722.
[26] See *Science of Taste*, pp. 90, 100, 141.

the multiple imagery was bewildering in its total effect and quite incompatible with any harmonious interior design. It was just that the individual motifs were badly misplaced; for one should certainly not be expected to preserve a courteous poise in the presence of a life-size tiger or to converse with ease beneath walls from which great birds might momentarily descend. It was obvious to the decorator that "nothing within doors should suggest that one is out of doors." Such was the first dictate of "Common Sense"; and "Common Sense" was of prime importance, "for not only [was] taste unable to proceed without it, but owing to its non-cultivation, material prosperity [was] impeded."

In *Hard Times* Dickens caricatured the literalist, the man of Common Sense, who deplored Sissy Jupe's lack of taste: "You are not to have, in any object of use or ornament, what would be a contradiction in fact. You don't walk upon flowers in fact; you can not be allowed to walk upon flowers in carpets. . . . This is the new discovery. This is fact. This is taste." Yet Dickens himself throughout his novels strove to achieve the factual accuracy of an anti-romantic "realism"; he was quite as intent upon following with scrupulous care the exact procedures of Chancery[27] as he was eager to chronicle in minute particulars a child's first view of Mr. Peggotty's grounded ark. For a concern with circumstantial detail obsessed the "maker" of literature no less than the designer of household ornament; and the reader of novels and poems and plays expected to find in his favorite author the proper respect for fact. Charles Kean was, therefore, disturbed by the anachronisms and logical inconsistencies of Shakespeare's *Winter's Tale*—so much disturbed, indeed, that, when producing the play in 1856, he not only clarified the plot but transferred the scene from a vague "Bohemia" to a definite Bithynia in Asia Minor, while his associate George Scharf designed settings which reproduced "the vegetation peculiar to Bithynia . . . adapted from his private drawings, taken on the spot."[28]

Writing in an age of analytic science, the Victorian poet felt less free than Shakespeare to depart from the literal truths of inanimate nature. Sydney Dobell, for all his "Spasmodic" rhapsodies, took pains to make his observations incontestably precise.[29] Once on a night journey, for instance,

[27] Cf. William C. Holdsworth, *Charles Dickens as a Legal Historian* (New Haven, 1928), esp. pp. 79-81.

[28] See John Mason Brown, "Children of Skelt," *Saturday Review of Literature*, Vol. XXX, No. 1 (1947), 23.

[29] See Dobell, *Thoughts on Art*, p. 83.

he noted for future poetic use the five main shifts in light and coloring before dawn, "the following symptoms of the dissolution of Night in the following order. . . ." And Browning, though not primarily a nature poet, delighted his admirers with ample evidence of his keen perceptions, his awareness of the tiny leaves round the elm-tree bole, and the short sharp broken hills, and the bell of the wild tulip "like a thin clear bubble of blood." But it was Tennyson who above all jealously guarded his reputation as a master of physical detail, as an unequaled recorder of sense impressions drawn from the natural world. Since, when in the Pyrenees, he had verbally sketched the cataract before him "Slow dropping veils of thinnest lawn," he was greatly irritated by a reviewer who objected to the image, claiming that the poet should not have gone "to the boards of a theatre but to Nature herself for his suggestions."[30] Again, while reading *Maud,* he is reported to have paused long enough to ask an authoress in his audience what sort of birds in a high hall garden would call, "Maud, Maud, Maud, Maud." When the embarrassed lady faltered that they might be nightingales, he impatiently rebuked her ignorance: "What a cockney you are! Nightingales don't say Maud. Rooks do, or something like it. Caw, caw, caw, caw, caw"—and then the reading continued.[31]

Though such self-conscious regard for exact detail helped discipline Tennyson's imagination, it frequently betrayed him —as it betrayed other Victorian writers—into the "ornate," the baroque style so distasteful to Walter Bagehot. The element of the ornate was, to be sure, utterly absent from many of Tennyson's most characteristic poems, especially from his personal epistles, which unfolded with a Horatian grace and purity of idiom. But it was disastrously present in a work like *Enoch Arden* (1864), where a desire for full literal presentation brought so much detail into sharp focus that the hero himself was barely distinguishable against the elaborated background. The "ornate" might thus be born of the will to document all the individual "realities" of a "romantic" setting; for in verse, as in the plastic arts, a reverence for the particular fact could often destroy the aesthetic unity.

George Eliot, whose *Romola* was sufficiently replete with factual data, insisted that the painter's imagination no less than the writer's should be rooted in the literal and the con-

---

[30] See H. Tennyson, *Memoir,* I, 259. But wherever the image occurred to Tennyson, the reviewer might have replied, it was still "artificial" in inspiration.

[31] Anecdote from Ritchie, *Tennyson, Ruskin, Browning,* p. 8.

crete. Even a picture of the Last Judgment should, she felt, be composed of details drawn "from real observation"; it should deal in "the veriest minutiae of experience" heightened by "ideal association."[32] To the representative Victorian painter such demands seemed only reasonable, since the canvas that lacked "truth to nature" could betoken only the artist's spiritual inadequacy or his technical incompetence. Frith, for example, attained his conspicuous popular success largely through his prolonged studies of setting, costume, and gesture and his careful selection of models who were eager to contribute their individual charms to his animated tableaux. His "Claude Duval," which illustrated an incident from Macaulay concerning a seventeenth-century highwayman, portrayed, against the "blasted heath" of a real Devonshire, an actual antique stagecoach which had been preserved at the estate of Lord Darnley; so grounded in fact, the painting derived little from a "creative" imagination. And his "Derby Day," which transcribed in paint the average man's response to an excited holiday crowd, was likewise characteristically objective. It was intended to reproduce a familiar scene not as it might strike an artist's unique vision, but rather as it might appear to the alert eyes of any spectator; and when the Prince Consort questioned the placement of certain shadows, Frith was naturally glad, in the interests of complete accuracy, to make all desirable changes.[33]

Though the Pre-Raphaelites had in general a far ampler concept of artistic truth than the "literalists," they were hardly less concerned with precise realistic detail. Millais used a magnifying glass when sketching veined leaves and tendrils; Rossetti burned wine and chloride to obtain the proper color for the flames about the feet of the Archangel Gabriel; and Holman Hunt journeyed to the Holy Land partly to pose his "scapegoat" against an authentic Dead Sea background. Most of the Pre-Raphaelites worked patiently with a medium over which they had little technical control; they painted, repainted, and overpainted layer upon layer of pigment; and in so doing they frequently altered their whole design after a long-pondered picture had been well begun. By blending a slow-drying varnish into their oils, they were able to match colors over protracted periods during which they could proceed deliberately with their innumerable revisions. They paid

[32] See George Eliot, "False Testimonials," *Impressions of Theophrastus Such* (1879; New York, n.d.), p. 155.
[33] See Frith, *Autobiography*, I, 201; on his own respect for detail, cf. I, 213-14.

little heed to the fact that, with the darkening of the resin mixed into the very colors, their pictures so produced would eventually deteriorate beyond reclaim; for they were enabled by slow painting to attain, for a time at least, the illusion of a carefully transcribed reality.[34]

Insofar as they wished to achieve "a pretty mocking of the life," all Victorian painters, including the Pre-Raphaelites, were fighting a losing battle against mechanical means of reproducing the actual with consummate "realism." During the fifties the daguerreotype became so fashionable that Lady Morley scarcely expected the sun to shine elsewhere when it was "fully occupied every day in taking likenesses in Regent Street."[35] And by 1870 the camera had completely outdistanced the pencil and the brush as a recorder of factual detail. Charles Landseer spoke a sadder truth than he knew when he told Frith that science had at last produced "a *foe-to-graphic art*."[36]

But, however devoted he might be to a pictorial "naturalism," the successful painter could not content himself with a mere transcript of observable experience. In order to reach a public insensitive to the simple effects of line and shade, he often adapted each carefully depicted fact to a "literary" pattern—to the purposes of storytelling or moral instruction. Draftsmen like Landseer, Egg, Harvey, and Phillip, who derived their greatest popularity from the "subject-picture," diligently sought out topics for illustration, scenes from literature, history, and contemporary life, richly informed with narrative content. Calderon established his reputation with "Broken Vows" (1857), a piece of documented sentimentalism which portrayed the shock of a pure maiden as she glimpsed her perfidious lover (in the act of flirtation) through a chink in the kitchen-garden wall. And Frith, who considered subject always of prime importance, moved from triumph to triumph, financially at any rate, with such canvases as "Ramsgate Sands" and "The Railway Station," sprawling panoramas packed with dramatic incident, and "The Road to Ruin" and "The Race for Wealth," mildly Hogarthian sequences, animated tales of fallen virtue.

[34] See Richard D. Buck, "A Note on the Methods and Materials of the Pre-Raphaelite Painters," *The Pre-Raphaelites* (catalogue, 1946, Fogg Museum of Art, Harvard University), pp. 14-18.
[35] See Sir Algernon West, *Recollections, 1832-1886* (London, n.d.), p. 169.
[36] See Frith, *Autobiography*, I, 149. Sir Charles Landseer was a brother of the more popular Sir Edwin.

From the forties onwards, most avowed "lovers of art" were skilled picture-readers with a keen appetite for character and episode and a will to find story values, even in the works of masters quite unconcerned with anecdote and parable. Kingsley, for instance, drew many "a sharp sermon" from Bellini's portrait of a Venetian doge; for in the doge he saw the sort of man who would most surely fight the inhumanities of Victorian capitalism as he had once resisted "those tyrannous and covetous old merchant-princes who had elected him—who were keeping their own power at the expense of everyone's liberty, by spies and nameless accusers, and secret councils, tortures and prisons, whose horrors no one ever returned to describe."[37] Even the major Pre-Raphaelites, whose appreciation of fine art was rather more sophisticated than Kingsley's, refused to regard a picture as essentially a problem in graphic design. If they scorned the "anecdotage" of Frith and the obvious appeals of "lettered" painting, Rossetti and Burne-Jones, nonetheless, surrounded their dream figures with literary—or at least "poetic"—symbols chosen to lend spiritual significance to each ornate detail.

Like the painter, the ornament maker found realistic reproduction not sufficient in itself. For men of "refined taste" self-consciously demanded of *décor* some "dash of allegory . . . imperceptible only to the uncultivated multitude."[38] The multitude, to be sure, had little difficulty in divining the "symbolic" import of the hens that nested on their egg warmers, or the cows that adorned their butter pots, or any other of the motifs, like animal paws or cherubs, promiscuously carved to suggest the abundant vitality of nature. But the cultivated few, to whom the allegorical was no secret, sought subtler associations of thought and feeling in plastic forms. They placed urns on their gateposts as tokens of affluence, and they pointed the railheads of their fences like spears and arrows, to represent the pride of possession and the will to defend the rights of property. They read "animation" into the serpentining curves of baroque furniture. They believed that a green wall might be the proper setting for pictures since green was nature's background. And they carefully calculated the "Rembrandt effects" of tasteful chiaroscuro to be attained by placing windows and lamps on one side of a room only. In general, though they allowed no common principle to

[37] See Kingsley, "The National Gallery," *Politics for the People,* May 20, 1848, pp. 39-40.
[38] *Science of Taste,* pp. 81-89.

dominate their individual prejudices, they showed a deep interest in the types and symbols of older and more coherent styles. Instead of creating their own "allegories," they drew eclectically on motifs to which time had attached complex connotations.

Interior *décor* could be readily adapted to suit changing fashions in ornament, and its excesses, indeed, may often be ascribed to the decorator's awareness that it was profitable to encourage successive vogues for old patterns newly minted. But architectural design was of its essence more durable. And it was, therefore, the architect rather than the ornament maker who left the most permanent reminders of the confusions and conflicts that vitiated Victorian taste. In *The Water Babies* Kingsley described the home of Sir John Hartover; it was a most eclectic manor house, "built at ninety different times, and in nineteen different styles," including the Anglo-Saxon, the Norman, the Cinquecento, the Doric, and the Boeotian, and bearing traces of the Parthenon, the Pavilion at Brighton, and the Taj Mahal at Agra. Though admittedly bewildering in its aspect, the house nonetheless "looked like a real live house" that had had a history and accumulated many forms as it aged. And this was more than Kingsley could say of most Victorian buildings, finished as they were to look old at birth, that they might trail the clouds of vanished glories into a world of machine-made façades. Reluctant to break with established structural traditions, the academic architects, unlike Joseph Paxton, refused to shape their plans in accordance with the new materials which industry was making available to them. They preferred to compound their styles of many influences, and they gave themselves wholeheartedly to the various "revivals"—to the Renaissance of Barry and the neo-Greek of Cockerell, but, above all, to the Gothic.

At the Great Exhibition, Owen Jones deplored the omnipresence of Gothic motifs: "I mourn over the loss," he said, "which this age has suffered, and continues to suffer, by so many fine minds devoting all their talents to the reproduction of a galvanized corpse."[39] But by the fifties the revival of Gothic had already advanced so far on so many levels that protest was in vain. Thanks to the efforts of the Pugins and of Gilbert Scott, it was becoming "an intricate science of styles,"[40] of Saxon, Norman, and Lancet, Perpendicular and

[39] *Lectures on the Great Exhibition*, 2d ser., p. 291.
[40] See Chambers, *History of Taste*, p. 225.

Tudor, each of which found its earnest supporters. After an initial Protestant revulsion to a "Catholic" architecture, many a Victorian professed to see in Gothic the embodiment of a philosophy of life and work which his generation might do well to regain. In the offices of George Edmund Street, one of the most successful "Gothicists," young apprentices called to each other in Gregorian chants.[41] And from their drawing boards came many of the hybrid designs that were to be inflicted en masse upon the whole English-speaking world throughout the sixties and seventies. Yet it is unlikely that the borrowed spires and gargoyles, the scrolls and trefoils and traceries, the symbols once, perhaps, of the bountiful earth and the hopes and terrors of the aspiring soul, awakened in the factory worker, the industrialist, or the city clerk much of the emotion that may have stirred the heart of medieval man. Certainly most of the sham-Gothic mansions and colleges and stables, like the pseudo-Gothic furniture of Charles Eastlake,[42] conveyed little more than a nostalgia for the past and a feeling for the picturesque, alien to the best design of the Middle Ages and quite unworthy the demonstrable vitality of the Victorian era.

Convinced that the nineteenth century could not approach a true architecture until it had clarified its moral and social objectives, Ruskin strove to reawaken the ideal which he felt must have guided the original Gothic craftsmen. In so doing, much of his energy was misspent on a vain repudiation of the machine—which, for better or for worse, had long since established itself as an inescapable force in Victorian society. Yet he at least made it clear that a vital style in building was inseparably related to the environment that produced it. Aware that the best in Gothic had arisen from a trained regard for "function," he recalled his contemporaries to a serious consideration of the uses of art; and, almost in spite of himself, he thus prepared the way for the "functionalist," whose designs were to reveal rather than to hide the purpose of his structures.

As his ablest disciple, William Morris was likewise handicapped by an inability to see that the new building—and indeed the applied arts generally—must accept all the conditions and resources of an industrial system. But he succeeded, all the same, by precept and example, in attacking the most flagrant examples of bad taste and in suggesting the essen-

[41] See Sir Reginald Blomfield, *Richard Norman Shaw, R. A.* (London, 1940), p. 15.
[42] On Eastlake, see Wellman, *Victoria Royal*, pp. 83-91.

tials of sound design. His Red House of 1859, built in collaboration with Philip Webb, represented not only the first modern attempt to shape a commodious home entirely from native building materials, but also the first effort to plan both exterior and interior as a single unit.[43] His furniture, though unduly cumbersome in its massive lines, dispensed with much unnecessary embellishment. And his flat patterns, based on a careful reworking of stylized motifs, supplied an effective antidote to the misapplied naturalism of household *décor*. If his emphasis on the handicrafts led certain ingenious manufacturers to mass-produce articles artificially roughened to look handmade,[44] it yet went far to broaden public concern for thorough workmanship. More than any other decorator, Morris helped clear the Victorian home of the ugly, the ornate, and the inorganic; for more clearly than all, he provided a standard of intelligent selection and a will to carry into practice the first principles of his creed: "Have nothing in your houses which you do not know to be useful or believe to be beautiful."

By 1880, when Morris turned his attention from art to socialism, Victorian taste had noticeably improved. The architect had grown impatient with imitative revivalism. The designer had learned to sacrifice florid ornament. The painter had come to prefer pattern of composition to the portrayal of incident in photographic detail. And the prose writer had mastered an urbane middle style freed from sentimental diction and turgid rhetoric. Yet Victorian taste had never been a static entity. From the beginning it had reflected the restless activity that was driving the whole era towards new horizons. But its "progress" had depended upon the curbing of an exuberance reluctant to undergo a civilizing discipline; and even as it gained in discretion and self-conscious tact, it lost something in spontaneity. Though the late Victorian could deride the absurdities of Prince Albert's Exhibition, he was uncomfortably aware that the splendor of the Queen's Jubilees might seem as contemptible to a new century. Whatever the extravagances of early Victorian culture, it had committed its sins with a religious intensity which a more disillusioned age could not recover; and it had called forth to denounce its follies earnest souls endowed with a range of enthusiasm and a capacity for synthesis which the narrow specialists of a later generation could not but envy.

[43] See Behrendt, *Modern Building*, pp. 54-56.
[44] See John Gloag, *English Furniture* (London, 1934), p. 134.

There is no better short summary of the long-range significance of Pre-Raphaelitism and aestheticism than Yeats's account, in this 1913 essay, of his own rootedness in that movement. "I had learned to think in the midst of the last phase of Pre-Raphaelitism." In writing, Yeats says, he followed the principles advanced by Arthur Hallam who, in reviewing Tennyson's 1830 *Poems*, associated Tennyson with Shelley and Keats, as poets of sensation, of the aesthetic school, in contrast to Wordsworth, who was a poet of "reflection." Thus, Yeats draws a line from Shelley and Keats through early Tennyson and the Pre-Raphaelites (who preferred early Tennyson) to the poets of the nineties and the twentieth-century poetry of Yeats himself.

In reaction to later Tennyson and the other Victorian poets, who "condescended to moral maxims, or some received philosophy," Yeats and his friends of the nineties wanted to empty their poetry of content. But Yeats remained dissatisfied with the poetry of pure sensation as still too self-conscious and specialized, as still unlike the careless old pre-Renaissance poetry. To escape the exclusive reliance on private sensation, Yeats sought his symbols in the real folklore and mythology of Ireland.

Pre-Raphaelite means for Yeats pre-Rennaissance. And since the Renaissance, our culture has cared for the pulpit rather than the altar—cared for moral ideas and reform rather than for art's proper concern: those rituals and symbols by which we remake our souls. Although Yeats and his friends thought they were turning away from all ideas, Yeats came to understand that there iş an ancient community of symbols more profound than any system of ideas; so that far from standing alone and communicating nothing, the poet communicates most profoundly when he brings to life again the ancient symbols in the idiom of his own age. It is this new understanding of how thought can be reintegrated with emotion, and content with poetry, that constitutes Yeats's "more profound Pre-Raphaelitism"—or what we nowadays call Symbolism.

W. B. YEATS

Art and Ideas

Two days ago I was at the Tate Gallery to see the early Millais's, and before his *Ophelia,* as before the *Mary Magdalene* and *Mary of Galilee* of Rossetti that hung near, I recovered an old emotion. I saw these pictures as I had seen pictures in my childhood. I forgot the art criticism of friends and saw wonderful, sad, happy people, moving through the scenery of my dreams. The painting of the hair, the way it was smoothed from its central parting, something in the oval of the peaceful faces, called up memories of sketches of my father's on the margins of the first Shelley I had read, while the strong colours made me half remember studio conversations, words of Wilson, or of Potter perhaps, praise of the primary colours, heard, it may be, as I sat over my toys or a child's story-book. One picture looked familiar, and suddenly I remembered it had hung in our house for years. It was Potter's *Field Mouse.* I had learned to think in the midst of the last phase of Pre-Raphaelitism and now I had come to Pre-Raphaelitism again and rediscovered my earliest thought. I murmured to myself, "The only painting of modern England that could give pleasure to a child, the only painting that would seem as moving as *The Pilgrim's Progress* or Hans Andersen." "Am I growing old," I thought, "like the woman in Balzac, the rich bourgeois' ambitious wife, who could not keep, when old age came upon her, from repeating the jokes of the concierge's lodge where she had been born and bred; or is it because of some change in the weather that I find beauty everywhere, even in Burne-Jones's *King Cophetua,* one of his later pictures, and find it without shame?" I have had like admiration many times in the last twenty years, for I have always loved those pictures where I meet persons associated with the poems or the religious ideas that have most moved me; but never since my boyhood

W. B. Yeats, ESSAYS AND INTRODUCTIONS (New York: Macmillan, 1961), pp. 346-55. Reprinted by permission of the publisher, copyright © 1961 Mrs. W. B. Yeats. See also Graham Hough, *The Last Romantics* (London, 1947); Frank Kermode, *Romantic Image* (London, 1957).

have I had it without shame, without the certainty that I would hear the cock crow presently. I remembered that as a young man I had read in Schopenhauer that no man—so unworthy a thing is life seen with unbesotted eyes—would live another's life, and had thought I would be content to paint, like Burne-Jones and Morris under Rossetti's rule, the Union at Oxford, to set up there the traditional images most moving to young men while the adventure of uncommitted life can still change all to romance, even though I should know that what I painted must fade from the walls.

II

Thereon I ask myself if my conception of my own art is altering, if there, too, I praise what I once derided. When I began to write I avowed for my principles those of Arthur Hallam in his essay upon Tennyson.[1] Tennyson, who had written but his early poems when Hallam wrote, was an example of the school of Keats and Shelley, and Keats and Shelley, unlike Wordsworth, intermixed into their poetry no elements from the general thought, but wrote out of the impression made by the world upon their delicate senses. They were of the aesthetic school—was he the inventor of the name?—and could not be popular because their readers could not understand them without attaining to a like delicacy of sensation and so must needs turn from them to Wordsworth or another, who condescended to moral maxims, or some received philosophy, a multitude of things that even common sense could understand. Wordsworth had not less genius than the others—even Hallam allowed his genius; we are not told that Mary of Galilee was more beautiful than the more popular Mary; but certainly we might consider Wordsworth a little disreputable.

I developed these principles to the rejection of all detailed description, that I might not steal the painter's business, and indeed I was always discovering some art or science that I might be rid of: and I found encouragement by noticing all round me painters [2] who were ridding their pictures, and

---

[1] ["On Some of the Characteristics of Modern Poetry, and on the Lyrical Poems of Alfred Tennyson," reprinted in *The Writings of Arthur Hallam*, ed. T. H. Vail Motter (New York and London, 1943), pp. 182-98.—Ed.]

[2] This thought, which seemed a discovery, was old enough. Balzac derides in a story a certain Pierre Grassou who attained an immense popularity by painting a Chouan rebel going to his death. (1924)

indeed their minds, of literature. Yet those delighted senses, when I had got from them all that I could, left me discontented. Impressions that needed so elaborate a record did not seem like the handiwork of those careless old writers one imagines squabbling over a mistress, or riding on a journey, or drinking round a tavern fire, brisk and active men. Crashaw could hymn Saint Teresa in the most impersonal of ecstasies and seem no sedentary man out of reach of common sympathy, no disembodied mind, and yet in his day the life that appeared most rich and stirring was already half forgotten with Villon and Dante.

This difficulty was often in my mind, but I put it aside, for the new formula was a good switch while the roads were beset with geese; it set us free from politics, theology, science, all that zeal and eloquence Swinburne and Tennyson found so intoxicating after the passion of their youth had sunk, free from the conventional nobility borne hither from ancient Rome in the galley that carried academic form to vex the painters. Among the little group of poets that met at the Cheshire Cheese I alone loved criticism of Arthur Hallam's sort, with a shamefaced love—criticism founded upon general ideas was itself an impurity—and perhaps I alone knew Hallam's essay, but all silently obeyed a canon that had become powerful for all the arts since Whistler, in the confidence of his American *naïveté,* had told everybody that Japanese painting had no literary ideas. Yet all the while envious of the centuries before the Renaissance, before the coming of our intellectual class with its separate interests, I filled my imagination with the popular beliefs of Ireland, gathering them up among forgotten novelists in the British Museum or in Sligo cottages. I sought some symbolic language reaching far into the past and associated with familiar names and conspicuous hills that I might not be alone amid the obscure impressions of the senses, and I wrote essays recommending my friends to paint on chapel walls the Mother of God flying with Saint Joseph into Egypt along some Connacht road, a Connemara shawl about her head, or mourned the richness or reality lost to Shelley's *Prometheus Unbound* because he had not discovered in England or in Ireland his Caucasus.

I notice like contradictions among my friends who are still convinced that art should not be "complicated by ideas" while picturing Saint Brandan in stained glass for a Connemara chapel, and even among those exuberant young men who make designs for a Phallic Temple, but consider Augustus John lost amid literature.

III

But, after all, could we clear the matter up we might save some hours from sterile discussion. The arts are very conservative and have a great respect for those wanderers who still stitch into their carpets among the Mongolian plains religious symbols so old they have not even a meaning. It cannot be they would lessen an association with one another and with religion that gave them authority among ancient peoples. They are not radicals, and if they deny themselves to any it can only be to the *nouveau riche,* and if they have grown rebellious it can only be against something that is modern, something that is not simple.

I think that before the religious change that followed on the Renaissance men were greatly preoccupied with their sins, and that to-day they are troubled by other men's sins, and that this trouble has created a moral enthusiasm so full of illusion that art, knowing itself for sanctity's scapegrace brother, cannot be of the party. We have but held to our ancient Church, where there is an altar and no pulpit, and founded, the guide-book tells us, upon the ruins of the temple of Jupiter Ammon, and turned away from the too great vigour of those who, living for mutual improvement, have a pulpit and no altar. We fear that a novel enthusiasm might make us forget the little round of poetical duties and imitations—humble genuflexions and circumambulations as it were—that does not unseat the mind's natural impulse, and seems always but half-conscious, almost bodily.

Painting had to free itself from a classicalism that denied the senses, a domesticity that denied the passions, and poetry from a demogogic system of morals which destroyed the humility, the daily dying of the imagination in the presence of beauty. A soul shaken by the spectacle of its sins, or discovered by the Divine Vision in tragic delight, must offer to the love that cannot love but to infinity, a goal unique and unshared; while a soul busied with others' sins is soon melted to some shape of vulgar pride. What can I offer to God but the ghost that must return undisfeatured to the hands that have not made the same thing twice, but what would I have of others but that they do some expected thing, reverence my plans, be in some way demure and reliable? The turning of Rossetti to religious themes, his dislike of Wordsworth, were but the one impulse, for he more than any other was in reaction against the period of philanthropy and reform that created the pedantic composure of Wordsworth, the rhetoric of Swinburne, the passionless sentiment of Tennyson. The saint does not claim to be a good example, hardly even to tell men what to do, for is he not the chief of sinners, and of how little can he be certain whether in the night of the soul or lost in the sweetness coming after? Nor can that composure of the moralists be dear to one who has heard the commandment, that is for the saint and his brother the poet alike, "Make excess ever more abundantly excessive," even were it possible to one shaken and trembling from his daily struggle.

IV

We knew that system of popular instruction was incompatible with our hopes, but we did not know how to refute it and so turned away from all ideas. We would not even permit ideas, so greatly had we come to distrust them, to leave their impressions upon our senses. Yet works of art are always begotten by previous works of art, and every masterpiece becomes the Abraham of a chosen people. When we delight in a spring day there mixes, perhaps, with our personal emotion an emotion Chaucer found in Guillaume de Lorris, who had it from the poetry of Provence; we celebrate our draughty May with an enthusiasm made ripe by more meridian suns; and all our art has its image in the Mass that would lack authority were it not descended from savage ceremonies taught amid what perils and by what spirits to naked savages. The old images, the old emotions, awakened again to overwhelming life, like the gods Heine tells of, by the belief and passion of some new soul, are the only masterpieces. The resolution to stand alone, to owe nothing to the past, when it is not mere sense of property, the greed and pride of the counting-house, is the result of that individualism of the Renaissance which had done its work when it gave us personal freedom. The soul which may not obscure or change its form can yet receive those passions and symbols of antiquity, certain they are too old to be bullies, too well-mannered not to respect the rights of others.

Nor had we better warrant to separate one art from

another, for there has been no age before our own wherein
the arts have been other than a single authority, a Holy
Church of Romance, the might of all lying behind all, a
circle of cliffs, a wilderness where every cry has its echoes.
Why should a man cease to be a scholar, a believer, a ritualist
before he begin to paint or rhyme or to compose music,
or why if he have a strong head should he put away any
means of power?

V

Yet it is plain that the casting out of ideas was the more
natural, misunderstanding though it was, because it had
come to matter very little. The manner of painting had
changed, and we were interested in the fall of drapery and
the play of light without concerning ourselves with the meaning, the emotion of the figure itself. How many successful
portrait-painters gave their sitters the same attention, the
same interest they might have given to a ginger-beer bottle
and an apple? And in our poems an absorption in fragmentary sensuous beauty or detachable ideas had deprived us
of the power to mould vast material into a single image.
What long modern poem equals the old poems in architectural unity, in symbolic importance? *The Revolt of Islam,
The Excursion, Gebir, Idylls of the King,* even perhaps *The
Ring and the Book,* which fills me with so much admiring
astonishment that my judgment sleeps, are remembered for
some occasional passage, some moment which gains little
from the context. Until very lately even the short poems
which contained as clearly as an Elizabethan lyric the impression of a single idea seemed accidental, so much the
rule were the "Faustines" and "Dolores" where the verses
might be arranged in any order, like shot poured out of a
bag. Arnold when he withdrew his *Empedocles on Etna,*
though one had been sorry to lose so much lyrical beauty
for ever, showed himself a great critic by his reasons, but
his *Sohrab and Rustum* proves that the unity he imagined
was a classical imitation and not an organic thing, not the
flow of flesh under the impulse of passionate thought.

Those poets with whom I feel myself in sympathy have
tried to give to little poems the spontaneity of a gesture or
of some casual emotional phrase. Meanwhile it remains for
some greater time, living once more in passionate reverie,

to create a *King Lear,* a *Divine Comedy,* vast worlds moulded by their own weight like drops of water.

In the visual arts, indeed, "the fall of man into his own circumference" seems at an end, and when I look at the photograph of a picture by Gauguin, which hangs over my breakfast-table, the spectacle of tranquil Polynesian girls crowned with lilies gives me, I do not know why, religious ideas. Our appreciations of the older schools are changing too, becoming simpler, and when we take pleasure in some Chinese painting of an old man meditating upon a mountain path, we share his meditation, without forgetting the beautiful intricate pattern of the lines like those we have seen under our eyelids as we fall asleep; nor do the Bride and Bridegroom of Rajput painting, sleeping upon a housetop, or wakening when out of the still water the swans fly upward at the dawn, seem the less well painted because they remind us of many poems. We are becoming interested in expression in its first phase of energy, when all the arts play like children about the one chimney, and turbulent innocence can yet amuse those brisk and active men who have paid us so little attention of recent years. Shall we be rid of the pride of intellect, of sedentary meditation, of emotion that leaves us when the book is closed or the picture seen no more; and live amid the thoughts that can go with us by steamboat and railway as once upon horseback, or camelback, rediscovering, by our reintegration of the mind, our more profound Pre-Raphaelitism, the old abounding, nonchalant reverie?

Chronology of Major Events

1832	Reform Act.
1833	Factory Act. Abolition of Slavery.
1834	New Poor Law. Houses of Parliament burned.
1837	Accession of Queen Victoria.
1841	Peel Prime Minister.
1842	Income Tax. Mine's Act, excluding from underground work women and boys under ten. Chartist riots.
1846	Potato famine. Repeal of Corn Laws.
1851	The Great Exhibition in Hyde Park.
1852	New Houses of Parliament opened.
1853	Death Duties (Inheritance Taxes).
1854-56	Crimean War.
1857	Indian Mutiny.
1858	Abolition of property qualification for M.P.'s. Jews admitted to Parliament. Powers and lands in India, of East India Company, transferred to Crown.
1859	Darwin's *Origin of Species*.
1861	Death of Prince Consort Albert.
1862-64	Lancashire cotton famine caused by American Civil War.
1866	Hyde Park riots.
1867	Disraeli Prime Minister. Reform Act.
1869	Disestablishment of Irish Church (Anglican). Suez Canal opened.
1870	Elementary Education Act, establishing government responsibility for education.
1871	Abolition of purchase of Commissions in the Army. Trades Union Act, legalizing Unions. Buchanan's article, "The Fleshly School of Poetry," attacking D. G. Rossetti and Swinburne.
1872	[Secret] Ballot Act.

1876	Queen Victoria becomes Empress of India.
1880	Compulsory elementary education.
1885	Death of Gordon and fall of Khartoum (Sudan).
1886	Gladstone Prime Minister. His Irish Home Rule Bill defeated in Commons.
1887	Queen's Jubilee.
1890	Parnell divorce case.
1891	Death of Parnell. Free compulsory elementary education.
1892	Gladstone Prime Minister. Gladstone's second Irish Home Rule Bill passed by Commons, rejected by Lords.
1895	Oscar Wilde imprisoned for homosexuality.
1897	Queen's Diamond Jubilee.
1899-1902	Boer War.
1900	Queen's visit to Ireland.
1901	Death of Queen Victoria. Accession of Edward VII.

Notes on Authors Reprinted and Discussed

ANNAN, Lord Noel, born 1916, England. Vice-Chancellor, University of London, retired.

ARNOLD, Matthew (1822–88), born England. Son of Broad-Church leader, Thomas Arnold, great head master of Rugby. M. Arnold was a leading poet and principal Victorian literary critic; writer on social, educational and religious questions; Inspector of Schools from 1851; Professor of Poetry at Oxford, 1857–67.

BROWNING, Robert (1812–89), born England. A leading Victorian poet. In 1846 married the poet, Elizabeth Barrett, and lived with her in Italy, mainly Florence, until her death in 1861, after which he settled in London.

BUCKLEY, Jerome Hamilton, born 1917, Canada. Professor of English, Harvard University.

CARLYLE, Thomas (1795-1881), born Scotland. Literary critic, who began by publishing essays on German literature; social and political philosopher, historian. In *The French Revolution* (1837) and other writings, he warned the English to mend their ways lest they suffer revolution as in France.

COLERIDGE, Samuel Taylor (1772–1834), born England. A leading poet and principal critic and philosopher of English romanticism. Wordsworth's friend and collaborator on *Lyrical Ballads* (1798). Helped introduce German literature and philosophy into England. His prose writings influenced Victorian thought.

DICKENS, Charles (1812–70), born England. Most famous Victorian novelist in Britain and abroad. Suffered crucial boyhood experience when his father was imprisoned for debt in Marshalsea Prison and he was forced to work for six months in a blacking warehouse (shoe-wax factory). Starting in 1836, most of his fiction appeared serially. In 1842, he visited America; from 1850, he was co-owner and editor of a weekly periodical; from 1858, he gave public readings from his works, which he continued during his second visit to America in 1867–68.

ELIOT, George, pseudonym for Mary Ann or Marian Evans (1819–80), born England. A leading Victorian novelist. Translated from German Strauss's *Life of Jesus* (1846) and Feuerbach's *Essence of Christianity* (1854); worked for *Westminster Review* (1850–53); published first fiction in 1857. In 1854, common-law union with G. H. Lewes until his death in 1878. Married J. W. Cross in 1880.

ELIOT, Thomas Stearns (1888–1965), born U.S.A. Settled in England, 1914; became British subject and Anglican, 1927. A leading poet, principal critic, most successful writer of verse plays, during first half of twentieth century. Also wrote on social and religious questions. Nobel Prize 1948.

ENGELS, Friedrich (1820–95), born Rhineland, Germany. Son of a textile manufacturer, visited England in 1843–44 and settled there in 1849 to manage Manchester branch of his father's firm. Closest collaborator of Karl Marx; wrote with Marx *The Communist Manifesto* (1848).

FORD, George H., born 1914, Canada. Professor of English, University of Rochester.

HARDY, Thomas (1840–1928), born England. A leading late-Victorian novelist, influential twentieth-century poet. His native Dorset is the Wessex of his Wessex novels. Practiced ecclesiastical architecture, 1856–67. In 1859, began writing verse and essays; published first short story in 1865; novels from 1871–95; poetry from 1898.

HOLLOWAY, John, born 1920, England. Professor of Modern English, Cambridge University; Fellow of Queens' College.

HOWE, Irving, born 1920, U.S.A. Professor of English, City University of New York at Hunter College; editor of *Dissent* and contributing editor of *The New Republic*.

KITSON CLARK, George Sidney Roberts (1900-1975), born England. Reader in Constitutional History, Cambridge Unversity; Pralector and fellow of Trinity College.

LANGBAUM, Robert, born 1924, U.S.A. Professor of English, University of Virginia.

MACAULAY, Thomas Babington, first Baron Macaulay (1800–59), born England. Essayist, poet, historian, Whig M.P.

MILL, John Stuart (1806–73), born England. Son of the Benthamite James Mill by whom he was educated with a strenuousness that made him phenomenally precocious. Logician, economist, social and political philosopher, literary critic, J. S. Mill gradually modified the Benthamite Utilitarian doctrine. His *On Liberty* (1859) is a classic of Victorian liberalism. Liberal M.P. 1865–68.

RUSKIN, John (1819–1900), born England. Wrote on painting, architecture, social questions and, starting with *Unto This Last* (1862), on economics, attacking classical laissez-faire economists. The first of the Victorian prophets to address himself specifically to workingmen, Ruskin has been considered the father of Fabian Socialism and of present-day welfare economics. In 1854 his marriage to Effie Gray annulled for non-consummation; she married his friend, John Everett Millais, Pre-Raphaelite painter. Ruskin was Slade Professor of Fine Art at Oxford (1870–79; 1883–84). From 1878, he suffered recurrent attacks of madness.

SOUTHEY, Robert (1774–1843), born England. Poet and prose writer, became Poet Laureate in 1813. Settled in Lake District from 1803. With Wordsworth and Coleridge, known as one of the Lake poets who moved from the radicalism of their youth to Toryism.

TENNYSON, Alfred, first Baron Tennyson (1809–92), born England. The most popular of the leading Victorian poets. In 1850, after the publication of *In Memoriam* which was much admired by Prince Albert, Tennyson succeeded Wordsworth as Poet Laureate.

VAN GHENT, Dorothy (1907-1967), born U.S.A. Taught at Universities of Kansas and Vermont.

WILLIAMS, Raymond, born 1921, Wales. Professor of English, Cambridge University; Fellow of Jesus College.

YEATS, William Butler (1865–1929), born Ireland, divided his time between Ireland and England. Son of John Butler Yeats, painter, friend of Pre-Raphaelites. Considered by T. S. Eliot and others "the greatest poet of our time," W. B. Yeats participated in occultist societies and the Irish nationalist movement. One of the founders in 1899 of the Irish national theater, he wrote many plays in verse and prose. His prose writings include fiction, autobiography, literary criticism and the socio-historical-occultist *A Vision* (1925; 1937), which offers a key to the symbolism of the later poems. In 1922, Yeats was made a member of the Irish Senate. Nobel Prize 1923.

YOUNG, George Malcolm (1882–1959), born England. Member British Standing Commission on Museums and Galleries, Historical Manuscripts Commission, Trustee of British Museum.

SOME NOTEWORTHY BOOKS SINCE
THE LAST EDITION

GENERAL

Josef L. Altholz, ed., *The Mind and Art of Victorian England* (Minneapolis, 1976)

Richard Altick, *Victorian People and Ideas: A Companion for the Modern Reader of Victorian Literature* (New York, 1973)

Asa Briggs, *Victorian People: A Reassessment of Persons and Themes 1851-67*, Revised Edition (Chicago, 1970)

Carol T. Christ, *The Finer Optic: The Aesthetic of Particularity in Victorian Poetry* (New Haven and London, 1975)

David J. DeLaura, *Hebrew and Hellene in Victorian England: Newman, Arnold, and Pater* (Austin and London, 1969)

Sandra M. Gilbert and Susan Gubar, *The Madwoman in the Attic: The Woman Writer and The Nineteenth-Century Literary Imagination* (New Haven and London, 1979)

Richard Jenkyns, *The Victorians and Ancient Greece* (Cambridge, Mass., 1980)

U.C. Knoepflmacher, *Laughter and Despair: Readings in Ten Novels of the Victorian Era* (Berkeley, Los Angeles, London, 1971)

George P. Landow, *Victorian Types, Victorian Shadows: Biblical Typology in Victorian Literature, Art, and Thought* (Boston, London and Henley, 1980)

George P. Landow, ed., *Approaches to Victorian Autobiography* (Athens, Ohio, 1979)

Robert Langbaum, *The Modern Spirit: Essays on the Continuity of Nineteenth-and Twentieth-Century Literature* (New York, 1970)

George Levine, *The Boundaries of Fiction: Carlyle, Macaulay, Newman* (Princeton, 1968)

George Levine and William Madden, eds., *The Art of Victorian Prose* (New York, 1968)

J. Hillis Miller, *The Form of Victorian Fiction* (Notre Dame and London, 1968)

Frank M. Turner, *Between Science and Religion: The Reaction to Scientific Naturalism in Late Victorian England* (New Haven and London, 1974)

ENGELS

Steven Marcus, *Engels, Manchester, and the Working Class* (New York, 1974)

MILL

J.B. Schneewind, ed., *Mill: A Collection of Critical Essays* (Garden City, N.Y., 1968)

MACAULAY

John Clive, *Macaulay: The Shaping of the Historian* (New York, 1973)

CARLYLE

G.B. Tennyson, *Sartor Called Resartus* (Princeton, 1965)

ARNOLD

A. Dwight Culler, *Imaginative Reason: The Poetry of Matthew Arnold* (New Haven and London, 1966)

Park Honan, *Matthew Arnold: A Life* (New York, 1981)

RUSKIN

Elizabeth K. Helsinger, *Ruskin and the Art of the Beholder* (Cambridge, Mass. and London, 1982)

Robert Hewison, *John Ruskin: The Argument of the Eye* (Princeton, 1976)

John Dixon Hunt, *The Wider Sea: A Life of John Ruskin* (New York, 1982)

George P. Landow, *The Aesthetic and Critical Theories of John Ruskin* (Princeton, 1971)

DICKENS

John Carey, *The Violent Effigy: A Study of Dickens' Imagination* (London, 1973)

Harvey Peter Sucksmith, *The Narrative Art of Charles Dickens: The Rhetoric of Sympathy and Irony in his Novels* (Oxford, 1970)

TENNYSON

James R. Kincaid, *Tennyson's Major Poems: The Comic and Ironic Patterns* (New Haven 1975)

Robert Bernard Martin, *Tennyson, The Unquiet Heart* [biography] (Oxford and New York, 1980)

Christopher Ricks, *Tennyson* (New York, 1972)

W. David Shaw, *Tennyson's Style* (Ithaca and London, 1976

BROWNING

Isobel Armstrong, ed., *Robert Browning* (London, 1974)

Harold Bloom and Adrienne Munich, eds., *Robert Browning: A Collection of Critical Essays* (Englewood Cliffs, N.J., 1979)

William Irvine and Park Honan, *The Book, The Ring, and the Poet: A Biography of Robert Browning* (New York, 1974)

Herbert F. Tucker Jr., *Browning's Beginnings: The Art of Disclosure* (Minneapolis, 1980)

Maisie Ward, *Robert Browning and His World: The Private Face* [*1812-1861*]; *Two Robert Brownings?* [*1861-1889*] (New York, 1967, 1969)

ELIOT

George R. Creeger, ed., *George Eliot: A Collection of Critical Essays* (Englewood Cliffs, N.J., 1970)

Gordon S. Haight, *George Eliot: A Biography* (New York and Oxford, 1968)

Barbara Hardy, ed., *Critical Essays on George Eliot* (London, Boston and Henley, 1970)

Ruby V. Redinger, *George Eliot: The Emergent Self* [biography] (New York, 1975)

HARDY

Donald Davie, *Thomas Hardy and British Poetry* (New York, 1972)

Robert Gittings, *Young Thomas Hardy; Thomas Hardy's Later Years* (Boston, 1975, 1978)

J. Hillis Miller, *Thomas Hardy: Distance and Desire* (Cambridge, Mass., 1970)

Michael Millgate, *Thomas Hardy: A Biography* (New York, 1982)

AESTHETICISM THROUGH YEATS

Harold Bloom, *Yeats* (New York, 1970) [ch. 2, "Late Victorian Poetry and Pater"; ch. 3, "The Tragic Generation"]

Barbara Charlesworth, *Dark Passages: The Decadent Consciousness in Victorian Literature* (Madison and Milwaukee, 1965)

Richard Gilman, *Decadence: The Strange Life of an Epithet* (New York, 1979)

Robert Langbaum, *The Mysteries of Identity: A Theme in Modern Literature,* Revised Edition (Chicago and London, 1982) [Part III, Yeats: The Religion of Art]

Gerald Monsman, *Walter Pater's Art of Autobiography* (New Haven and London, 1980)

INDEX

(Darker type shows page where the
term is explained.)